ISBN: 978129010635

Published by:
HardPress Publishing
8345 NW 66TH ST #2561
MIAMI FL 33166-2626

Email: info@hardpress.net
Web: http://www.hardpress.net

ENGLAND IN TRANSITION
1789 - 1832

ENGLAND IN TRANSITION
1789-1832

A STUDY OF MOVEMENTS

BY

WILLIAM LAW MATHIESON

HON. LL.D. ABERDEEN

LONGMANS, GREEN, AND CO.

39 PATERNOSTER ROW, LONDON

FOURTH AVENUE & 30TH STREET, NEW YORK

BOMBAY, CALCUTTA, AND MADRAS

1920

To C. M. M.

PREFACE

No other period of equal length has witnessed so great a change in the political and social life of England as that which extends from the outbreak of the French Revolution to the passing of the Reform Bill ; and the object of this work is to distinguish and illustrate the forces—the economic, but especially the spiritual and intellectual forces—which combined to bring about that result. I have endeavoured to trace the development in earlier years of a liberal and humane spirit, and, whilst indicating the general features of transition, to show how this spirit was crushed but not extinguished in the struggle with Republican France, revived in the more spacious atmosphere of the Napoleonic War, was again imperilled by the disorder and repression which followed the Peace, and finally, in the last ten years of the period, came rapidly to fruition.

As on a former occasion, I have to acknowledge my indebtedness to the Carnegie Trust for the Scottish Universities.

EDINBURGH, *September* 1920.

CONTENTS

INTRODUCTION

CHAPTER I

WAR AND REPRESSION, 1789–1802

CHAPTER II

WAR AND PROGRESS, 1803–1814

CHAPTER III

DISILLUSIONS OF PEACE, 1814–1820

CHAPTER IV

THE LIBERAL SPIRIT, 1820–1828

CHAPTER V

THE TRIUMPH OF REFORM, 1828–1832

ENGLAND IN TRANSITION

1789-1832

A STUDY OF MOVEMENTS

INTRODUCTION

AT the close of the eighteenth century England was emerging from a survival of mediæval conditions into the latest phase of its modern life. The French Revolution contributed materially to this process, not as the parent of democracy which in England was of earlier and native growth, but because it called in question the permanence of all institutions and re-constituted politics on a conservative and a liberal basis. In the reaction caused by this event forces hitherto little more than latent in the Church were roused to an activity which under Evangelical or sacerdotal auspices has continued ever since ; the first popular agitation directed' to a wholly humanitarian aim was at the same time in progress ; and lastly, the industrial organisation, urban and rural, with all that this meant to the mass of the people, was then being moulded into its present shape. It need hardly be said that none of these forces—political, religious, philanthropic and social—had sprung suddenly into being ; and our first task must be to trace and account for their growth.

The political movement which culminated at the close of our period did not definitely assert itself till the early years of George III, but was an outcome of the state of things which had been established when James II was deposed in 1689. The importance of that settlement consists not so much in the limitation of the kingship as in the career opened to Parliament, and especially to the House of Commons, under a line of sovereigns who could not claim the divinity associated with hereditary right. This was the effect rather of circumstances than of design ; for, if James II's son had not been born under conditions which made it possible to put him aside as supposititious, and if the two daughters who succeeded him on the throne had not both died childless, it is more than probable that the old passion of loyalty, consecrated as it was by the Church, would soon have revived. But such a sentiment could not attach itself to a foreign ruler, such as George I, who was more interested in Hanover than in England, and was a stranger to the customs and even to the language of his subjects ; and thus the executive functions of the Crown—which had been little curtailed at 'the Revolution and have not since been abridged— came to be engrossed by Ministers acting in accord with the legislature, or rather with that branch of it which by withholding supplies could at any moment drive them from power. The Commons were not, however, in reality an independent body, most of the borough members, who formed a large majority of the House, being practically nominated either by the Crown or by a few great landowners ; and from 1714 to 176c England was ruled by a group of Whig nobles, whose power was great but precarious, since it depended on the Jacobitism of their opponents and the depression, on the one side, of the King and, on the other, of the people.

Of the two forces which the Whigs were keeping in subjection, it was natural and indeed inevitable that the monarchy should be the first to revolt ; for the King had merely to recover power, whilst the people—

at least in modern times—had never attained to its possession. George II had been over thirty years of age when his father ascended the British throne ; but the grandson who took his place in 1760 had lived all his life in England ; he had been brought up in the belief that he was entitled to as much personal authority as the law allowed ; and the Tories, whose Jacobitism had long been extinct, were now eager to transfer their adulation of royalty from a Catholic and foreign Pretender to a Protestant and home-bred King. George III had, therefore, the opportunity as well as the inclination to strike a blow at those who, in the words of a contemporary statesman, had " kept his grandfather in chains and were determined to make a mere pageant of the throne:" The Whigs, in default of more acceptable politicians, might still have their share of office, but it was to be a share only, and they were no longer to be recognised as a political corps, armed in their own defence with the Crown patronage, and led by an accredited chief. In other words, party government, with its attendant corruption, was to be discontinued ; the King was to rule as well as to reign ; and his Ministers, with no collective responsibility, were to be his agents in administration and his advisers in council. But it was not easy to dislodge the Whigs, entrenched as they were within so many ramparts of territorial and borough influence ; and George found it necessary, despite his abhorrence of corruption, to organise a party which became known as the " King's friends," because it was their function, at a hint from their master, to dissociate the personal from the official kingship. How far he had succeeded by such means in capturing the House of Commons became apparent, as we shall see, in 1763, and still more in 1770 on the accession to power of Lord North, who disclaimed even the title of Prime Minister and preferred to call himself the King's agent or man of business.

Meanwhile, though the people had not yet asserted themselves, there were signs that the period of their quiescence; if not of their subjection, was drawing to a close. Walpole had been induced by an agitation raised and fomented by his opponents throughout the country to withdraw his Excise Bill in 1733 and, contrary to his own judgment, to declare war against Spain in 1739. It has frequently been remarked that the growth of a popular spirit in the latter part of Elizabeth's reign was due to an advance in wealth, and consequently in social importance, of the middle class. A similar movement had been in progress during the twenty-six years of comparative peace which followed the Treaty of Utrecht in 1713 ; and, just as Puritanism had combined with commerce to excite impatience of Tudor and Stewart despotism, so in the eighteenth century the Methodist revival of religion was inimical both in its spirit and in its practice to the continuance of oligarchical rule. Unlike the Puritans, the Methodists took no part in politics ; but the excitement they produced amongst the vast multitudes assembled to hear them in the open air could not fail sooner or later to make itself felt in the political sphere ; and the democratic tendency of their preaching was well expressed by an indignant duchess who taxed them with " endeavouring to level all ranks " and declared it " monstrous to be told you have a heart as sinful as the common wretches that crawl on the earth." Nor can it be dismissed as a mere coincidence that there had arisen at this period amongst the Whigs a statesman, unconnected with any of the great families, whom the voice of the nation as well as his own genius had constrained them to recognise as their actual, if not their nominal, chief. Pitt, indeed, was never tired of contrasting the potency of public opinion with the quite inadequate means for its expression provided in Parliament ; and George II announced his conversion to this view in his memorable reply to Pitt when the latter was entreating him to pardon Admiral Byng on the ground that the Commons were disposed to show mercy : " Sir, you have taught me to look for the sense of my subjects in another place than the House of Commons." Hallam has remarked that the Whigs themselves constantly complained of " the democratic spirit, the insubordination to authority, the tendency to republican sentiments which they alleged to have gained ground among the people " ; and Fielding, writing as a contemporary in 1760, declared " that the constitution of this country is altered from its ancient state and that the power of the commonalty has received an immense addition." [1]

The Whigs indeed at this period were far from participating in Pitt's respect for public opinion ; and their humiliation might have excited as little general sympathy as interest if it had not been accompanied by the rise of Bute, a Scottish peer whose sudden elevation could be ascribed neither to birth nor merit, and by the conclusion on what were deemed inadequate terms of a highly successful war. On the prorogation of Parliament in April 1763, George III referred to the Peace of Paris as honourable to his Crown and beneficial to his people ; and the speech was violently attacked by John Wilkes, member for Aylesbury, in a paper which he had established to exploit the national prejudice against the Scots and had ironically termed the *North Briton*. The King's speech had long been regarded in its present light as the composition of his Ministers ; but this was just the admission which the new sovereign could not afford to make ; and Wilkes was committed to the Tower on a charge of seditious libel. He soon recovered his freedom on the ground of his privilege as a member of Parliament, and the warrants issued for his apprehension and for the seizure of his papers

[1] Jephson, *The Platform, Its Rise and Progress*, i. 8, 9.

were both declared illegal. The two Houses did their utmost to counteract these decisions—the Commons, in order to admit of his being brought to trial, contracting their privileges, and the Lords expanding theirs in regard to certain indecent parodies, privately printed by Wilkes at his own house, which concerned them only in so far as they professed to be edited by a bishop. On this pretext for interference they procured a charge of blasphemy in addition to that of libel. In proportion to the wrath of King, Ministers and Parliament was the riotous exultation of the people; but popularity, as Wilkes well knew, could only aggravate his offence; and, having stood his ground long enough to prevail in an action for damages against the Government, he fled to France, and in his absence was expelled from Parliament, convicted and outlawed.

He returned—after two secret visits—just in time to offer himself as a candidate at the general election of 1768, and, though too late in the field to poll more than 1200 votes for the City of London, was returned for Middlesex, after a contest which occasioned the wildest disorder and resulted in London being illuminated for two nights at the bidding of the mob. Wilkes, though a forcible writer and a famous wit, was known to have no parliamentary talent, and the Duke of Grafton, who was then at the head of a weak and divided Ministry, would gladly have allowed him to take his seat; but, George being inexorable, he was sentenced to twenty-two months' imprisonment and a heavy fine; and the new House of Commons resorted, like its predecessor, to a vote of expulsion. The county of Middlesex at once re-elected its member, who was then declared incapable of sitting in that Parliament; and, after Wilkes had been returned a third time, a young officer of the Guards was induced to oppose him, and, though he received only a small minority of the votes, was declared duly elected.

No subsequent crisis in our political history has produced so sudden and so complete a change as was occasioned by the course of events which has just been reviewed. The state of things in which a group of nobles and their dependents engrossed the administration and manipulated Parliament, with nothing to disturb them but their own dissensions, whilst the kingship was in abeyance and the people looked on with no more interest than might have been shown by the spectators in a theatre, had passed away. The King was now the dominant influence in politics ; two forces, Tory and Whig, contended for the mastery in Parliament ; and the people had begun to realise that what went on at Westminster was not a mere drama evoking their censure or applause, but a struggle of real life in which their interests were at stake. So clearly indeed was this discerned that public opinion, which had hitherto been expressed only by individuals in the form of pamphlets, now sought to organise itself as a collective force calculated to prevail less by argument than by pressure. The Middlesex electors held a great meeting at Mile End to protest against the violation of their rights ; in many other counties the freeholders assembled to vote addresses for the dissolution of Parliament ; and a meeting for this purpose in Westminster Hall is said to have been attended by about 7000 persons.

That the object of this agitation was to recall the House of Commons to a sense of its representative character was made manifest in the doctrine, now widely avowed, that its members were mere delegates, liable to be instructed and called to order by their constituents, and in proposals for its reform. But Wilkes was a man of unusually dissolute and extravagant habits ; and the necessity of raising money to uphold him in his struggle with the Court caused his supporters to take a further step in political organisation by forming themselves into clubs. Many of these had already been instituted in London and were distinguished by the names of the taverns at which they met, when in February 1769, after Wilkes had been excluded as well as expelled from Parliament, a new and more select body assembled at the London Tavern and gave proof both of its liberality and its wealth by subscribing more than £3000. At their second meeting the members assumed the name of the Supporters of the Bill of Rights, declared that their object was to assist all those who had suffered contrary to law, and, in order to attest the catholicity of their public spirit, resolved that the name of Wilkes should never be proposed as a toast at their meetings. Wilkes naturally resented this disclaimer, and, preferring his needs to his obligations, was by no means satisfied when a sum of £12,000 had been raised to release him from debt. He had sufficient influence to defeat a motion for the relief of a rival claimant ; and the minority who had supported this proposal then seceded and formed a new association " to exist only upon the public ground." These were probably the more moderate as well as the more " respectable " members ; for the original society, a few months after their departure, pledged itself to promote, not only the prevention of corrupt influence, but annual Parliaments and the full and equal representation of the people.[1]

We have seen that the Whigs had built up their power on a system which involved the effacement of the people as well as of the King ; and this sudden irruption of a popular element into politics caused them as much embarrassment as surprise. In so far as Wilkes had suffered for his resistance to arbitrary power, they had of course no difficulty in espousing his cause ; for their traditions were those of the Revolution Settlement and much of their support was derived from the commercial

---

[1] Stephens's *Memoirs of John Horne Tooke*, i. 163–175 ; Veitch's *Genesis of Parliamentary Reform*, pp. 29–32.

classes and Dissenters as opposed to the country gentlemen and the Church. Thus they dilated on the iniquity of a general warrant—a warrant which mentioned no names and authorised the arrest of several or many persons in order to secure the discovery of one ; and they contended that, though the House of Commons might expel one of its members, it could not exclude him, if re-elected, without altering by its own authority the election laws and so making one branch of the legislature do the duty of all three. But Wilkes as the victim of oppression and Wilkes as the advocate of a reformed legislature were in their opinion two very different persons ; and here they fell back on a distinction which was eventually to cause the appearance of a new type of politician—the Radical as opposed to the Whig. Knowing that the useless offices, the sinecures and pensions which they had used in former days to uphold their own ascendancy in Parliament, would not long be tolerated and meanwhile had been wrested from them by the King, they were ready, as their own historian puts it, to " abandon the cause of corruption " [1]; but for the most part they opposed or sought greatly to minimise such changes in the franchise or in the representative system as would have deprived them of the influence they still enjoyed as the owners of decayed boroughs. It is not easy to recognise the homely features of this policy as transfigured in the glowing rhetoric of Burke, who had to disguise as best he could the exploitation of Parliament by the Whig nobles, whilst exposing the same system as practised by the King.

Riots, meetings, associations and the growth of a really popular party—all the factors, in short, which never wholly ceased to operate till their object was attained in 1832—were a remarkable result to be achieved mainly by a man who was no orator and who may well seem to have been less fitted for agitation than any one

[1] Cook's *History of Party*, iii. 197.

who has followed him in that path. The son of a London distiller and excluded as a Dissenter from the English Universities, Wilkes had nevertheless been welcomed as an associate by the most dissolute nobles. By natural inclination he was rather a man of taste and fashion than a demagogue, and he had a grace and charm of manner as well as a buoyancy and humour which more than atoned for his "unhappy physiognomy" and his squint. Amidst all his dissipation he found time to study French and Italian literature, to translate Anacreon, and to edit Greek and Latin texts. "Mr. Wilkes," said Lord Mansfield, "is the pleasantest companion, the politest gentleman and the best scholar I know." And even George III, when in 1775 he made the personal acquaintance of his old enemy as chief magistrate of the City and the bearer of a very unwelcome address, confessed that he had never seen "so well-bred a Lord Mayor." But Wilkes was too closely associated with the mob to be accepted in Parliament as a reputable politician. Pitt denounced him as " the blasphemer of his God and the libeller of his King," and declared that he " did not deserve to be ranked among the human species." Lord Temple, the brother-in-law of Pitt, had encouraged and befriended Wilkes ; but even Temple deserted him when he refused to submit in silence to the terms, so far from flattering to himself, in which his cause was advocated by the leading Whigs. Disowned by Pitt, now Earl of Chatham, as a follower of whom he had entered Parliament, he became a candidate for municipal honours, having indeed been elected an alderman before his discharge from prison ; and in this sphere by using the privileges of the City to combat those of the Commons he achieved one of his greatest triumphs—the free publication of parliamentary debates. At the next general election, that of 1774, he was again returned for Middlesex, and this time, though the vote of incapacitation was not erased from the journals till 1782, he was allowed to take his seat.

Wilkes was not long in bringing before Parliament the proposals for its reform which had been put forward under his influence by the Supporters of the Bill of Rights. His scheme provided for an extension of the suffrage wide enough to include "the meanest mechanic, the poorest peasant and day-labourer," and a re-distribution of seats on a scale sufficient to give members to the unrepresented towns and the more populous counties. "The disfranchising the mean, venal and dependent boroughs would," he said, with an eye both on the King and on the Whigs, "be laying the axe to the root of corruption and treasury influence as well as aristocratic tyranny."

These words were uttered in 1776, about three months before the declaration of American Independence ; and the failure of Lord North's Government to put down the colonists and to deal successfully with the intervention of France gave rise to a powerful agitation against the waste and misuse of public money at a time when so much of it was needed for the prosecution of the war. This movement was in several respects an advance on the Middlesex agitation, for it raised no personal issue, was free from disorder, and, if less democratic, was also more widely diffused. The freeholders of Yorkshire in 1780 led the way in complaining to Parliament of an increase in "sinecure places, efficient places with exorbitant emoluments, and pensions unmerited by public services, whence the Crown has acquired a great and unconstitutional influence" ; and the example of Yorkshire was followed by twenty-eight other counties, including Middlesex, and by a dozen considerable towns. At a conference in London, attended by delegates from the various local associations, it was resolved to petition for shorter Parliaments and a more numerous representation of counties ; but this addition to the original programme was distasteful to the main body of the Whigs ; and, when these politicians were called to office under

Lord Rockingham on the resignation of North in 1782, they contented themselves with disfranchising revenue officers, excluding Government contractors from Parliament and cutting down the pension list. Meanwhile, however, the Society for Promoting Constitutional Information had been instituted in 1780; and the guinea subscriptions of its members were applied to the printing, for free distribution, of pamphlets in favour of annual Parliaments, manhood suffrage and vote by ballot.

Several of the Whig aristocracy, such as the Duke of Richmond, the Earls of Derby and Effingham, and the future Dukes of Norfolk and Roxburgh, were members of this society; but the reformers derived more encouragement from the fact that a certain section of the Whigs, though far from keeping pace with these enthusiasts, was disposed at least to move in the same direction. Lord Chatham, who died in 1778, whilst not prepared to cauterise the rotten boroughs, had proposed to neutralise their baleful influence by a large addition to the county membership; and in 1782 his second son, William Pitt, moved for a committee to inquire into the state of the representation—a motion which came nearer to success, being defeated by only twenty votes, than any similar proposal till 1831. A fortnight later, at a meeting in the Thatched House Tavern, Pitt concurred with such thorough-going reformers as the Duke of Richmond, Wilkes and Major Cartwright, one of the founders of the Society for Constitutional Information, in a resolution that " the Collective Body of the People in their respective districts " should be incited to petition for "a substantial reform of the Commons' House of Parliament."

When Rockingham died, after less than four months of office, in 1782, the Whig nobles chose as their chief the Duke of Portland; but their real leader was Fox, who had for some time been at variance with his colleague, the Earl of Shelburne, leader of the Chathamite Whigs. Both were reformers, but Fox in that capacity inspired much less confidence, not so much on account of his own opinions, though these were open to suspicion, as because they were known to be shared by but few of his friends ; and Shelburne, on being called upon to reconstitute the Government, made Pitt his Chancellor of the Exchequer. The Shelburne Ministry had, however, but a brief career owing to the unexpected reconciliation of Fox and North, who combined to eject it and to bring themselves into power under the Duke of Portland ; and it was consequently as a private member that Pitt returned in May 1783 to the question of reform. The resolutions he proposed on that occasion were rejected by 293 votes to 149 ; but the King soon succeeded in getting rid of what he described as " the most unprincipled coalition the annals of this or any other country can equal " ; and Pitt had been Prime Minister for a year and four months, to the great satisfaction of his fellow-reformers, when, in April 1785, he made his third and last effort in the common cause. This took the form of a Bill for the gradual and voluntary extinction of thirty-six rotten boroughs under the influence brought to bear on their owners by a growing compensation fund, and was rejected at the first reading by seventy-four votes. This defeat, aggravated by the disunion resulting from the Coalition and from the rivalry of Fox and Pitt, was accepted as all but conclusive ; and by the end of the year most of the committees and associations had been dissolved. It was natural indeed that an agitation which had originated as a protest against the corrupt and autocratic influence of the Court should be assuaged by the accession to power of a Minister who was equally acceptable to the nation and to the King. But the glowing embers of popular enthusiasm were stirred again into a flame by the means taken to celebrate the centenary of the English Revolution in 1788 ; and this effect was intensified for a time by the much greater revolution which next year broke out in France.

The cause of reform had hitherto been supported

mainly by the county freeholders ; and, unfortunately for its prospects of success, the representation of this class was far less substantial than even its limited membership would lead one to expect. The counties of England returned only eighty members to the House of Commons, whilst the close or nomination boroughs returned more than four hundred ; but three-fourths of the counties were either strangled by aristocratic, clerical or Government influence or were virtually put out of action by an agreement amongst the squirearchy that the Whigs and Tories should each nominate one of the two members. The remainder, with some notable exceptions, such as Yorkshire and Warwickshire, were situated in what was then pre-eminently the industrial part of England, Norwich and Taunton, centres of the woollen manufacture, being at the two extremities and London in the middle. This area, extending from Somerset to Kent and thence by way of Hertfordshire to Suffolk and Norfolk, was the real home of English freedom, as it had been in the days of Charles I ; for here the yeomanry with their minimum qualification of a forty shilling freehold were more or less dominant, and the industries carried on around them had no doubt quickened their political spirit. Hertfordshire, despite the Salisbury influence, had maintained its independence in ten successive Parliaments, and Wiltshire had even succeeded about 1770 in returning a yeoman member. But landowners, whether great or small, have seldom been favourable as a class to constitutional innovation ; and we have seen that the movement of 1780, which originated amongst the 20,000 freeholders of Yorkshire, had been directed, under Whig auspices, to administrative rather than organic reform.[1]

[1] Oldfield's *Representative History of Great Britain and Ireland*. The yeomanry had greatly declined before the Revolution of 1688 ; but at that date more than half the farmers of England—160,000 out of 310,000—were still cultivating their own lands ; and Mr. Rae in the *Contemporary Review* for October 1883 has shown that the number did not seriously diminish till after the Peace of 1815.

So far the agitation for reform, as described in these pages, had been as practical and as insular as the most typical Englishman could desire. The House of Commons had expelled one of its members, had refused to admit him when re-elected, and finally had adjudged his seat to an unsuccessful opponent ; and this affair had suggested the re-modelling of a representative system which no longer fulfilled its purpose. But within this movement was another which was avowedly a movement of thought.

In the latter half of the seventeenth century Hobbes and Locke had carried political speculation from its theological into its metaphysical phase by maintaining against those who upheld the divine right of kings that government had originated in mutual consent—a surrender of rights on the part of men emerging from a state of nature which Hobbes regarded as complete and final and Locke as limited to certain ends and as binding only in so far as these were attained. The idea of a social compact was intended in Locke's case to provide a philosophical basis for the revolution which his countrymen had accomplished, or were about to accomplish, in 1688 ; and as developed by Rousseau, who borrowed from both Locke and Hobbes, it was to inspire, ten years after his death, another and far greater revolution in France. Rousseau derived from Hobbes his idea of a complete surrender of individual rights ; but, whilst Hobbes imagined this sacrifice to have been made to a person or to an assembly, Rousseau maintained that it could be made only to the general will. He thus arrived at his conception of a sovereign people ; and in asserting that men retained their natural liberty so far as consistent with common action, that authority entrusted to individuals could be no more than a temporary delegation, and that there was no contract of subjection in a state but only the original contract of association, he formulated the three ideas—liberty, equality and fraternity—which were to be the watchwords of an emancipated France. His system was obviously a fusion of the popular element in Locke with the despotic element in Hobbes ; and he carried the former so far as to deny the lawfulness of representation and to insist on the nullity of any law which had not been submitted to a direct popular vote. In his opinion the English were a free people only " during the election of members of Parliament. When these are chosen, they become slaves again."

We are all agreed now that, if liberty were our birthright, there could be, or at least there ought to be, no such thing as government, which in itself involves the idea of compulsion ; but in those days, when despotism was all but universal in Europe, men were not likely to regard subjection to the majority of their fellows as an infraction of their natural freedom, especially as they were supposed to have sanctioned it vicariously in the persons of prehistoric—not to say unhistoric—ancestors. Even Locke himself, however, laid almost as much stress on expediency as the warrant for forming and submitting to government as on the social compact ; and Francis Hutcheson, who before the middle of the century had greatly developed this part of his teaching, may be said to have foreshadowed the reconstruction of political science on a purely utilitarian basis. Hutcheson went so far in this direction as to insist that, as " the public happiness is the sole end of all civil power, rulers are not entitled to retain their power if it gives rise to fears and suspicions which, however groundless, they are unable to remove." It was indeed from Hutcheson that Bentham derived at second hand his famous formula " the greatest happiness of the greatest number " ; and the connecting link was Joseph Priestley, better known as a liberal theologian, a man of science and the discoverer of oxygen than as a political philosopher, whose " Essay on the First

Principles of Government " was published in the year of the Middlesex election, 1768. Priestley maintained that "every man retains and can never be deprived of his natural right " to relieve himself " from everything that has been imposed upon him without his own consent," and that the restriction of this right consequent on his entering into a state of society can be justified only if he receives as compensation a share of political power. He admitted the unwelcome necessity of delegation which Rousseau denied, and there was this further difference between the two thinkers, that, whilst Rousseau looked to government as a means of levelling all that obstructed the return of man to his original state of nature, Priestley exulted in it as an instrument of progress, and declared that, " whatever was the beginning of this world, the end will be glorious and paradisaical beyond what our imagination can now conceive." In this attitude he was at one with the best thought of an age in which much had been gained, and still more was expected, from the enlightenment of rulers. " The young are indeed happy," wrote Voltaire in 1764, " for they will see great things."

Another and more influential writer of the same school was Richard Price, whose " Observations on Civil Liberty and the Justice and Policy of the War with America " was published in 1776. Price's object in this tract is to combat the idea that the colonies were not entitled to independence ; but he moves to the attack on so wide a front that many other positions are assailed by him in the course of his advance. All civil government, he holds, is the creature of the people and can be exercised in its perfection only in small states where the citizens vote in person. The election of delegates chosen by all and restricted to the terms of their commission is, however, a satisfactory substitute ; but, "if a State is so sunk that the majority of its representatives are elected by a handful of the meanest persons in it whose votes are always paid for, and if also there is a higher will on which even these mock representatives themselves depend and that directs their voices, it will be an abuse of language to say that the State possesses liberty "; and the writer affirms that in Great Britain, with nearly six millions of inhabitants, 5723 persons, mostly of the humblest rank, elect one half of the Commons and 364 persons choose a ninth part. That the members of a separate community, several thousand miles distant, should be subject to the decrees of such a legislature he naturally regarded as the worst servitude of all.

The political movement for reform in the first half of George III's reign, and the much slighter speculative movement, have now been reviewed ; and they have been reviewed as one because they both aimed at a reform of the legislature as a condition precedent to all further progress. We have now to consider the philanthropic movement which either made no demand for legislative aid or asked only for such assistance as even an unreformed Parliament might be expected to afford. The line of continuity in this case is not very substantial or clearly marked, but it commences with the century and suffers no interruption at its close ; and one cannot but remark that, whilst the political movement was the belated outcome of conditions established at the Revolution, the philanthropic movement originated in a conjunction of religious aspirations and social needs which was then making itself felt. Religion, though far from embracing all the objects aimed at by philanthropy in the eighteenth century, was at all times its principal motive ; and we shall find that in this connexion it passed through three phases—High Church, Methodist and Evangelical. The first of these phases carries us back to a time when the Church of England was threatened with a coalition of Catholics and Dissenters, and was consequently impelled to emphasise those beliefs and usages which marked out her path as a *via media* between Rome and Geneva. The bias of her clergy was, however, much more to the former of these extremes than to the latter, and was strongest in the small number—known as Nonjurors because they refused to take the oaths to the new Government—who, having helped to get rid of James II as an enemy to the Church, would have liked to restore him as essential to their idea of a divinely constituted State. As early as 1678 some young men of the middle class in London had formed themselves into a society which was designed to promote, not only the personal piety of its members, but the institution of daily services and frequent communions. Their example was soon followed by others; and, when the movement culminated in the High Church enthusiasm of Queen Anne's reign, no fewer than forty-two of these societies were meeting weekly in London, in addition to those which had been formed in other towns, and "greater appearances of devotion were diffused through the city than had been observed in the memory of man." It was at this time, after the fall of the Whigs in 1710, that Parliament voted a sum of £350,000 for church building in London. Fifty new churches were projected, but only a fifth of that number were actually built.[1]

Meanwhile, if religious persuasion had sufficed to give an air of devoutness to the City, nothing short of legal compulsion had been found necessary, at a time of industrial progress, to reform its morals. Under the Stewart dynasty, despite civil and ecclesiastical contentions and ten years of actual civil war, there had been a steady advance in material wealth; and it was estimated in 1670 that the merchants and shipping had doubled within the previous twenty years. From that period to 1690 the country was enriched by an

---

[1] Secretan's *Life and Times of the Pious Robert Nelson*, pp. 91, 142; Hutton's *English Church*, p. 305.

immigration of something like 80,000 Huguenot refugees, who established many new industries and gave so great an impetus to the silk manufacture that in 1698 the importation of spun silk had ceased to be allowed. During the last decade of the century the annual value of the imports, favoured by a new coinage and the development of banking, rose from about £2,000,000 to little short of £7,000,000. Most of the new capital and labour was concentrated in London, which had half a million inhabitants or more than a third of the whole urban population[1]; and the growth of an unregenerate London, coinciding as it did with the religious revival, caused Church and Dissent in 1692 to unite in Societies for the Reformation of Manners. The object was to collect facts and money for the prosecution of those who broke the laws against swearing, drunkenness, immorality and desecration of the Sabbath; and, great as was the activity of these societies, it was almost equalled by their success. As many as seventy or eighty " common swearers " were sometimes prosecuted in a week; Sunday markets were suppressed; hundreds of brothels were closed, and thousands of " lewd persons " were fined, imprisoned, transported or scourged. It soon appeared, however, that, whilst the members of these societies were men of substance and might even be nobles, bishops or judges, their victims were usually of the lowest rank; and for one person who objected to the co-operation of Churchmen and Dissenters there were many who detested such unneighbourly practices as eavesdropping and spying.[2] Yet the societies continued to exist, if not to flourish, till 1730, and were even resuscitated for nine years under Methodist auspices in 1757.[3]

[1] Lecky's *History of England*, cabinet edition, i. 240–242; *Social England*, iv.
[2] Secretan's *Nelson*, p. 96; *Social England*, iv. 592–594.
[3] Tyerman's *John Wesley*, ii. 468.

The nature of these associations, devotional and moral, would hardly have brought them within the scope of this survey, if they had not prepared the way for another, in which modern philanthropy as something more than a purely religious interest may be said to have had its rise. The Society for Promoting Christian Knowledge was established, mainly through the exertions of the Rev. Thomas Bray, in 1698, and proposed to carry out its design by means of missionaries in the colonies, and at home by diffusing religious literature, and especially by promoting a movement for the institution of parish schools. Bray and the four laymen who formed the original membership were zealous sons of the Church, and their principal object was to extend its influence amongst the poor. The master of a school must not only be a Churchman, but one who " frequents communion " ; he was to be approved by the parish minister before being presented for licence to the bishop ; and his chief business was to teach the Church Catechism and to bring his pupils twice to Church on Sundays and holidays. But the scheme went much further than this ; for not only was there the usual elementary instruction, but girls were taught sewing, knitting and spinning, and boys were apprenticed to trades. In some cases evening classes were held to teach grown people to read. In the majority of these seminaries—the so-called " Blue Coat " schools—the children were clothed as well as taught, and all of them were known as " charity schools," because they received no assistance from public funds and were based on the principle of voluntary contribution. We are told that a clergyman would suggest the setting up of such a school to some of his parishioners or they to him ; that a list of those willing to become annual subscribers would then be opened and sent round ; and that the object would usually be attained in seven or eight months. Within the fifteen years ending in 1712 as many as 117 charity schools were established in London and more than 500 throughout England and Wales. The number of scholars who had been placed as apprentices or female servants was then 2250, and in 1735 it had risen to 16,000. Addison considered these schools " the glory of the age we live in," and Defoe called them " the best and most glorious parts of Christian charity that had been set on foot in this part of the world " since the reign of Edward VI. The children thus cared for, though poor, were not of the lowest class ; for it was proposed by one of the keenest supporters of the scheme—a layman whose devoutness so far exceeded even the professional standard that he was known as " the pious Robert Nelson "—to extend its benefits to " the children commonly called black-guard boys," who would thus become " more useful in their little stations as well as less wicked and profane " [1]

Soon after founding the Society for Promoting Christian Knowledge, Bray left England on a mission to Maryland ; and some years earlier, finding that only clergymen too poor to buy books were available for such service, he had initiated a scheme which was to occupy him for the rest of his life—that of providing parish libraries for the colonies and for the more poorly endowed cures at home, in over two thousand of which the income of the incumbent was no more than £30. At his death in 1730 sixty-seven private libraries for the use of individual clergymen and eighty-three lending libraries had been established in England, whilst fifty donations of books had been sent out to America and the West Indies. In this part of his work he had the assistance of a separate body known as his " Associates." On his return from Maryland he founded in 1701 the Society for the Propagation of the Gospel in Foreign

---

[1] Secretan's *Nelson*, pp. 100, 122, 149 ; *Life and Designs of Dr. Bray ; Account of Charity Schools,* 1709 ; Lee's *Defoe,* iii. 157 ; *Social England,* iv. 594 ; Lecky, iii. 132.

Parts, and also induced the Christian Knowledge Society,
now relieved of its mission duties, to interest itself in
prison reform. A committee was appointed in 1702
to visit the London gaols ; and in a report [1] drawn up
by Bray himself we find the following amongst many
other useful suggestions : that hardened criminals on
their discharge should be detained for a time in workhouses, and, even after they had entered on " an honest
employment," should be kept under supervision ; and
that criminals who had behaved well during their confinement should be assisted by a public notice exhorting
people "to help them in getting a livelihood in their
trades that they may not return to their old courses."
The state of the gaols was again forced on his attention
in 1727, when he succeeded in raising funds to provide
the Whitechapel prisoners with a substantial meal on
Sundays and occasionally throughout the week, and
also obtained for them the ministration of missionaries
intended for America, who were thus employed in order
" to inure them to the most distasteful parts of their
office." [2]

At this period, when he was busy not only with prison
reform but with schemes for converting the negroes,
his career merges in that of the man who was to carry
on his work. James Oglethorpe now became one of
Bray's " Associates " ; and in 1729, when one of his friends
had died in a sponging-house through deliberate exposure to smallpox, this chivalrous soldier and politician,
whose " great benevolence of soul " is commemorated
by Pope, prevailed upon the Commons to appoint a
Prison Visiting Committee with himself as Chairman.
The horrors, suspected rather than known, were now
fully revealed and certain remedies devised ; but Oglethorpe, in concert with Bray, had a larger scheme in
view and proposed to attack the prison problem as one

[1] Hepworth Dixon's *John Howard*, p. 10.
[2] Bray's *Life* ; Secretan's *Nelson*, p. 138.

of prevention rather than cure. The territory of North America lying between South Carolina and the Spanish settlement of Florida had long been an object of contention to Great Britain and Spain; and the British colonists, exposed to the inroads of Spaniards, Indians and fugitive slaves, were anxious that a new settlement should be made on their southern frontier. This opportunity was seized by Oglethorpe as a means of rehabilitation for those who were either the inmates of a debtors' prison or through misfortune or loss of means were clearly on their way thither. In 1732 he obtained a royal charter empowering himself and twenty other persons to found a colony in the disputed area, which in honour of the King was to be called Georgia. Meanwhile Dean Berkeley, the mental philosopher, had just returned from America, where he had hoped to found a college for the education of Indian missionaries. Parliament had encouraged him with a grant of £20,000 ; but most of the funds out of which this sum was to have been paid had been given as a marriage dowry to the Princess Royal, and the remainder, with the Dean's consent, was assigned to the Georgian project. The public had responded liberally to Berkeley's appeal, and, undeterred by its failure, were not indisposed to support another which had a religious as well as a social and patriotic object ; for Oglethorpe also proposed to convert the natives, and for this purpose selected the two Wesleys and Whitefield. The first batch of settlers sailed with Oglethorpe in 1732 ; and it may suffice here to say that he succeeded in establishing his colony and won a considerable military reputation by defending it against the Spaniards in the war which broke out in 1739.[1]

Philanthropy was still indebted for most of its progress to the religious enthusiasm in which it had originated at the Revolution. The *Catechetical Lectures* which first brought Bray into notice were dedicated to Bishop

[1] Wright's *Life of Oglethorpe.*

Lloyd, one of the seven prelates who had incurred the wrath of James II ; Nelson, who died in 1715, was for some time associated with the Nonjurors ; Berkeley had prejudiced his early career by a *Discourse of Passive Obedience* preached in 1712 ; and Oglethorpe was one of the few Tories in the House of Commons, suspected as a Jacobite and with a sister at the exiled Court. Bray died in 1730, and the movement seems to have been fairly well maintained during his life. Mandeville, author of the " Fable of the Bees," who published a pamphlet against the charity schools in 1724, admitted that they were still in " uncommon vogue and unanimously approved of and admired among all sorts and conditions of people."[1] A company which had been formed in 1707 to assist the poor and tradesmen who had got into difficulties was ruined through the embezzlement of its funds in 1731, but meanwhile its capital had increased from £30,000 to £600,000 ; and we have seen that Oglethorpe's emigration scheme was launched as late as 1732. None the less is it true that philanthropy of the Anglican or High Church type was now becoming a spent force. This was due partly to an imputation of Jacobitism which militated against the religious societies and even caused disorder when collections were made in church for the charity schools, but much more to the fact that the religious revival was a bequest to the eighteenth century from the troublous but more inspiring years which had brought its predecessor to a close. " Those years," it has been well said, " gave the world a new calculus, a new astronomy and physics, a new psychology, a new system of government, a new and more brilliant strategy."[2] There was now to be a period of exhaustion, intellectual as well as political. Hume complained that the " Treatise on Human Nature," his first and greatest work, " fell dead-born from the press " in 1739 ; the poet Gray said

[1] *Fable of the Bees*, 3rd edition, pp. 313, 321, 357.
[2] Benn's *English Rationalism*, i. 160.

in 1754 that " the mode of freethinking had given place to the mode of not thinking at all " ; and the apathy of the nation during the Jacobite crisis of 1745, and about ten years later at the outbreak of the Seven Years' War, was viewed by its rulers with equal astonishment and dismay.

Meanwhile the community found it imperative to deal with certain evils which had become a danger to its corporate life. One of the worst of these was drunkenness. This vice, whether or not it originated in the association of English soldiers with the Dutch in Elizabeth's reign, had long been prevalent ; but till the Revolution it had been confined mainly to those who could afford to purchase the imported wines, rum and brandy which were then the chief, or at least the readiest, means of its indulgence. The popular beverage was beer, and, though enormous quantities were consumed—about a third of the arable land being devoted to barley—it does not seem to have been generally abused. In 1689 the importation of foreign spirits was prohibited, whilst the home production was encouraged ; and thenceforth the use of gin increased till in the course of a generation it had almost supplanted that of beer. In 1727 the average of British spirits distilled had risen from half a million gallons in 1684 to over three and a half millions, and it went on increasing till in 1750 it amounted to eleven millions. The annual consumption at this period has been reckoned at six gallons per head of the population as compared with one gallon at the present day.[1] Every facility was offered to the poor, not so much for drinking, as for making themselves drunk ; and Fielding predicted that, if gin continued to be consumed at this rate for another twenty years, there would by that time be very few of the common people left to drink it. In 1736 an almost prohibitive excise duty was imposed, and the price of a retail licence was raised to £50 a year ; but the

[1] *Social England,* v. 50.

only permanent effect of this measure was to give a great impetus to illicit sale—so great indeed that, thirteen years later, there were 17,000 unlicensed ginshops in and around London, and 14,000 cases of illness, most of them likely to prove fatal, were directly attributed to gin. An Act which achieved more satisfactory results was, however, passed in 1751.

The tendency of " these accursed spirituous liquors," as a bishop called them, " to destroy the very race of people themselves " must have been counteracted to some extent by the facilities provided—frequently on the same premises—for getting married as well as drunk. In those days the only essentials to marriage were a priest in orders and a stamped licence. The latter could be dispensed with, without affecting anybody but the priest, and even he was liable only to a penalty for defrauding the exchequer which could be evaded for at least a year. A host of disreputable clergymen—most of them detained for debt in the Fleet prison—contrived in this way to make an income, in some cases even a fortune ; the number of those who sought their services increased yearly with the popularity of gin ; and almost every public house in the neighbourhood is said to have had a " Fleet parson " within call. One such divine is said to have married 173 couples in a single day. An effective remedy for this evil was found in Lord Hardwicke's Act of 1753 which introduced the present marriage law.[1]

Bishop Horsley remarked, with special reference to this period, that sermons had degenerated into moral essays, and that the clergy were content to " come abroad one day in the seven dressed in solemn looks and in the garb of holiness to be the apes of Epictetus,"[2] and the author of " Tom Jones " was reproached in some quarters with having resolved the whole moral law into

---

[1] Lecky, ii. 98–104, 223.
[2] Overton's The Evangelical Revival, p. 147.

the dictates of a kindly disposition and a generous heart.
If this was the sort of teaching inculcated by preachers
and novelists, we have some reason to believe that it was
not without effect. At least ten London hospitals were
founded between 1740 and 1760,[1] and various attempts
were made to secure a better provision for the poor.
The project of a foundling hospital had originated as
early as 1708, was kept alive by several persons who
remembered it in their wills, and at length, owing mainly
to Thomas Coram,[2] a merchant captain, resulted in the
opening of a house for this purpose in 1739. But so
many of the children died in the first year—66 out of
136—that steps were at once taken to erect a building
outside London. The popularity of this institution
promised for a time to rival that once enjoyed by the
charity schools ; large sums were raised by Handel, who
offered his services as a musician and presented to the
governors an organ and the score of his *Messiah* ; and
Parliament for many years voted sums amounting in all
to over half a million on condition that all infants under
a certain age should be received. Institutions of this
nature had long existed on the Continent—fortunately
for Rousseau, who was in the habit of sending his children
there as soon as they were born ; but public opinion was
not prepared to sanction such a practice when it showed
signs of developing in England. In 1771 all assistance
from the Treasury was withdrawn ; and admission to
the hospital was thenceforth regulated according to the
funds available by a monthly ballot.[3]

Two men now come before us, distinguished for their
endeavours to ameliorate respectively the condition
of paupers and criminals—Jonas Hanway and John
Howard. The former was a merchant who, after various

---

[1] Colquhoun's *Police of the Metropolis*, p. 573.
[2] Hence the " Tattycoram " of Dickens's *Little Dorrit.*
[3] Pugh's *Remarkable Occurrences in the Life of Jonas Hanway*,
1787, pp. 155–168,

adventures in Russia and Persia, had returned home in 1750 to recruit his health and do—as he quaintly expressed it—" as much good to himself and others as he was able." In 1758 be became a Governor for life of the Foundling Hospital, where he may have met Oglethorpe, who was, or at least had been, one of the General Committee ; but he had already won distinction as the executor, if not the originator, of philanthropic ideas. His usual method was to take up a scheme which had been suggested but not carried out ; to publish a pamphlet in its favour ; and then to bring together those whose interest he had aroused. In this way he founded the Marine Society projected by Fowler Walker—a society which was the means of obtaining and fitting out for the Navy during the Seven Years' War over 10,000 idle youths and " vagabond boys "—and also enabled Robert Dingley to realise the project he had long entertained of a Magdalene home. There was, however, one scheme—" the most arduous and splendid of all his public undertakings "—which from start to finish was entirely his own work. In order to qualify himself as an authority on pauperism, Hanway undertook an exhaustive inspection of workhouses both in England and abroad ; and he soon discovered that, in his own country at least, the fate of parish infants was too often the same, whether they were nominally taken care of or were left to die. When the facts he had collected and published were met with incredulity, he did not hesitate to give the name of every parish officer under whom many infants had died. As a temporary expedient, he contrived to get a number of these victims transferred to the Foundling Hospital ; and at last, after labours continued " for day after day and year after year," he succeeded in making it compulsory, first that every London parish should keep an annual register of infants received, discharged and dead, and then that all infants should be sent a certain distance out of London, there to be nursed under guardians appointed for the purpose till they were six months old. The success of this measure as shown by the registers was quite phenomenal, and the poor are said to have called it " The Act for keeping children alive." Many other projects almost equally beneficial were initiated or promoted by this noble worker, whose industry is attested by more than sixty books and pamphlets, some of them in two or even three volumes. At the time of his death in 1786 he had a Bill before Parliament for the protection of young chimney-sweepers ; and, unwilling that even death should put an end to his usefulness, he expressed a wish that his body should be dissected.[1]

The task of prison reform, attempted by Bray in 1702 and by Oglethorpe in 1729, was carried on by James Neild when he came to London as a jeweller's assistant in 1760. It was not till 1770 that Neild started in business for himself, but by that time he had visited many English and even French prisons. In 1772, as the result of an eloquent pulpit address, over £80 was collected for the rescue of imprisoned debtors. An appeal to the general public added largely to this sum ; and by May 1773, when a society was formed with Neild as treasurer for the discharge of prisoners whose debts did not exceed £10, nearly 10,000 of these captives had been set free.[2] In this year a Bill to provide gaolers with salaries paid out of the rates, and so to put an end to the detention of prisoners for non-payment of fees, was brought into Parliament by a member named Popham.

---

[1] Pugh's *Life of Jonas Hanway*, pp. 119, 141, 169, 185, 200, 211. Hanway was the first person to use an umbrella in London, and persisted in that practice for nearly thirty years before it became general. His hardships as a " martyr to the Persian trade " had made him very thin and so susceptible to cold that he wore fur-lined clothes and usually three pairs of stockings. Cheerful but not mirthful, he always left his companions when they became " too merry to be happy or to let me be happy." Having no great opinion of the art of conversation as practised in English society, he had his reception rooms so curiously decorated as to provide subjects for talk during the time which preceded card-playing.

[2] Nicols's *Literary Illustrations*, ii. 689.

Meanwhile, Howard, quite unconnected with this movement and merely in the course of his duties as High Sheriff of Bedfordshire, was entering on the career as a prison reformer which was to make his name known and revered all over Europe. As he published two large works on the subject, and as his life has been more than once written, the cruelties and abuses he brought to light are comparatively well known; but one case may be mentioned as showing what evils of this nature could be charged to an Anglican prelate as late as 1768. The gaol of Ely, which belonged to the bishop, had been allowed to fall into decay ; but, instead of its being repaired, the cheaper but barbarous device had been adopted of chaining the prisoners on their backs to the floor with a spiked iron collar round their necks and a heavy iron bar over their legs. At the instance of one of the magistrates who appealed to the King, Bishop Mawson, an aged but very wealthy prelate, had been compelled to rebuild his prison six years before Howard visited it in 1774 ; but the philanthropist found it in a deplorable state—an unsalaried keeper dependent on the fruits of extortion, no fixed allowance of food, no provision for sick debtors, no straw for bedding, and a courtyard for felons without water and traversed by an open sewer. Bishop Mawson had died in 1770 ; but his successor seems to have paid no attention to the strictures of Howard who, when he visited this gaol for the last time in 1782, found that there was now no separate accommodation for debtors and felons. Popham's Bill, after Howard had given evidence in its support, became law in 1774 ; and another measure was passed requiring the walls and ceilings of prisons to be whitewashed at least once a year and the rooms to be properly ventilated and regularly cleaned.[1]

Both Hanway and Howard were deeply religious men—the one a Churchman, the other an Independent;

[1] Howard's *State of the Prisons in England and Wales*, 4th edition, p. 291.

but their piety, unlike that of their predecessors and successors, bore the impress of no particular school. When Hanway returned to England in 1750, such religious enthusiasm as ventured to assert itself was of the Methodist type ; and this takes us back in unbroken sequence to the High Church movement which had culminated in Anne's reign. The long life of John Wesley dates from 1703, the second year of Queen Anne, and both he and his brother Charles—not to mention Whitefield—were conspicuous at first only for their Anglican zeal. Their father, the rector of Hepworth in Lincolnshire, though himself at one time a Nonconformist, had warmly defended the Schism' Act which was intended to put down Dissenting schools ; and the society, nicknamed " The Methodists," which they formed at Oxford, was modelled on the devotional societies instituted in 1678,[1] one of which indeed their father had established in his parish. John Wesley was wont in those days to look for guidance to the Nonjuror, William Law, and, when in Georgia, was so faithful to his master's teaching that he excluded one Dissenter from communion unless he would consent to be re-baptised and denied to another the rites of burial.[2] In 1738, however, he experienced the completion of a change from sacramental to personal religion which had begun three years earlier through his intercourse with some of the Moravian sect ; and thenceforth he devoted himself to propagating throughout Britain the tenet of conversion or the " new birth." This dogma, avowed in the theology of the Church but discountenanced in its ritual, had fallen into general neglect, and the clergy soon refused to tolerate within their walls the popular excitement and panic to which its assertion too often gave rise ; but in response to the Methodist agitation, conducted in the open air, in meeting-houses and especially by Whitefield in Lady Huntingdon's drawing-room, it

---

[1] See p. 19.
[2] Southey's *John Wesley*, i. 96.

slowly but steadily revived. At the outset of his mission in 1738 Wesley could mention only ten clergymen whom he believed to be Evangelical preachers. In 1764, when he sought to form a union of such incumbents, he wrote to about fifty, only three of whom, however, replied. Nineteen years later, we find him writing in his Journal, " The tide is now turned ; so that I have more invitations to preach in churches than I can accept of"; and soon after his death in 1791 the number of parish ministers akin to him in spirit, if not in doctrine—for he had long ceased to be a Calvinist—was estimated at five hundred.[1]

What concerns us here is the effect produced within the Church by this re-kindling of zeal ; for few of the Methodists themselves had the wealth or social position which would have enabled them to take the initiative in philanthropic work. Wesley indeed had a theory of education, or at least of moral discipline, which he sought to carry out to the letter in a school, intended mainly for the sons of his itinerant preachers, which he built at Kingswood, near Bristol, in 1748. The twenty-eight boys selected for this experiment were all under twelve years of age. They were to begin their day at four in the morning with an hour for private and another for public prayer ; when not occupied with their lessons— which accounted for eight hours—they were to sing, or meditate, or walk, or work in the garden, but were on no account to play ; they were always to be under supervision, were to have no holidays, and no boy was to leave the school, even for a day, till he left it for good. All went well at first, the school being " a resemblance of the household above " ; but another sort of "resemblance" was suggested by its condition three years later. Only eleven children remained ; four or five of these had become " wicked " ; the rest were becoming " wilder and wilder " ; and not only did they all play, but one of the masters played with them. Wesley can hardly have mended

---

[1] Tyerman's *Wesley*, ii. 509 ; iii. 390 ; Lecky, iii. 124, 125.

matters in 1757 by appointing as matron a bigamist or rather a " trigamist " ; for Sarah Ryan, though "unquestionably a converted woman," was still so embarrassed by her past as to have three living husbands. The next glimpse we have of the school is in 1783, when Adam Clarke—who was to rise to distinction as a Methodist scholar—declared it to be " perfectly disorganised " and " the worst he had ever seen." The founder of this singular institution seems, however, to have succeeded at last in realising his ideal ; for in 1786 he found it "in excellent order " ; and three years later he thus records his satisfaction : " I went over to Kingswood : sweet recess ! where everything is now just as I wish." [1]

The greatest service rendered to humanity by the Evangelical revival was the abolition of the slave trade ; and the first man to devote himself to this object was now entering on his task. Sir John Hawkins, the Elizabethan sea-captain, won the distinction in his own age and the infamy in ours of having initiated the English slave trade, when in 1563 he captured some three hundred negroes at Sierra Leone, shipped them across the Atlantic and sold them to the Spaniards of San Domingo ; and it is a curious satire on the entry of Englishmen into this traffic, no less unwise than cruel, that the two principal ships with which he sailed on his second expedition in 1564 were called the *Solomon* and the *Jesus*. Hawkins indeed so little anticipated the verdict of posterity that he assumed as his crest " a manacled Moor." The England of Queen Elizabeth did not succeed in obtaining a permanent foothold in the New World ; but in 1620, fourteen years after its foundation by Captain John Smith, Virginia received from a Dutch warship its first batch of negroes [2] ; and these twenty slaves were the nucleus of a black population which in 1750 numbered about a quarter of a million. At the Peace of Utrecht

---

[1] Tyerman's *Wesley*, ii. 10, 121, 286–288 ; iii. 398–400.
[2] Bancroft's *History of the United States*, 13th edition, i. 176.

in 1713 the right of supplying Spanish America with slave labour was transferred from France to Great Britain. The contract was for an annual consignment of 4800 and continued till 1739 ; and during those years, when she monopolised both her own and the Spanish market, Britain gained a supremacy, which was never lost, as the great slave-trading Power. Chatham during the Seven Years' War made it a principal object of his policy to extend the trade, which was regarded as the mainstay of our shipping ; and about 1770, on the eve of American Independence, it was prosecuted from Liverpool, London, Bristol and Lancaster with a fleet of 192 vessels. In 1791 the total annual exportation of negroes from West Africa was 74,000 ; and of these, 38,000 were the property of British merchants.

It cannot be necessary to enlarge on so familiar a theme as the diabolical character of the slave trade, which indeed may be inferred from the fact that only fifty per cent. of its victims lived to become effective labourers. Readers of such a book as Thackeray's "Virginians" may, however, be surprised to learn that the British slave-owners, at all events in the West Indies, had the reputation, even with their own countrymen, of being more merciless than those of any other nation.[1] The reason may have been, as suggested by Dean Tucker, that our planters had a greater number of slaves than their foreign rivals and consequently were more exposed to the danger of revolt ; that more of them were absentees, leaving their estates to be managed by overseers ; and that the British sugar islands had much greater powers of self-government than were permitted to those of France and Spain.

There had always been protests against slavery—not

---

[1] Burke, Paley and Tucker agree on this point. Sir Spenser St. John, however, in his *Hayti or The Black Republic*, p. 31, says that French slavery was much the worst and Spanish slavery the mildest of all.

to mention the slave trade—since Pope Leo X denounced it as an outrage on " not the Christian religion only, but human nature itself "; and it is curious to observe how variously both the institution and the means of recruiting it were regarded by religious people in all but the last twenty years of the eighteenth century. Berkeley, when he resided in America, owned slaves and intimated his dissent from a prevalent opinion that their conversion would entitle them to freedom. Oglethorpe considered slavery " a horrid crime," and he and his fellow trustees forbade its introduction into Georgia ; but Whitefield, thinking slave labour essential to the cultivation of lands belonging to his Orphan House,[1] procured or helped to procure the repeal of this law in 1749 ; and amongst the " goods and chattels " which he bequeathed to the Countess of Huntingdon were a large number of slaves. Lord Dartmouth, the Countess's intimate friend, nicknamed " The Psalm-Singer " and celebrated by Cowper as " one who wears a coronet and prays," declared, when Secretary of State in 1775, that the colonies could not be allowed " to check or discourage in any degree a trade so beneficial to the nation " ; and the Society for the Propagation of the Gospel not only owned an estate in Barbadoes which was cultivated by slaves, but refused as late as 1784 the earnest recommendation of Bishop Porteus that means should be provided for their Christian instruction.[2] The Bishop had consequently to form a separate society for the conversion of negroes in the West Indies. On the other hand, a full exposure of the slave trade was made by Newton, the well-known Evangelical divine ; and his pamphlet was the more

[1] Clarkson is quite mistaken in saying that it was Whitefield's successors in the management of the Orphan House who " soon after his death . . . bought slaves and these in unusual numbers."— *History of the Abolition of the Slave Trade*, i. 171.

[2] One of the missionaries even attempted to prove that " the African Trade for Negro Slaves is consistent with the principles of humanity and revealed religion."—Hoare's *Granville Sharp*, p. 262, and Appendix No. IX.

effective as he himself had been nine years in the trade and for the last three of these had been captain of a slave-ship.[1] Wesley in his Journal refers to "that execrable sum of all villainies, commonly called the slave trade." In 1774 he published his "Thoughts on Slavery"; and in 1791, writing just before the lapse into unconsciousness which preceded his death, he exhorted Wilberforce to include in his attack, not only the slave trade, but "even American slavery, the vilest that ever saw the sun." Hutcheson, Principal Robertson, Adam Smith, Dr. Johnson, Dean Tucker, Paley, Bishops Warburton, Porteus and Watson, all expressed themselves in one form or another to the same effect as Wesley [2]; but none of them endeavoured to restrain in practice the power of slave merchants or owners; and it was reserved for a young man, then comparatively unknown, to attempt, and in some measure to accomplish, this task.

The early career of Granville Sharp has some resemblance to that of James Neild; for, though his grandfather had been Archbishop of York and his father was Archdeacon of Northumberland, he was apprenticed in 1750, at the age of fifteen, to a linen-draper in London, and continued in that employment till in 1758 he obtained some post preliminary to a clerkship in the Ordnance Office. During those years he acquired sufficient command of Greek and Hebrew to win for him the reputation of a Biblical scholar, and—what is more singular—sufficient legal knowledge to vindicate the claim to a dormant peerage of another linen-draper, the father-in-law of his first employer.

He soon had reasons of a more public kind for continuing his study of the law. Slave owners who brought any of their human property to England had

---

[1] *Thoughts upon the African Slave Trade*, 1788, pp. 3, 4.

[2] Bancroft's *History of the United States*, i. 172; iii. 409, 416, 426, 448; Lecky, ii. 248, 249; Tyerman's *Whitefield*, ii. 169, 206; Tyerman's *Wesley*, iii. 61, 115, 183; Hodgson's *Bishop Porteus*, pp. 85–90; *Life of Wilberforce*, i. 297.

at one time great difficulty in keeping it intact, especially as the idea prevailed here, as in America, that the slave could emancipate himself by becoming a Christian. Unwilling to risk the consequences of an adverse decision in the courts, they sought and obtained in 1729 from the law officers of the Crown—one of whom was the future Lord Hardwicke—a full recognition of their rights; and under cover of this opinion there sprang up " a slave trade carried on in the streets of Liverpool and London." Not only were fugitive slaves advertised for in the newspapers, and rewards offered for their capture, but slaves who had not run away were openly disposed of, with other property of their masters, at auction sales. An incident which occurred in 1765 directed the attention of Sharp to this abuse; and seven years later, after a course of litigation which consumed the whole of his leisure and small private means, he had the satisfaction of hearing Lord Mansfield deliver the famous judgment that slavery could not be enforced at law within the bounds of England. At a subsequent time we find him co-operating with Oglethorpe in an attempt to procure a similar decision against the impressment of seamen, and re-publishing, with an introduction, the General's very popular work, " The Sailor's Advocate."[1]

Meanwhile a singular coincidence had brought him into touch with Anthony Benezet, a Quaker schoolmaster, who was then the slave's best friend in America; for, coming across one of Benezet's publications on a London bookstall, he had reprinted it; and shortly afterwards Benezet, unaware of the compliment that had been paid to *his* pamphlet, reprinted one of Sharp's.

[1] This is the last we shall see of Oglethorpe, who died at the age of eighty-nine in 1785. " His faculties were as bright as ever and his eye was undimmed; ever ' heroic, romantic and full of the old gallantry,' he was like the sound of the lyre as it still vibrates after the spirit of the age that sweeps its strings has passed away."—Bancroft, iii. 448.

The English philanthropist was soon in frequent communication with those of a like spirit in America, including Benjamin Franklin as well as Benezet ; and, finding that the colonists in general disapproved of the slave trade and were anxious to have it abolished, he encouraged them to disown in this matter the authority of Parliament, as they had already disowned it in matters of taxation, and to address their petitions solely to the King. On the outbreak of war with the colonies in 1775 he obtained leave of absence from the Ordnance Office, and ultimately resigned his post ; but it must have been a grievous disappointment to him, if he ever heard of it, that in the Declaration of American Independence as originally drafted there was an anti-slavery clause, believed to have been written by, or at least borrowed from, Paine,[1] which was subsequently struck out. Having sacrificed his capital to the African, and his salary to the American, cause, he was dependent on a provision made for him by two of his brothers[2] till in 1787 he entered into possession of an estate in Essex which had been left to him by General Oglethorpe's widow.

The Yorkshire agitation of 1780 for parliamentary reform was actively supported by Sharp, who advocated annual as opposed to triennial parliaments ; and in 1787, being a zealous Churchman and rigidly orthodox,

---

[1] Paine was all but the first writer in America to attack the slave trade, which he called " the most horrid of all traffics, that of human flesh," and his essay, which appeared in the *Pennsylvanian Journal*, led to the formation of the first American anti-slavery society. In 1779 he wrote the preamble to an Act which abolished slavery in the State of Pennsylvania. His services to this cause have been persistently ignored.—Conway's *Life of Paine*, pp. x, 41, 52, 80, 154.

[2] The Sharps had a genius for philanthropy. Their father had maintained in Northumberland at his own expense at least five unsectarian schools. The eldest son, John, who succeeded him as Archdeacon, was believed to have spent some £10,000 in converting Bamborough Castle into a combination of school, hospital and lighthouse ; and James and William, an iron merchant and a surgeon, who thought it an honour to support Granville, were both eminently philanthropic.

he was the chief means of obtaining the consecration in England of an independent American episcopate. But he had still work to do as the patron of several hundred slaves to whom Lord Mansfield's judgment had opened no better career than that of begging in the London streets. Their number was increased after the war by the discharge of negro soldiers and sailors ; and there were rumours that Parliament might prohibit the landing of slaves from the colonies, except under security that their masters would take them back. Alarmed by the prospect of a measure which would extinguish the freedom he had won for such refugees, Sharp undertook, partly at their own suggestion, to establish for them a settlement in Africa ; and the result was the colony of Sierra Leone, founded mainly through his exertions in 1787, and, twenty years later, taken over by the Crown.[1]

Allusion has been made from a political standpoint to the economic expansion which took place in England during the last quarter of the eighteenth century—an expansion so vast that it is commonly known as the industrial revolution. The term is misleading if it is taken to mean that industry was not organised on the present basis till mechanical invention had suddenly enlarged its scope. Capitalist production, the dependence of workmen on an employer who supplies the raw material and disposes of it when manufactured, was no new thing ; and in some cases the artisans had even ceased before 1760 to work in their own homes. Adam Smith said that all over Europe only one workman in twenty was independent. The staple industry of England had for centuries been the manufacture of woollen cloth. The chief centres were at Norwich and in the south-west at Frome, Stroud, Taunton and Stourbridge. Cloth of a coarser kind was made in the West Riding of Yorkshire ; and the cotton manufacture, small as it then was,

[1] Hoare's *Granville Sharp*, passim.

had its headquarters at Manchester and Bolton. At Norwich and also in the south-west district Defoe in 1725 found many rich merchants owning a considerable number of looms [1]; and, though most of the work was done in dwelling-houses, some of it was executed in large sheds under the eye of a master. What the industrial revolution did was to make general this "large scale industry," to concentrate it in localities and ultimately in premises adapted to the new machines, and in consequence to alter—one might almost say, to reverse—its geographical distribution. [2]

The earlier phase of this movement was governed by two factors—the discovery, or rather the re-discovery, about 1750 that coal could be used instead of charcoal for the smelting of iron, and the substitution in the textile industries from 1769 of water-driven machinery for hand labour. The iron-works, hitherto confined to woodland districts such as the Weald of Sussex and little encouraged owing to their "voragious" consumption of timber, [3] now shifted to the midland and northern coalfields ; Staffordshire, where Wedgwood was making his famous stoneware, began to assume its present aspect of the "Black Country"; and the cotton trade of Manchester, to which the new inventions were first applied, enormously increased. Meanwhile the cutting of canals, which began in 1761, by connecting the various

[1] As early as the sixteenth century, the ". wealthy clothiers " of Somerset, Gloucestershire and Devon had " mightily increased, their houses frequented like kings' courts."—Webb, *Trade Unionism*, p. 28.

[2] Hobson's *Evolution of Modern Capitalism*, p. 59 ; Meredith's *Economic History*, p. 621.

[3] Every ton of pig-iron required for its production four loads of timber converted into charcoal, and every ton of bar-iron required three additional loads. Timber was not only essential to ship-building, but was long preferred in London for domestic purposes to coal, which was thought to be poisonous and bad for the complexion. The Sussex iron-mills developed with the use of cannon, and were at the height of their prosperity towards the end of Elizabeth's reign, when, according to Raleigh, the Spaniards fought us at sea with guns of our own make. There is a most interesting account of these mills in Smiles's *Industrial Biography*, chap. ii.

centres and bringing them within easy reach of London
and the sea, greatly stimulated production ; and finally
a new era of expansion was opened after 1791, when steam
as a motive power in industry began to supplant water.
Weaving continued, on the whole, to be a domestic
occupation till certain improvements on the power-
loom effected in 1803 brought it very gradually into
general use ; but spinning, especially cotton spinning,
had been confined mainly to factories before the close
of the century.

Statistics are our best resource if we wish to realise
the magnitude of such changes as these. Before 1751
the largest decennial increase of population had been
about five per cent. ; but from that period, and especially
from 1781, it rose rapidly till in 1801 it had become
14 per cent. In 1783 commodities were exported to
the value of £14,000,000 and imported to that of
£11,000,000. In 1800 the values were respectively
£34,000,000 and £28,000,000.[1]

We have seen that this expansion had been anticipated
on a small scale in the latter years of the previous century,
when various new industries were established owing to
an immigration of foreign skilled labour ; and the Church,
being confronted in both cases with the same problem,
sought to dispose of it in the same way. In 1692 William
and Mary had issued a proclamation against vice ;
and a similar proclamation was issued by George III
in 1787. In that year as in 1692 was instituted a Society
for the Reformation of Manners. Now as then there
was the same enthusiasm for the instruction, not wholly
religious, of the young and for missions. In place of
charity schools we have Sunday schools ; and by way
of supplement to the Societies for Promoting Christian
Knowledge and for Propagating the Gospel, which still
flourished, we have the Religious Tract Society and the

---

[1] *Political History of England.* x. 268 ; H. de B. Gibbin's *Industry
in England* ; Toynbee's *Industrial Revolution*, chap. viii.

London Missionary Society. Church building on a much larger scale than that of 1712 was indeed deferred till the close of the war; but as early as 1798 Arthur Young advocated the erection of a large number of churches in the form of a theatre, with galleries and boxes for the wealthier people and benches and thick mats for the poor.[1] And in William Wilberforce, the intimate friend of Pitt, the later revival had a lay representative no less devout and energetic and far more influential than "the pious Robert Nelson." Clapham, with its "villa-cinctured common," has been called the Mecca of Evangelicalism; for here resided not only Wilberforce, but his brother-in-law, James Stephen; Henry Thornton, whose father, John, the associate of Hanway, had "anticipated the disposition and pursuits of the succeeding generation"; Zachary Macaulay, Lord Teignmouth and Granville Sharp. We shall find, however, that this revival of religion was, as one would expect from its antecedents, a far bigger affair than its prototype, and that, whilst the earlier movement had seen its best days before the Peace of 1713, the later movement was still far from its maturity at the close of the Napoleonic War in 1815.

The Sunday school of that age was a more substantial institution than that which still perpetuates its name, and the credit of having originated it is justly ascribed, to Robert Raikes. It had indeed occurred to others that Sunday might be utilised for teaching children, and here and there the idea had actually taken shape; but Raikes was the first to advocate as well as to practise it, and it has been truly said of him that he "raised Sunday teaching from a fortuitous rarity into a universal system." Raikes, like Oglethorpe, began his philanthropic career as a voluntary inspector of prisons, and was thus led on in the same way from the punishment of debt and crime to the means of their prevention.

[1] Mr. and Mrs. Hammond, *The Town Labourer*, p. 234.

Finding that the streets of Gloucester, where he owned and edited the principal newspaper, were made hideous every Sunday by a host of profane and noisy children, he first induced some of them to accompany him to early morning service and then paid a shilling each to four women for teaching them the Church Catechism. This was the origin of his four schools ; and, after the scheme had been in operation for more than three years, he began in November 1783 to set forth its advantages in the *Gloucester Journal,* a medium which he had previously employed to expose the condition of the county and city gaols. He must have been astonished as well as gratified with the success of his effort. Within nine months Wesley was writing in his Journal, " I find these schools springing up wherever I go." [1] In 1785 a Sunday School Society was formed, Hanway and Henry Thornton being amongst its promoters. In two years it had helped to establish more than two hundred schools, and the total number of scholars then receiving instruction was estimated at 250,000.

The new institution had the benefit of some wise but friendly criticism from Dr. Beilby Porteus, Bishop of Chester and subsequently of London, the first prelate to countenance, if not quite to identify himself with, the Evangelical movement. He urged that great care should be taken to maintain Sunday as a day of pleasant rest by allowing the scholars " sufficient time for cheerful conversation and free intercourse with each other, and above all for enjoying the fresh and wholesome air and sunshine in the fields or gardens with their relatives and friends." The latter part of this advice may have been a counsel of perfection so far as the great industrial centres were concerned ; but the promoters of the scheme appear to have acted on Wesley's maxim that to work is to play. According to the rules adopted at Gloucester and afterwards widely extended, the hours

---

[1] Tyerman's *Wesley,* iii. 414.

of schooling were from eight to half-past ten in the morning and from half-past five to eight in the evening, and the children were expected to attend in the interval both the morning and the afternoon service. When we consider that many of the pupils were employed in factories for twelve or fourteen hours a day, one cannot wonder that certain bribes were needed to procure so great a sacrifice of their Sunday leisure—such as a hat and coat for the boys, a Sunday hat for the girls, sweets and gingerbread, and, above all, an occasional penny, which last, said a grave divine, " operates very power-fully." It should, however, be remembered that for most of the children the difficulty was not to repeat the catechism, but to learn to read it ; and some parents, thinking rightly enough that one day in seven was not sufficient for general education, provided additional instruction for their unhappy offspring at the breakfast and dinner hours during the week. The Sunday-school teacher was in those days a paid official, receiving a shilling to two shillings a day. Unpaid teaching was introduced by the Methodists—who took a great interest in the movement—as early as 1785 at Bolton,[1] and in 1810 had become general at Gloucester. These schools were too limited in scope to have the same social value as the charity schools ; but they covered a far wider area, and are said to have raised enormously the stan-dard of demeanour and conduct. An employer, when questioned as to the behaviour of the children in his works, declared that the change could not have been more extraordinary had they been transformed from the shape of wolves and tigers to that of men ; and Adam Smith said, " No plan has promised to effect a change of manners with equal ease and simplicity since the days of the Apostles." [2]

[1] Tyerman's *Wesley*, iii. 501.
[2] Gregory's *Robert Raikes, a History of the Origin of Sunday Schools,* passim.

It may be supposed that no two forces in Europe could be less likely to come into contact than the French Revolution and an English Sunday School ; but we shall find that even in this sphere the Revolution made itself felt ; and there can be no better illustration of the pervasive and ineluctable influence which was to be exerted by that great movement on all the activities which have passed before us in this survey.

CHAPTER I

WAR AND REPRESSION, 1789–1802

IT will probably appear from what has been said in the opening pages of this work that there was little scope in England for the French Revolution as a creative force. The democratic agitation which elsewhere sprang up under its influence, and notably in Scotland, had here been in progress for twenty years ; there was nothing new in the demand for annual parliaments and universal suffrage ; and in England as well as in France political speculation had been dominated by abstract notions and the idea of natural rights. But Englishmen, though they had little to learn from the Revolution, were more or less susceptible to its spirit ; and the movement for parliamentary reform, which latterly had been but a sluggish stream, assumed a very different character when it had been joined by the torrent of enthusiasm from Paris.

Hitherto comprehensiveness rather than equality had been the watchword of reform, the object being to broaden the basis of a constitution believed to be almost ideal.- Cartwright regarded the English constitution—of which, as he conceived it, universal suffrage was merely a lapsed feature—as constructed throughout on the principles of the common law, and the excellence of that law could not be better " expressed than by its well-known definition of being the perfection of human

reason." Priestley had, indeed, a quarrel with those
who thus extolled the constitution, but only because
they thought it so good that it could not be improved.
Far from objecting to hereditary kingship, he thought
its advantage, if not its necessity, had been proved by
experience; and he suggested that the higher offices
should be reserved for " persons of considerable fortune "
and that " the lowest classes of the people " should have
votes only " in the nomination of the lowest officers." [2]
Price was even more moderate, holding that " an
hereditary council consisting of men of the first rank "
might be a useful check on the representatives of the
people. [3] Very different was the language of Thomas
Paine, whose " Rights of Man " was adopted as their
text-book by the societies which had been formed or
reorganised in sympathy with the Revolution. Had
Paine been disposed to congratulate his fellow-country-
men—he was an American and a French citizen as well
as a British subject—on the excellence of their constitution, he could not have done so, for he denied that
they had one; but he had nothing but contempt for
the " strange chaos " of customs and traditions which
passed under that name. England in his opinion was
practically a republic—a shapeless and corrupt republic
which would need to be rebuilt on a regular plan. The
Crown, ever since its functions had been engrossed by
Ministers, was " a metaphor shown at the Tower for
sixpence or a shilling a piece " ; Parliament was a
burlesque of hereditary wisdom and " the filth of rotten
boroughs " ; and there is a premonition of social as well
as political upheaval in Paine's allusions to the Game
Laws, and to the law of primogeniture as one which
permits all the children of a nobleman except the
eldest son to be " cast like orphans on a parish to

[1] *Life and Correspondence*, i. 90.
[2] *First Principles of Government*, pp. 16–18.
[3] *Civil Liberty*, p. 12.

be provided for by the public, but at a greater charge."[1]

The difference between the earlier and the later agitation for reform is, however, by no means exhausted when we have seen that the one was constitutional and the other revolutionary in spirit. There was an element of scepticism in the later movement which gave it a wider range and was indeed to make it an epoch in the emancipation of thought. Anything that had yet appeared of this nature amounted to no more than an irreligious or heretical bias. The man who did most to secure the return of Wilkes for Middlesex was Horne— afterwards Horne Tooke—the vicar of Brentford. Horne had so little respect for his orders that he thought it necessary to apologise for having " suffered the infectious hand of a bishop to be waved over me, whose imposition, like the sop given to Judas, is only a signal for the devil to enter "; and, on leaving Paris in 1767, he asked Wilkes to take charge of the lay garments he had worn on the Continent, with the remark, " They too as well as yourself are outlawed in England and on the same account—their superior worth."[2] Two other leading reformers were also beneficed clergymen ; but Chrystopher Wyvil had become a great landowner when he organised the Yorkshire agitation in 1779, and Jebb, the associate

---

[1] It has been well said (*Encycl. Brit.*) that those who know the *Rights of Man* " only by hearsay as the work of a furious incendiary will be surprised at the dignity, force and temperance of the style." Paine is one of the few examples in our history of a man who has been accepted by posterity at the valuation put upon him by un-scrupulous opponents during his life. The task of rehabilitation was successfully accomplished by Mr. Moncur Conway nearly thirty years ago ; and the excuse of ignorance can no longer be pleaded for the depreciation of one who associated on equal terms with the leading statesmen of America and France, who was a philanthropist, a man of science and an inventor as well as a politician, and whose essays and pamphlets are probably the most influential of their kind that ever issued from the press. Mr. Conway's *Life of Thomas Paine* appeared in 1892, and had been anticipated to some extent by Mr. J. M. Robertson in his *Thomas Paine : An Investigation*, published in 1888. [2] Stephens's *Memoirs of Horne Tooke*, i. 76, 83.

E

of Cartwright, had by that time deserted divinity for medicine. Price was, and Priestley [1] had been, an Independent minister ; both of them, as well as Wyvil and Jebb, were Unitarians ; and Cartwright might have been characterised, like one of greater fame, as " an honorary member of all religions," having already professed thirty, and seeing no reason why he should not yet profess thirty more.

The orthodox had more reason to be alarmed in 1789, and for the origin of their fears we must return, by way of Locke, to Paine. Locke had based, or rather had staked, his system of ethics on the existence of a God so interested in human progress that He had revealed for its guidance certain principles and rules of conduct ; but the acceptance of this revelation was with him a matter of rational belief, not of simple or mystical faith ; and consequently, if the revelation should be found to contain statements contrary to reason, it could not be accepted as divine. This was the inference drawn, not by Locke himself, but by his unwelcome disciple, Toland, the first of a line of thinkers known as Deists. Deism, though politically barren in England, developed quite another character in France, where its arguments were effectively used by Voltaire to discredit a religion which had become the patron of every political and social abuse.[2] It was in this form, as part of the general unrest excited by the French Revolution, that Deism now returned to its original home. That Paine had adopted the tenets of this school [3] must have been

[1] " Ce penseur bizarre, cet héretique de profession, déterministe, matérialiste, négateur de la divinité de Jésus, et cependant, prêtre chrétien, d'ailleurs historien fécond, agitateur politique, grand chimiste, ' Priestley-Protée.' "—Halévy's *Radicalisme Philosophique*, i. 31. " Proteus-Priestley " was Bentham's epithet.

[2] " There is not one of the arguments of the French philosophers in the eighteenth century which cannot be found in the English school of the beginning of the century."—Morley's *Voltaire*, p. 91.

[3] One of the strangest articles of " the Paine mythology " is that Paine was an atheist. " Religion," he said, " has two principal enemies, Fanaticism and Infidelity."

apparent to most readers of the " Rights of Man " ; but he was not content to leave the matter in doubt ; and in 1794 and 1796 he published in two parts " The Age of Reason "—a work which still retains some of the immense popularity it achieved, and is remarkable not only as a distinct advance in Biblical criticism, the standpoint being rather that of legend than imposture, but as insisting that theology implies a conception of our earth irreconcilable with its utter insignificance as disclosed by science. " The two beliefs cannot be held together in the same mind, and he who thinks that he believes both has thought but little of either." Paine had some pretensions to be an astronomer, having seriously studied that subject in his youth ; and, writing more than twenty years before the discoveries of Herschel, he put forward the conjecture that each of the fixed stars " is also a sun, round which another system of worlds or planets, though too remote for us to discover, performs its revolutions." [1]

When we consider the notoriety of Paine's writings, the cheap editions that were issued and the efforts made by Government to suppress them, there can be no doubt that the Revolution had a considerable following amongst the small tradesmen and more intelligent mechanics. But the populace whose anti-foreign passions and prejudices had been fully aroused, were as far as possible from idolising Paine as in 1763 and 1768 they had idolised Wilkes. The cry had then been ' Wilkes and Liberty.' It was now ' Church and King ' ; and when rioting occurred, it was not the enemies of reform that suffered but its friends. The worst outbreak was caused by a meeting at Birmingham in 1791 to commemorate the taking of the Bastille ; and Priestley, whose house, books, manuscripts and laboratory were destroyed in the commotion, declared that " the same bad spirit

---

[1] Conway's *Life of Paine*, pp. 234, 243 ; Bury's *History of Freedom of Thought*, p. 170.

pervaded the whole kingdom." Next year there was a similar disturbance on a small scale at Manchester; and an attempt to disseminate the " Rights of Man " at Leeds resulted in Paine's effigy being paraded and burnt, as it was also on the fifth of November throughout Northumberland and Durham.[1]

The Sedition and Treason Bills of 1795, which prohibited unauthorised public meetings and brought speaking and writing within the law of treason, were much resented by friends of the Revolution in London; and the Whigs, believing that the same temper prevailed amongst the freeholders of Yorkshire—the largest constituency in England and one which the growth of the woollen manufacture had " multiplied beyond all precedent "—called upon the High Sheriff to summon a meeting at York, and on his refusal endeavoured to forestall their opponents by an informal gathering on Tuesday, December 1. "Come forth, then, from your looms "—so ran their appeal—" ye honest and industrious clothiers; quit the labours of your fields for one day, ye stout and independent yeomen; come forth in the spirit of your ancestors and show you deserve to be free." Wilberforce, one of the two members for the county, was then at Westminster. On his way to church on Sunday morning he received word that his presence was needed to counteract this design; and, having started at once, despite his reluctance to travel on Sunday, he drove into York just as the meeting was being held and succeeded in making it a triumph, not for the Opposition, but for the Government. His strength lay—where one would hardly have expected to find it— in the industrial centres of Leeds, Halifax, Wakefield, Huddersfield and Bradford. Three thousand weavers from the West Riding, mounted on the ponies which carried their cloth to market, were said to have ridden

---

[1] Lecky, vi. 474; Veitch's *Genesis of Parliamentary Reform*, p. 233; Trevelyan's *Lord Grey of the Reform Bill*, p. 63.

through Halton turnpike on the previous day; and they were long known as " Billymen " on account of the enthusiasm they had shown on this occasion for " Billy Pitt." At Leeds " the bells were ringing till midnight " in celebration of the event, and " Twenty King's men to one Jacobin " was the popular cry.[1]

The north of England was now undergoing, as we have seen, an industrial transformation, which in less than twenty years was to convert it into a forcing-house for democratic ideas ; but in some parts of this region the instinct for politics—if not indeed for civilisation— had yet to be developed. Francis Place, describing the townspeople of Lancashire as they were before 1792, said that a stranger walking through their streets was liable to be hooted as an " outcomling " ; that the term " Lancashire brute " was common and appropriate ; and that a meeting of five hundred persons could not have been held without the likelihood of a raid on bakers and butchers' shops. Societies to promote reform were established in several northern towns ; but, except at Sheffield, famous for its cutlery since the days of Chaucer and a stronghold of Dissent, they were but the struggling offshoots of an organisation which was unpopular enough even at its headquarters in London.[2]

One must admit, even when due allowance is made for the outbreak of war with France in 1793, that the measures taken by Pitt to repress the activity of his old associates in reform, such as the Sedition and Treason Acts, were unnecessarily severe. Indeed, it has been said with pardonable exaggeration that he was " using

---

[1] *Life of Wilberforce*, ii. 4, 117–131. The total number of petitions against the Sedition and Treason Bills is said to have been 94.— Stanhope's *Pitt*, ii. 362. We shall find that four years earlier as many as 517 petitions had been presented against the slave trade. " Infamous as these laws were, they were popular measures. The people—ay, the mass of the shopkeepers and working people may be said to have approved them without understanding them."—Francis Place, quoted by Veitch, p. 327.

[2] Wallas's *Francis Place*, p. 146 ; Veitch, p. 195.

a sledge-hammer to crush a wasp." [1] Public opinion, at first friendly to the Revolution, was estranged by its excesses long before these had deepened into crimes.

It is not, however, to be supposed that the arrest of a movement in sympathy with the Revolution was due wholly to the crimes and follies perpetrated at Paris, or that the reaction could have succeeded on this scale if it had not concurred with other forces which were then reaching the maturity of their power. The whole philosophy of liberalism in the eighteenth century was vitiated and imperilled by the want of any sound historical basis ; and this is the more surprising as it was an age of great historians, and as early as 1760 De Brosses—to whom we owe the word " fetichism "—had initiated the study of primitive peoples. The same ignorance of history which made it possible for men to picture their savage ancestors as engaged in constitutional discussions caused them to overlook the fact that stability is more essential than uniformity to the constitution of a state, and that changes in the constitution are likely to be beneficial only in so far as they can be adjusted to the underlying social structure, which is not a mechanism but a growth. And it so happened that the friends of progress at this crisis were confronted by a man to whom the past was as great a source of inspiration as the future was to them. Burke indeed, when it suited his purpose, could be as false to the spirit of history as any of those who had not yet awakened to its claims. In his " Reflections on the French Revolution " his whole object is to magnify the excesses and outrages attendant on the liberal movement in France— which when he wrote in 1790 had not been serious— without ever stopping to inquire how it was that the French people, whose lives and fortunes had been for centuries at the disposal of arbitrary power, were in a temper and in a condition so far from favourable to

[1] Oman's *History of England*, p. 580.

patience and self-control ; and even this injustice need not surprise us in one who was capable of arguing that, if the English people had once possessed the right of dismissing their ruler for misconduct, they had abjured it in 1689 " to the end of all time," because the Lords and Commons in an address to William and Mary " do most humbly and faithfully submit themselves, their heirs and posterities, for ever." On the other hand, no finer tribute has ever been paid to the principle of historical development than the famous passage in which Burke reminded his philosophical opponents, whose formulas and metaphysical distinctions he frankly abhorred, that they had no more than a life interest in the commonwealth ; that they could have no right " to cut off the entail or commit waste on the inheritance " and ought to beware of such hazardous experiments as might " leave to those who come after them " a ruin instead of a habitation ; and whilst conceding to them that " society is indeed a contract," showed that he conceived this idea in a far higher sense than theirs as a " chain and continuity " which links generation to generation and without which " men would become little better than the flies of a summer." [1] The training of the reformers had not fitted them to cope successfully with what Paine called " the disorderly cast " of Burke's genius—" a genius at random and not a genius constituted " [2]; and, though the anti-reformers were naturally delighted with one who found a political value in the habits, and even in the prejudices and superstitions, with which they were only too plentifully endowed, there were forces at work which secured for Burke's appeal a wider and more disinterested response.

What has come to be known in literature as Romanticism—a love of the abnormal and the picturesque and consequently of the semi-barbarous times prolific

[1] *Reflections*, edited by Payne, p. 112.
[2] *Writings*, edited by Conway, ii. 134.

in such themes—was now rapidly gaining ground.   In the early years of the century Lord Shaftesbury, a moralist of the free-thinking or Deist school, had deplored a tendency to mediævalism in the public taste and had compared his age to Desdemona, whose "greedy ear" for tales of adventure had betrayed her to the Moor. Not unrepresentative of such an age were the enthusiasm excited by Anson's voyage round the globe, the admiration of Wesley for Mary Queen of Scots and the delight of Chatham in Spenser's "Faerie Queen."   In 1764 we find Lord Egmont soliciting a grant of St. John's Island with a view to the revival of feudal tenures, and rebuilding his country house in the guise of a moated castle.   Horace Walpole, who records and ridicules this foible, had himself converted his house at Strawberry Hill near Twickenham into something more like an abbey than a baronial keep ;   and in the same year he published "The Castle of Otranto," which professed to be a translation into English of an old Italian romance and the issue of which may be said to have inaugurated the modern romantic revival.   Twenty years later, General Oglethorpe was "gravely lamenting" to Hannah More that he could not prevail upon her to read the old romances, and assuring her that it was "the only way to acquire noble sentiments."[1]   Any political bias shown by the movement was at first rather Whig than Tory, Dr. Johnson, the critic of Ossian, being its keenest opponent ; but Burke himself, as revealed in his familiar lament, "The age of chivalry is gone,"[2] was obviously in some measure a product of this school ; and he it

[1] Wright's *Memoir of General Oglethorpe*, p. 56.

[2] "If I were called upon," said Dr. Arnold, "to name what spirit of evil predominantly deserved the name of Antichrist, I should name the spirit of chivalry—the more detestable for the very guise of the 'Archangel ruined,' which has made it so seductive to the most generous spirits—but to me so hateful, because it is in direct opposition to the impartial justice of the Gospel, and its comprehensive feeling of equal brotherhood, and because it so fostered a sense of honour rather than a sense of duty."—Stanley's *Life of Arnold*, chap. v.

was, as a recent writer has remarked, who brought Romanticism into politics as an auxiliary of the conservative cause.[1]

There was, however, another and a far greater movement so closely akin to that cause that it hardly needed to be annexed. Evangelicalism, which, as professed by the Methodists, had been extruded from the Church, was now promising, or threatening, to become at no very distant date the dominant religious force. Its leading doctrine was that all professions of Christianity were worthless which were not accompanied by such a change in disposition as could be effected only by supernatural means ; and it was consequently the bitter opponent of that humanism which was supposed to have discredited itself in the crimes of the French Revolution. The influence of Hannah More and Wilberforce secured for it a considerable foothold in fashionable life, and the upper classes were disposed, on the whole, to countenance it as a means of keeping the populace in check. It was indeed with a view to counteracting the political influence of Paine that Miss More published in 1792 her " Village Politics by Will. Chip, a Country Carpenter." Many thousand copies of this dialogue were purchased by the Government for free distribution ; it was translated into French, and even received the doubtful compliment of being reprinted in Italian, with certain emendations, by the Papal Court. Three years later, the same writer and two of her sisters provided an antidote to Paine's " Age of Reason " in the " Cheap Repository," a series of penny tales, ballads and religious tracts, issued at the rate of three a month. Committees were formed in London under episcopal patronage to disseminate this pious seed, and two million copies were sold in the first year.[2]

[1] Benn's *Modern England*, i. 43 ; *History of English Rationalism*, i. 127, 308.
[2] Thompson's *Hannah More*, 1838, pp. 135, 150.

The activities of Evangelicalism were, however, regarded at first with no small suspicion in quarters unfavourable to reform. One may think that nothing could be more natural at such a time than an attempt to introduce Christianity where it was still unknown ; and yet such an endeavour was a breach rather than an observance of Evangelical tradition. It is true, as we have seen, that the Societies for Promoting Christian Knowledge and for Propagating the Gospel had existed since about 1700 ; but, except for some co-operation with Danish missionaries in India, the province claimed by both of these societies was colonial rather than foreign, and the income of the latter in the course of almost a century had risen only from £1535 to £2608. It appears that the command of Jesus in the addition to Mark's narrative, "Go ye into all the world and preach the Gospel to every creature," was held to have been given only to the Apostles and to have been fulfilled when they received the Gift of Tongues ; and the growth of a wider interpretation has been ascribed with some plausibility to the enthusiasm for humanity and for nature as opposed to civilisation which was diffused by Rousseau.[1] But those who suspected the political bias of Evangelicalism had grounds for apprehension more relevant than this. The first foreign mission society was that of the Baptists, formed in 1792 ; but the London Missionary Society, initiated by Dr. Bogue in 1795, was supported by both Evangelicals and Dissenters ; and amongst the latter were many who had avowed their sympathy with the Revolution. Indeed, Dr. Bogue himself had preached and published a sermon in which he declared that government, as it existed in "most of the countries of Europe," was "little else than a conspiracy, not only against the happiness of man, but against religion and the cause of God." It was perhaps to be expected that the mechanism

[1] Warneck's *History of Protestant Missions*, third English edition, p. 77.

of the mission societies—their public meetings and their committees for correspondence—should excite alarm at a time when all popular agitation was so much discouraged ; but one is hardly prepared to find such an attitude assumed towards the very movement which had been started by Raikes to prevent the growth of a criminal and improvident class. Yet, just as the Charity Schools had been accused, possibly with some reason, of Jacobitism, so the Sunday Schools were accused, without reason, of Jacobinism ; and the imputation was countenanced by Bishop Horsley, the ablest but by no means the most liberal prelate of his day,[1] who declared that there was "much ground for suspicion that sedition and atheism are the real objects of some of these institutions rather than religion." Rowland Hill, whose Sunday school in connexion with Surrey chapel is said to have been the first established in London, thus ironically alludes to this charge : "Respecting the little army we are about to raise to overthrow the King and constitution, it should be considered that the children in these schools of sedition are, on the average, only from six to twelve years of age ; consequently they will not be able to take the field at least these ten years ; and, half of these being girls, unless we raise an army of Amazons, with a virago Joan at the head of them, we shall be sadly short of soldiers to accomplish the design."[2]

In many quarters, however, it was not the character of the education given to the children of the poor, but the idea that they were being educated at all, that excited alarm. Hitherto such a feeling had been almost unknown. When the public enthusiasm for charity schools was at its height, it had not been damped by any fear that the children trained in these institutions would prove a source

---

[1] It was he who said in the House of Lords that he " did not know what the mass of the people in any country had to do with the laws but to obey them."—Stanhope's *Pitt*, ii. 363.

[2] See *Church and Reform in Scotland*, 1797–1843, pp. 80, 88.

of trouble or discomfort to their superiors.[1]   On the contrary, as Nelson expressed it in regard to the "black-guard boys," the expectation was that they would become "more useful in their little stations."   Mandeville had indeed attacked the charity schools on the ground that they would make it impossible to find hands for "an abundance of hard and dirty labour"; but he confessed that the public could not be made to realise this danger, and he attributed their obtuseness to "an unreasonable vein of petty reverence for the poor that runs through vast multitudes"—to such an extent "that men cannot endure to hear or see anything said or acted against the poor."[2]   The panic caused by the French Revolution proved fatal to this kindly and unsuspicious spirit; and the alarmists were divided into two classes—those who held that the poor should be left wholly untaught, and those who proposed to teach them under such meagre and pious auspices that they should learn only to read, and should desire to read only the Bible.   Conspicuous in the latter class was Hannah More.   In 1789 she opened a Sunday school as well as a school of industry at Cheddar, and her scheme of education was soon extended to nine adjacent parishes.   It was not a liberal scheme.   The son of a farmer might be taught writing and cyphering as "beneficial and appropriate knowledge for the boy of this class"; but the children of a day labourer must be content with much less.   "I allow no writing nor any reading but the Bible, catechism, and such little tracts as may enable them to understand the Church service."   Unfortunately, despite these precautions, the master of Miss More's school at Blagdon developed Methodist tendencies which brought him into conflict with the local

---

[1] Brougham in 1820 referred to this as "a modern idea," and recalled that Pope Benedict in 1724 had issued a bull encouraging the establishment of schools on the ground that the source of all evils was ignorance, "presertim in illis qui egestate oppressi sunt."—Hansard, N.S., ii. 57.

[2] *Fable of the Bees*, pp. 356, 357.

curate ; and the result was " the Blagdon controversy," which was sufficiently portentous to embroil the two great obscurantist organs, the *British Critic* and the *Anti-Jacobin Review*, and in the course of which this devout lady was taxed with Jacobinism and with "not believing one word of Christianity." A few years later, we find Mrs. Trimmer, another educationist of the same type, objecting to the institution of an order of merit in certain schools lest the boys, when they grew up, should "aspire to be nobles of the land and to take the place of the hereditary nobility "; and it appears that as late as 1833 many of the largest contributors to Sunday schools were opposed to the children of the poor being taught to write.[1]

We have seen how Granville Sharp as the result of seven years' litigation had obtained from Lord Mansfield the decision which emancipated slaves brought by their masters to England. We have now to trace the movement for the abolition of the slave trade, which dates from another decision reluctantly pronounced by the same judge in 1783. On March 19 of that year a negro who had assumed the grandiloquent name of Gustavus Vasa came to Sharp with a report that a hundred and thirty of his countrymen had been thrown overboard from a British slave-ship, the *Zong* of Liverpool. Three days later, with his usual alacrity and courage, Sharp issued instructions for a charge of murder ; but an action brought by the underwriters of the vessel against the owners soon made it plain that the deed—which was not denied— far from being legally a murder, was not even a crime. A scarcity of water was the plea put forward by the defence ; but it was proved that the allowance of water had never been curtailed ; that the slaves had been sent

---

[1] Thompson's *Hannah More*, pp. 93, 100, 193 ; Sydney Smith's *Works*, i. 168 ; Mr. and Mrs. Hammond's *The Town Labourer*, p. 58. Though her health was always precarious, Hannah More usually spent about thirteen hours every Sunday in visiting her schools.

to their death in "parcels" of fifty-four, forty-two and thirty-six on three successive days ; that on the second day there was a plentiful rainfall ; and finally that the captain had proposed the massacre to his subordinates on the ground that, if the slaves died of sickness, as seemed probable, the loss would fall on the owners, whereas if it should appear that a certain number had been got rid of in order to save the rest, the underwriters would be liable at the rate of £30 a head.   The Solicitor-General, on behalf of the owners, went so far as to repel not only the "suggestion of cruelty," but even a "surmise of impropriety in the transaction" ;   and Lord Mansfield reluctantly admitted that the only question he could put before the jury was one of necessity, the affair being the same as if horses had been thrown overboard.   "It is," he added, "a very shocking case."[1]

Sharp spared no effort to give publicity to "this most inhuman and diabolical deed," sending a full account of it to the newspapers, memorialising the Lords of the Admiralty and the Duke of Portland, and circulating as widely as possible a shorthand report of the trial.   The result was to elicit the first general outcry against the slave trade that had yet been raised.   Bishop Porteus, just before Sharp apprised him of the *Zong* disclosures, had preached a sermon to the Society for the Propagation of the Gospel in which he referred to its three hundred slaves in Barbadoes ;   and he now began a more systematic attempt—fruitless, as we have seen—to have this anomaly mitigated, if not removed.   A sermon which made a powerful and lasting impression at Cambridge was delivered to the University by Dr. Peckard.   Amongst those who published essays or pamphlets were Gilbert Wakefield, Dr. Gregory, Thomas Day, author of "Sandford and Merton," and, above all, James Ramsay.   The first and second knew the slave trade

---

[1] Hoare's *Sharp*, pp. 236–241.

from having lived for some time at Liverpool,[1] its principal base ; but the last had the knowledge and authority of one who had come into close personal contact with its operation and effects in the West Indies. Ramsay was a Scotsman, who had served in the Navy, first as surgeon and then as chaplain, and had combined both these qualifications in pastoral work on the island of St. Christopher's, where he made himself very unpopular by his efforts to protect and Christianise the negroes ; and he was now Rector of Teston in Kent. For several years he had been engaged in the preparation of a work on the treatment and conversion of West Indian slaves, and this at the request of Bishop Porteus he published in 1784. A long and bitter controversy ensued, which did much to enlighten the public, but proved so vexatious to the author that he is said to have died of its effects in 1789.[2]

Dr. Peckard followed up his sermon by a step which was to call into the field an opponent of the slave trade who had all Ramsay's courage, and in addition the vigour and enthusiasm of youth. In 1785, as Vice-Chancellor of the University of Cambridge, he proposed the question whether men could lawfully be made slaves as the theme of a Latin essay ; and one of those who entered for the competition was Thomas Clarkson, son of a schoolmaster at Wisbeach. Knowing nothing of the slave trade except that Dr. Peckard had preached against it and would probably expect it to be dealt with, he was much at a loss for information ; but Benezet's " Historical Account of Guinea," made known to him through a newspaper advertisement, supplied almost all his wants ; and the subject as presented in this book so impressed itself on his imagination that he was completely overcome by

[1] " Had I command of the elements," said Paine, " I would blast Liverpool with fire and brimstone. It is the Sodom and Gomorrah of brutality."—*Works*, ii. 350.

[2] " Ramsay is dead—I have killed him," wrote a planter who had fiercely assailed him in the Commons.—*Life of Wilberforce*, i. 235.

its cruelty, sordidness and horror.[1] His essay, having been awarded the first prize, was translated, expanded and published ; and the author, after satisfying himself that many prominent men were prepared to support an agitation against the slave trade, resolved to forego the career he had chosen in the Church and to devote himself to this as the work of his life.[2]

Perhaps, however, the most important effect of the *Zong* case was the impression it produced on that small section of the community which Sharp described as " unhappily involved in the errors of Quakerism." In order to understand how this had come to pass, we have to go as far away as Pennsylvania and as far back as 1755, when the outbreak of war with France caused the Quakers who had hitherto been dominant in that colony to withdraw in increasing numbers from political life, and when from the same motive they imposed certain penalties on those of their number who were engaged in the slave trade. In 1774 the Society resolved that not only such persons, but all who possessed slaves and refused to emancipate them, should be expelled from its communion ; and, thirteen years later, it could claim that the anomaly of a Quaker slave owner had ceased to exist.[3]

This fine record, unsurpassed or rather unapproached by that of any other religious body, was due in great measure to five men—Burling, Sandiford, Lay, Woolman and Benezet—who laboured in succession to diffuse an abhorrence of slavery, and the influence of whose writings and reputation helped to promote a parallel movement in the home country. Indeed Woolman came himself to England and died there, a victim of smallpox, in 1772.

[1] " It was but one gloomy subject from morning to night. In the day-time I was uneasy. In the night I had little rest. I sometimes never closed my eyelids for grief."

[2] Clarkson's *History of the Abolition of the Slave Trade*, i. 204–230.

[3] Grahame's *History of the United States*, iii. 403–408 ; Hoare's *Sharp*, p. 396.

The English Quakers had concurred in censuring the slave trade as early as 1729 ; and in 1783 they not only presented to Parliament the first address for its abolition, but circulated many thousand copies of an appeal to the public which had been prepared by a committee and was entitled "The Case of our Fellow Creatures, the Oppressed Africans." In the same year six of the committee formed an association to secure space for articles on the subject in London and provincial newspapers ; and this body soon extended the scope of its activities by obtaining the permission of Bishop Porteus to print his sermon. It was a Quaker bookseller who undertook the publication of Clarkson's essay ; and to this irrepressible young man, then only in his twenty-fifth year, who had a genius for the sort of work—canvassing rather than propagandism—which one associates with an election agent, the Society for the Abolition of the Slave Trade was largely indebted for its formation in May 1787. Granville Sharp, as "father of the cause in England," was appointed chairman, though he could never be induced actually to take the chair [1] ; and all the twelve original members, except Sharp himself, Clarkson and Philip Sansom, were Quakers. The Society was, however, intended only to provide the funds and literature required for the conduct of a political campaign ; and Wilberforce, who directed its operations and eventually joined it, had undertaken to lead such forces as should be raised in Parliament.

The slave trade was not abolished till 1807 ; but we shall find that the issue of what was to prove a long and bitter struggle was practically decided as early as 1792. The chief business of the Society or, as it was usually called, "the London committee," was by means of correspondence and the printing of books and pamphlets

[1] Clarkson, i. 449. Sharp wished to decline the chairmanship because he had not time to discharge its duties. During the first four or five months he was never able to attend.—*Life of Cartwright,* i. 169.

to feed the fire of indignation against the slave trade which had been kindled by Ramsay, whilst Clarkson explored the sea-ports—and indeed the whole kingdom—for the requisite fuel. To find the persons he wanted, to overcome their reluctance to be examined, and to extort from them facts that they would allow him to divulge were the three great difficulties of his task. We are told that he boarded all the warships at Deptford, Woolwich, Chatham, Sheerness and Portsmouth in quest of a certain seaman, and found him on the fifty-seventh vessel. In one of his journeys he travelled nearly 2000 miles without securing a single witness, and retraced his steps from York to Edinburgh only to find that a person who had previously refused to see him would now give nothing but private information.[1] Nevertheless by the end of February 1798 enough had been disclosed to create a considerable stir. Meetings had been held in almost all the principal towns, and thirty-five petitions —the first instalment of over a hundred—had been presented to Parliament. But Wilberforce agreed with Pitt that, though the House of Commons might possibly be induced at this stage to express its abhorrence of the slave trade, an inquiry was essential if they aimed, as of course they did, at a statutory abolition ; and a committee of the Privy Council was consequently appointed to investigate and report.

The African merchants, staggering under the weight of public opprobrium, had now their chance. They complained loudly of the charges that had been brought against their character and occupation ; and, with no facts at their disposal, they had—what served them even better for a time—an unlimited command of lies.[2]

[1] Clarkson, ii. 176, 197.
[2] As this, for example : " On the voyage from Africa to the West Indies the negroes are well fed, comfortably lodged, and have every possible attention paid to their health, cleanliness and convenience."— Norris's *Short Account of the African Slave Trade*, 1789, p. 28. Very different was the testimony of one who had made four voyages as

Indeed Clarkson learned, to his astonishment and dismay, that his principal witness, "a host of himself," had come to London as one of the three delegates from Liverpool in defence of the trade.[1]   And, whilst the merchants were demonstrating on such evidence the humanity of their traffic, the planters were prepared to prove that, whether humane or cruel, it was all that stood between them and ruin.   The abolitionists had, however, no reason to be dissatisfied with the Privy Council report ; but it was not presented, in the shape of a large folio volume, till May 1789, when, after a debate initiated by Wilberforce, it was resolved that a further inquiry should be opened by the House itself.   Both Pitt and Fox expected that this supplemental investigation would be brief, occupying perhaps only one day ; but the merchants and planters succeeded in prolonging it into the next session ; and on April 23, 1790, when all the witnesses for the trade—and these only—had been examined, Lord Penryn, one of the members for Liverpool, proposed that no more should be heard.   This was negatived without a division ; but the abolitionists were unable to complete their case till April 5, 1791.   A fortnight later, the question which had hung in suspense for more than three years was brought to an issue ; and the slave-traders and their friends, though waging what one of their own number described as a war of the pigmies of the House against its giants, found themselves in a majority of nearly two to one—163 to 88.[2]   So far, all that had been wrung from them was Sir William Dolben's Act limiting the number of negroes that could be carried in a slave-ship.

Wilberforce had devoted to this cause an amount of time, energy and close personal attention which is

surgeon on a slave-ship : " It is not in the power of the human imagination to picture to itself a situation more dreadful or disgusting."— Falconbridge's *Account of the Slave Trade*, p. 25.

[1] Clarkson, i. 477.

[2] Pitt, Fox, Burke, Grey, Sheridan, Windham and Lord North were all in the minority.   Windham changed sides later.

barely credible in one of his slender frame, weak eye-
sight and utterly precarious health[1]; but he was as
far as possible from being discouraged by his defeat.
Realising that the success of its partisans in Parliament
had merely deepened the general abhorrence of the
slave trade, he resolved to give notice early in the next
session of a renewed attack, and then to elicit, or rather
to authorise, such an expression of public opinion as
should compel the House of Commons to reverse its
decision.   The Abolition Society had done much already
to assist him in this design.   In the previous year, 1790,
a great effect had been produced by a print of the interior
of the slave-ship *Brookes*, as occupied by the 450
negroes still permitted to a vessel of this tonnage by the
Dolben Act [2]—a vessel which on one of its voyages had
carried as many as 609.   The poet Cowper and Josiah
Wedgwood, the famous potter, had contributed to
confirm this impression—the one by his ballad, *The
Negro's Complaint*, which was set to music and sung in
the streets, the other by his cameo reproducing the seal
of the Society—a suppliant negro.   This was soon
generally adopted as an ornament on snuff-boxes,
bracelets and hairpins.   The Society now circulated
an abridgment of the evidence given in the House of
Commons against the trade and a report of the recent
debate ; and the effect of these fresh disclosures was at
once seen in a widespread resolution to abstain from the
use of West Indian sugar.   Clarkson, who made one of
his longest journeys at this time, estimated that some
300,000 persons had adopted this measure ; but

[1] Clarkson in his *History of the Abolition* makes so much of his
own exertions that the biographers of Wilberforce could not fail to
put those of their father in the strongest light ; but both men worked
so hard that there was little room in either case for exaggeration.
Clarkson's self-assertion must, however, have been a trial to his friends.
—*Life of Wilberforce*, i. 141 ; ii. 38, 52.

[2] The space allotted to each negro was one foot six inches wide.
In 1819 a considerable sensation was caused by the discovery that
in convict ships the space allotted to prisoners, soldiers and sailors
was only one foot one inch wide.—Hansard, xxxix. 89, 90.

Wilberforce, who was appealed to from all sides as director of the agitation, sought to discourage it as extreme, or at least premature. Meanwhile Newcastle had set an example which was followed by several other towns in forming an association similar to the original one in London [1] ; and petitions multiplied at such a rate that, according to Clarkson, there was not a week-day for three months on which five or six were not being initiated in different parts of the realm. The greatest enthusiasm of all was shown in Scotland, where we are told that, every sort of corporate body from a town-council to a kirk-session " united in denouncing the slave trade as immoral and unchristian." [2] Of five counter-petitions, only two were of any importance, and these came from Reading and Derby, not from Liverpool and Bristol. "Liverpool," wrote one of Wilberforce's correspondents in that city, " will never again, I think, petition on this subject ; conviction of the truth has spread amongst us widely.' [3] The petitions, when their number was complete, reached an unprecedented total. Scotland, in proportion to its population, was easily first with 187 ; but 310 were received from England and 20 from Wales.

Under these highly encouraging auspices, Wilberforce returned to the assault in April 1792. His motion for immediate abolition, though supported as before by all the leading statesmen, was converted into one for abolition in four years, and in this form was carried by 193 votes to 125. The leader, who had thus suffered a partial defeat, was overwhelmed with congratulations ; and, though "hurt and humiliated," he could not but see on reflection that he had gained all but the full measure of success. "No man hereafter," said Pitt, "can pretend to argue that the abolition of the trade ought not to take

[1] Edinburgh and Plymouth had long anticipated Newcastle in this respect.—Clarkson, ii. 29.
[2] Meikle's *Scotland and the French Revolution*, p. 77.
[3] *Life of Wilberforce*, i. 343.

place, however he may wish from motives of private interest to defer the day of its suppression." [1]

But the means which had enabled Wilberforce to advance thus far towards his goal were now to prove an obstacle to his further progress ; and here again we are confronted with that shadow of the French Revolution which in other fields had so often blighted, if not killed, the promise of reform. Down to May 1791 the question of the slave trade had been debated, and was then determined on its merits ; but the appeal to popular opinion with a view to reversing this decision coincided with the first serious alarm in regard to the spread of revolutionary ideas ; and for several reasons the two movements, humanitarian and political, could not be kept distinct. The mechanism of affiliated societies, meetings and petitions was common to both. Some of those who were most active against the slave trade, such as Cartwright, Wyvil and, to some extent, Sharp, had been known since 1780, and were still known, as extreme parliamentary reformers. Others, and especially Clarkson, made themselves conspicuous by their admiration for the new order in France. " You will see Clarkson," wrote Wilberforce to Lord Muncaster ; "caution him against talking of the French Revolution ; it will be ruin to our cause." [2]   In September 1792 Wilberforce learned that he had been elected a French citizen in company with Priestley, Clarkson and Paine ; and, dreading the effect of this on " our Abolition cause," he joined the committee for relief of the French emigrant clergy, " partly to do away French citizenship." [3]   Still further alarm was caused by a revolt in Western or French St. Domingo, by far the greatest and most flourishing of all the West Indian colonies [4]—a revolt

---

[1] *Life of Wilberforce*, i. 350.   [2] *Ibid.* p. 343.
[3] *Ibid.* p. 368.
[4] " An island which in its commerce with France employed more ships and tonnage than our whole West Indian trade."—*Life of Wilberforce*, ii. 92.

which, when it had spread from the whites and mulattoes to the negroes, quite eclipsed in ferocity and outrage the parent revolution at Paris. All these adverse conditions were, of course, aggravated by the outbreak of war with France in 1793. Burke, once favourable to the movement for abolition, told Wilberforce that he now regarded it as " a shred of the accursed web of Jacobinism "[1]; and Windham, whose attitude to Burke " was as if one went to inquire of the oracle of the Lord,"[2] said to Lady Spencer : " Your friend, Mr. Wilberforce, will be very happy any morning to hand your Ladyship to the guillotine." Popular opinion was equally panic-stricken and fickle. " People connect democratical principles with the abolition of the slave trade and will not hear it mentioned," was a report from Norfolk. The Commons never rescinded their resolution that the trade should cease in 1796, but, despite the exertions of Wilberforce, nothing was done to carry it into effect. Even the London Society was forced to relax and finally to suspend its efforts. During the first fourteen months of its existence it had held fifty-one meetings. From 1795 to 1797 it met only twice a year, and no further meeting was held till 1804.[2]

Hitherto we have been concerned with religion merely as an incentive to philanthropic effort, and in this respect the movement against the slave trade is a striking illustration of its power. Sharp and Wilberforce were the most devout of laymen ; Ramsay was a country parson ; and Clarkson, being in deacon's orders, had preached at Manchester in the course of his travels. But religion, and especially Evangelical religion, was in those days not only a moral force but a theological system ; and we are now entering on a period in which we shall have to distinguish between its services to humanity in the former capacity and its disserves in

---

[1] Hansard, N.S., xviii. 775.
[2] *Life of Wilberforce*, ii. 19, 72, 211.

the latter.   So far theology had not proved much of a
barrier to freedom of thought.   Woolston, the ablest and
least judicious of the Deists, was indeed prosecuted and
imprisoned for blasphemy in 1729, and a similar fate
befell Peter Annet, a late survivor of this school, in
1763 ; but Woolston had gone out of his way to insult
individually several of the bishops ; and Annet, who
had attacked the Resurrection with impunity in 1744,
would no doubt have ended his career unscathed if he
had not lived to see the rule of the Whigs displaced by
that of the pious and illiberal George III.   It seemed
for a time as if even the Evangelical revival—" terrible
and inevitable," as it has been called [1]—need not be
wholly obscurantist in spirit ; for Wesley in his later
days grew more and more liberal in doctrine, and came
at last to the conclusion " that right opinion is a slender
part of religion or no part of it at all."   In the ripening
and mellowing of disposition, which was a happy feature
of his indomitable old age, he at least entertained the
idea that all Churches, if not even all religions, were
but different aspects of the same truth, and proclaimed
with enthusiasm that he and his associates were pledged
to each other by no exclusive bond : " There is no other
religious society under heaven which requires nothing
of men in order to their admission into it but a desire
to save their souls. . . . The Methodists alone do not
insist on your holding this or that opinion, but they
think and let think." [2]

It was not, however, Wesley the Arminian, but Whitefield the Calvinist who had inspired the Evangelicalism
which at the time of the French Revolution was spreading
within the Anglican fold ; and the reaction caused by
the excesses at Paris was well calculated to strengthen
this element, particularly as its leader had not hesitated

[1] Morley's *Voltaire*, p. 91.
[2] On this point see the author's *Church and Reform in Scotland,*
1797–1843, pp. 39, 40, 49.

in more normal times to avow the extreme fanaticism of his faith. Speaking in the House of Commons as early as 1773, Burke had professed his readiness to tolerate men of every religious persuasion then existing in England, but as for " the others, the infidels," they were " never, never to be supported, never to be tolerated. These are the people against whom you ought to aim the shafts of law ; these are the men to whom, arrayed in all the terrors of government, I would say, You shall not degrade us into brutes. I would have the laws rise in all their majesty of terrors to fulminate such vain and impious wretches." [1] In 1787 Wilberforce had founded the Society for Reformation of Manners, usually known as " the Proclamation Society," because its activities were defined in the royal proclamation against immorality and vice.[2] To secure the Sabbath from profanation and the public from indecent literature seems to have been its principal task ; but in 1797 the spread of infidelity from France brought within its grasp one of the " vain and impious wretches " who had been marked for sacrifice by Burke. This was a bookseller named Williams, who had issued a cheap edition of Paine's " Age of Reason." Dr. Watson, the scholarly but absentee Bishop' of Llandaff, implicitly in his reply to Paine, and explicitly in his reply to Gibbon, had indicated his contempt for those who preferred force to argument in religious discussion ; but the hint was thrown away on Wilberforce and his associates ; and, without waiting for the Government to take action, they prosecuted Williams, with the result that he was convicted of publishing a blasphemous libel. Erskine, the leading Whig lawyer, had conducted their case. Having appealed to them in vain not to ask for sentence on a man who was thoroughly penitent, who had already been several months in gaol and whose wife and family were suffering from disease and want, he threw up his brief ;

---

[1] Morley's *Edmund Burke, A Historical Study*, p. 36.
[2] See p. 42.

but Wilberforce had the satisfaction of recording in his Journal " We firm."[1]

We need not pause to inquire whether Paine's "Age of Reason," unlike his " Rights of Man," made any great impression on the mass of the people ; but some allusion must be made here to a change in the economic outlook of Parliament which probably did much more than such writings to foster a democratic spirit.

The divorce of labour from capital had, as we have seen, originated in days long previous to the industrial revolution ; and in several industries it had produced that antagonism with which we are familiar as its natural, if not inevitable, result. One of these was the tailoring trade, in which only men of substantial means could afford to begin business in the fashionable parts of London, and to begin it in the twofold capacity of shopkeeper and craftsman which had become usual in these districts as early as 1680. Another and far more important example was the woollen manufacture. Whilst the Yorkshire weaver continued to be an independent producer, buying the material of his craft and selling the finished product, his fellow workmen in other parts of England, and especially in the south-west, had degenerated into mere wage-earners, working up in their own dwellings and with their own tools the material supplied to them by wealthy employers. In 1720 the master tailors of London complained to Parliament that their journeymen, " to the number of seven thousand and upwards, have lately entered into a combination to raise their wages and leave off working an hour sooner than they used to do." In 1718 the weavers and wool-combers of Somerset and Devon were rebuked in a royal proclamation for having formed certain " lawless clubs and societies which had

---

[1] *State Trials*, xxvi. 654 ; *Life of Wilberforce*, ii. 251. The sentence passed on Williams was a year's imprisonment with hard labour. His counsel had taken the bold line of justifying both the intention and argument of Paine's work.

illegally presumed to use a common seal and to act as Bodies Corporate " ; and it appeared in 1741 that this or a similar " sort of corporation " had for some considerable time been giving " laws to their masters as also to themselves—*viz.*, That no man should comb wool under 2s. per dozen ; that no master should employ any comber that was not of their club ; if he did, they agreed one and all not to work for him ; and if he had employed twenty, they all of them turned out, and oftentimes were not satisfied with that, but would abuse the honest man that would labour ; and in a riotous manner beat him, break his comb pots and destroy his working tools ; they further support one another in so much that they are become one society throughout the kingdom."

These early attempts at Trade Unionism were invariably held, in so far as they meddled with the question of employment or remuneration, to be an offence at common law ; nor was this attitude unreasonable so long as the workman could look for redress to the Elizabethan statute—itself a confirmation of much older usage—which prescribed the number and training of apprentices and provided for an annual revision of wages by the Justices of the Peace ; and in fact the only combinations which the law did allow were those which had been formed to enforce this Act. But the industrial expansion, which set in after the middle of the eighteenth century, soon convinced all but the workmen themselves how hopeless it was to apply mediæval regulations to modern economics. Production on a large scale necessitated a numerous staff and a wages bill determined rather by competition than custom. The use of machinery, owing to its minute specialisation, could be learned in as many months as under the old conditions it had taken years to train a complete craftsman ; and the factory system not only greatly facilitated the growth of Trade Unionism, and by way of protest was the immediate cause of its introduction into Yorkshire, but by stimulating production put the remedies it demanded still further out of reach.

Parliament being thus disposed to withdraw the protection it had hitherto afforded to the workers, it might have been expected that their claim to protect themselves by resorting to combination would now be recognised. But two influences arose in succession to defeat this claim. The publication of Adam Smith's "Wealth of Nations" in 1776 revealed to strenuous employers and baffled legislators a doctrine which—when it suited their purpose—they were only too ready to accept—that industry is its own best regulator when left free to adapt itself to the interaction of demand and supply ; and after 1792 Trade Unionism, in common with all other popular movements, was of course discredited as an outcome of the revolutionary spirit. The issue could not long be in doubt. Though the old regulations were not repealed till 1813 and 1814, they were suffered to fall into disuse ; and an Act was passed in 1799 which made it criminal for workmen under a penalty of three months' imprisonment to combine, or even as individuals to hamper in any way the action of their employers, whilst any similar laws against the latter were declared to be still in force. Next year the Act was replaced by another, more cautiously worded, but in substance equally comprehensive and severe.[1] Combination was not a weapon which the masters had much occasion to wield ; but, even if those of them who defied the law had been convicted—which they never were—the plight of their operatives could hardly have been less galling than it was. "A single master," said Lord Jeffrey, " was at liberty at any time to turn off the whole of his workmen at once—100 or 1000 in number—if they would not accept of the wages he chose to offer. But it was made an offence for the whole of the workmen

---

[1] 39 Geo. III, c. 81 ; 39 & 40 Geo. III, c. 106.

to leave that master at once if he refused to give the wages they chose to require." [1]

Even if Trade Unionism had been able to surmount the economic objection to its activity, if not to its existence, it would still have had to reckon with the temper which prescribed that the child of an artisan or labourer should be taught to read but not to write [2] ; and this disposition may be illustrated from the works of two famous men, one of whom referred the poor for compensation to a future life and the other sought to convince them that their lot was really preferable to that of the rich. Burke in the earliest of his treatises, published as far back as 1756, had expressed great sympathy with the poor or at least with those of them, such as miners and metal-workers, whose labour was both unwholesome and ill-paid, and had even ascribed their condition to "the blindness of mankind"; but, writing in 1790 against the French Revolution, he said that the masses "must respect that property of which they cannot partake. They must labour to obtain what by labour can be obtained ; and when they find, as they commonly do, the success disproportioned to the endeavour, they must be taught their consolation in the final proportions of eternal justice." Five years later, he had so far assimilated the new economic doctrine as to assert that the more avaricious the farmer, the more likely he was in his own interest to see that his labourers were in good condition.[3] Meanwhile Paley, though by no means an anti-Jacobin,[4] had come forward with the somewhat novel idea that poverty within certain bounds is more enjoyable than wealth. "Frugality itself is a pleasure. It is an exercise

---

[1] *History of Trade Unionism*, by Sidney and Beatrice Webb, *passim*.

[2] See p. 60.

[3] *Thoughts on Scarcity*, 1795.

[4] Paley in 1792 was reported to be " as loose in his politics as he is in his religion. . . . There is scarce one of his old friends here at Cambridge who is not disposed to give him up : and most say that he is mad."—*Life of Wilberforce*, ii. 3.

of attention and contrivance which, whenever it is success
ful, produces satisfaction. The very care and forecast
that are necessary to keep expenses and earnings upon a
level form, when not embarrassed by too great difficulties, are an agreeable engagement of the thoughts.
This is lost amidst abundance." And he goes on to argue
that the poor man, if healthy, upright and industrious,
will not " fail to meet with a maintenance adequate to
the habits with which he has been brought up and to the
expectations which he has formed." [1]

The author of " Reasons for Contentment " is said to
have regarded it as the most valuable of his works, and no
doubt it was known to many at Westminster ; but Parliament, though thus reassured as to the felicitous condition
of the working classes, had apparently some scruple in
putting down their combinations ; for the Act of 1800,
without restricting or blunting that of 1799, looks like
an attempt to make it less indecently unfair. Two
Justices of the Peace, and not one, were to be essential
to conviction ; the prohibition to the workman of certain
acts was qualified by a reference to motives ; the combination of masters was now expressly forbidden under
a penalty of £20 ; and it was provided that arbitration,
if proposed by one party to an industrial dispute, must
be accepted by the other. But all such provisions were
vain. Thousands of journeymen suffered under the Act,
but not one employer. [2]

As with capitalist production and Trade Unionism,
so with child labour. The third of these phenomena
was no more the offspring of the industrial revolution
than the first and second. We have had occasion to
notice the over-taxing of young minds in connexion with
the development of Sunday schools. However excellent
these institutions may have been, one cannot but be

[1] Morley's *Burke* in " English Men of Letters," p. 16 ; Hammond,
The Village Labourer, p. 208 ; *The Town Labourer*, pp. 199, 233.
[2] Webb, *History of Trade Unionism*, p. 64.

surprised, if not astonished, to find that children were expected to receive five hours of instruction and to attend two religious services on their only day of rest, and that parents sometimes added to these demands by providing them with more purely secular education at meal hours during the week. When Raikes opened his Sunday school at Gloucester in 1780, machinery had begun to take the place of hand labour ; and there is reason to believe that the overworking of children for industrial purposes was no novelty in the mills that were then established. Certain schools of industry for the training of pauper children were in operation during most of the eighteenth century ; and we are told that scarcely any of the inmates were more than eleven years old, that they worked with intervals for meals from six to six in summer and from seven to five in winter, and so enjoyed their exertions—at all events in one such school—that " content smiles on every little countenance." Defoe writes with evident admiration of a district in which there was " scarce anything of five years old " that did not earn its living in the woollen manufacture ; but the children so employed in the cottage of the weaver or spinner can hardly have worn the same cheerful expression. According to one authority, " The creatures were set to work as soon as they could crawl, and their parents were the hardest of task-masters." That such a state of things prevailed must seem likely enough when we remember that the scattered artisans could seldom afford to refuse the work and remuneration offered by the agent of the cloth merchant when he chanced to come their way in the course of his rounds.[1]

There was, however, one abuse of child labour for which the mill-owners were directly responsible ; and, strangely enough, it was the philanthropic efforts of Hanway that had enabled them to perpetrate this evil. We

[1] Hutchins and Harrison, *History of Factory Legislation*, pp. 2–5 ; Hobson's *Evolution of Modern Capitalism*, p. 195.

have seen that Hanway had procured an Act of Parliament requiring parish infants in London to be sent out to
nurse till they were six months old at a certain distance
from the City, and that the success of the measure had
caused it to be known amongst the poor as "The Act for
keeping children alive."   Before steam-power had been
discovered as a means of working the new machinery
devised for the cotton manufacture, the mills had necessarily to be erected on the banks of streams ; and, as the
sites thus indicated were frequently far from the centres
of population, the mill-owners were naturally attracted
to the children available for their purpose in the London
workhouses.[1]   A traffic thus sprang up between London
and Lancashire which—if we consider the difficulties of
communication in those days—was not unlike the slave
trade between West Africa and the West Indies.   The
children were apprenticed for a term extending from the
age of about eight to that of twenty-one ; and little or no
care was taken to ascertain the character of the employer
to whom they were sent or to secure their safe transit
and good treatment.   Their indentures had indeed to
be signed by two Justices of the Peace for Middlesex or
Surrey ; but these assumed no responsibility, and in many
cases even put their names to blank papers.   The result
was that the children could be, and sometimes were, sent
in gangs to a contractor who disposed of them to the
mill-owner ; and that bargains were made by which he
agreed to take one idiot with every consignment of twenty.
If the employer failed, his apprentices might be put up
for sale with the rest of his assets, but usually were simply
dismissed ; and in one instance they were actually taken
in a cart to a spot near the sea-shore and there turned
adrift.   The traffic, though discouraged by the gradual
introduction of steam-power and the transfer of industry

[1] Yet even as early as 1732 parish officers were blamed for trying
to save expense by putting children out as early as possible to " any
sorry master that will take them."—Hutchins and Harrison, p. 6.

to the towns, continued at the rate of about two hundred victims a year till 1816, when it was made illegal to apprentice parish children at a distance of more than forty miles from London. Happily, however, not more than half of the London parishes had ever adopted the system.[1]

The magistrates of Lancashire could not afford to be so callous in this matter as those of Middlesex and Surrey, for an outbreak of fever at Manchester in 1784 was found to have originated amongst the children employed in one of the adjacent mills ; and they then resolved on the advice of Dr. Perceval and other physicians not to countenance the use of parish apprentices in factories where they would be required to work during the night or for more than ten hours during the day. The recurrence of similar epidemics led to the formation of the Manchester Board of Health in 1795, the members of which, in view of " the excellent regulations which subsist in several cotton factories," recommended an application to Parliament in order to establish " a general system of laws for the wise, humane and equal government of all such works." Nothing, however, was attempted in this direction till Sir Robert Peel, father of the statesman and one of the largest cotton manufacturers, brought the matter before Parliament in 1802. Peel was advised by Dr. Perceval ; but his factories were at Blackburn, some twenty-five miles from Manchester, and appear to have been of the isolated class which could hardly have been centres of disease. In the account of his motives which he gave, thirteen years later, to a Select Committee,[2] of which he himself was chairman, he said that on the rare occasions on which he could find time to visit his factories he was struck with " the uniform appearance of bad health and often stunted growth of the children," and ascribed this to the system under which the overseer was paid according

---

[1] *Report of Committee on Parish Apprentices,* 1815 ; Hansard, xxxi. 625 ; Hammond, *The Town Labourer,* pp. 144, 145.
[2] *Committee on Children in Manufactures,* H. C., 1816, iii. 132.

to the work done and had consequently a motive for forcing or bribing the children to overtax their strength. The Act for the Preservation of the Health and Morals of Apprentices,[1] which was passed under his auspices, comprised all factories employing more than three children and twenty other hands ; but, with exception of a clause providing for white-washing and ventilation, it applied only to apprentices. These were not to work before six in the morning and after nine at night and for more than twelve hours, exclusive of meals. During the first four years of their apprenticeship they were to be instructed in reading, writing and arithmetic, and were to receive religious instruction on Sundays ; and the Justices of the Peace were to appoint two visitors yearly to see that these regulations were observed. The Act can hardly have been as ineffective as is generally supposed if Peel was at all justified in his claim that there was "a visible improvement in the health and general appearance of the children," and that "since the complete operation of the Act contagious disorders have rarely occurred." But too much was left to the discretion of the Justices, and we are told that "in some districts the very existence of the Act was unknown."[2]

We are now at the close of the first and most sombre phase of our subject ; but, if the friends of progress at this period were looking forward to a happier future, it must have been due to their hope of a termination of the war and not to a change in their actual condition. We have seen that all liberal and popular movements which the night of repression had overtaken on their march were sooner or later confronted and arrested by the spectre of revolution ; and there was as yet no sign of deliverance from this persistent and ubiquitous phantom. The Sedition Act, which practically prohibited all unauthorised public meetings, had indeed expired at the end of

---

[1] 42 Geo. III, c. 73.
[2] Hutchins and Harrison, pp. 7–11, 16–18.

1798 ; but the Treason Act, which made it a crime punishable in the second offence by transportation to criticise
in any hostile spirit the King, the Ministry or the constitution, and the Habeas Corpus Suspension Act, were
still in force ; and public and even popular opinion was
so much in favour of repression that the Government
was almost unchecked in the exercise of its exceptional
powers. We read of persons being apprehended and sent
on board a warship for laughing at the awkwardness of a
volunteer corps ; of one man being pilloried as the prelude
to five years' hard labour for calling out in the streets,
" No George, no war " ; of another sentenced to a year's
solitary confinement for having ventured on the impropriety of damning the King.[1] Fox, for proposing as
a toast at a meeting of the Whig Club " The Sovereignty
of the People," was expelled from the Privy Council ;
and Pitt had even consulted Dundas as to the expediency
of having him committed to the Tower.[2] It was at this
period that Bishop Horsley made his interesting discovery of the " sedition and atheism " which were taught
in Sunday schools. In short, the prevailing temper was
little better in England than it was in Scotland where, as
Lord Cockburn says in reference to the French Revolution, " Everything, not this or that thing, was soaked in
this one event." [3]

But the deeds of the Government fell short of its
designs. Pitt's mentors in religious affairs were Wilberforce and his own college tutor, Pretyman, whom he had
made Bishop of Lincoln ; and between the two he had
some chance of steering an even course ; for, whilst the
former was devoted to " the serious clergy," the latter
—and Pitt himself inclined to the same opinion—thought
them " great rascals." At the instigation of Pretyman
the Government in 1799 had resolved to bring in a Bill—
indeed they had already drafted it—for repealing the

---

[1] Veitch's *Genesis of Parliamentary Reform*, p. 335.
[2] Stanhope's *Pitt*, iii. 128.   [3] *Memorials*, p. 70.

Toleration Act in so far at least as it extended to itinerant preachers; and it was only with the greatest
difficulty that Wilberforce prevailed on the Prime Minister
to abandon this scheme. "I confess," he wrote, "I never
till then knew how deep a prejudice his mind had
conceived against the clergy to whom he knew me
to be attached."[1]

Whilst the civil government was enforcing and devising
measures to avert the danger of revolution, the military
authorities had a similar scheme in hand which they were
less anxious to avow. The peace army of England on
the home establishment had been some 20,000 men disposed in forty-three fortresses and garrison towns; but
at the end of the war in 1815 there were 163,000 men
accommodated in two hundred barracks; and there is
good reason to believe that the object aimed at in this
development was rather to occupy than to defend the
country. Pitt can hardly have been contemplating war
with France in the spring of 1792, for he reduced by 2000
the number of sailors in the Navy; and yet in the
following June, shortly after the issue of the proclamation
against seditious writings, a certain Colonel Delaney was
appointed as Barrackmaster-General to provide additional
accommodation for troops. The funds placed at his disposal were not voted specifically by Parliament but were
paid out of 'Extraordinaries of the Army'; and though,
as the result of an inquiry which was made in 1804, it
appeared that this official had received £9,000,000 of
which he could give no satisfactory account, had appropriated large sums to himself as personal expenses,
and had even appointed barrack-masters where there
were no barracks, he was allowed to retire with the
colonelcy of a dragoon regiment and a pension of £6 a
day. One can only acquiesce in the assumption that
Pitt, knowing that Parliament was not likely to sanction
any large scheme of barrack-building, had conceived it

[1] *Life of Wilberforce*, ii. 335, 360, 362.

his duty to proceed in the matter by stealth. Most of the infantry were disposed round the coast ; but detachments of cavalry, as more suitable for the breaking up of mobs, were stationed in manufacturing centres such as Nottingham, Northampton, Manchester, Coventry and Sheffield ; and it is significant that, of forty-eight barracks for cavalry, only two were built to contain as many as six troops.[1] The Opposition had obtained sufficient information to raise a debate in Parliament as early as 1793 ; and, three years later, we find one of them exclaiming in the course of his speech, "Good God, was every town to be made a citadel, and every village to be converted into a garrison ? "[2]

There was, however, a suspicion—which was amply confirmed during the food disturbances of 1795—that both regular soldiers and militiamen were as likely to support as to oppose the mob ; and hence recourse was had to Volunteers. These were always a more or less select corps, for few workmen could afford or obtain time for the term of drilling which procured exemption from the Militia ballot ; but, as their numbers increased, so did their sympathy with the people ; and the only section of them which could always be trusted was the mounted Yeomanry, which, being drawn from the upper ranks of the agricultural class, had nothing in common with the populace of the towns. A similar development may be noted in Scotland. There in 1792 persons willing to co-operate in maintaining "internal tranquillity " were invited to enrol themselves as Volunteers ; but in 1796, when fear of invasion coincided with the alarm which

---

[1] Fortescue's *History of the British Army*, iv. 903–907. The practice of billeting troops, which prevailed before the establishment of barracks, is said to have had a very bad effect on their morals—so bad, that in 1791, 1792 and 1793, out of every fourteen criminals executed in London, one was a Guardsman.—Hansard, N.S., x. 865.

[2] Hansard, xxxii. 929. Something very like the result thus apprehended was noticed by Louis Simond, a French visitor, in 1810.— Smart's *Economic Annals*, i. 316.

gave rise to the Sedition and Treason Bills, the response to this appeal assumed such dimensions that Principal Hill confessed to a friend that he dreaded the Volunteers more than the French. The First Edinburgh Regiment had, he said, consisted wholly of gentlemen ; but the corps now being raised in all the towns were "a promiscuous armed democracy." [1]

This elaborate system of repression, political and military, may well surprise us when we remember that the masses, at all events at the time of its inception, were decidedly hostile to the Revolution ; but their temper was not what it had been ; and the change would seem to have originated in the very "lean years" which brought the eighteenth century to a close. From 1794, the year before that in which the West Riding had displayed its enthusiasm for "Billy Pitt," [2] there was a series of poor harvests, culminating in that of 1799, which was so deficient that it amounted to little more than half a crop. [3] Throughout the eighteenth century the price of wheat had rarely exceeded 50s. a quarter ; but in February 1800 it was 101s. ; in July it had risen to 134s. ; and at the end of the year, after another poor harvest, it was again 130s. [4] The dearness of bread was not the only economic hardship which the lower classes had to face ; for the price of other necessaries, such as meat, butter, sugar, salt and soap, had enormously increased owing to the war taxation ; and in the southern half of England the poor rates had doubled since the beginning of the war. There had of course been a rise in wages, but not at all in proportion to their purchasing value. It was found, for example, that a Suffolk labourer who, some

---

[1] *Church and Reform in Scotland*, 1797–1843, p. 118.

[2] See p. 53.

[3] "Season uncommonly backward," wrote Wilberforce on June 8 ; "scarce a beginning of leaves on our oaks."

[4] "The two-penny loaf in London, August 1783, weighed twenty-one ounces. In March 1801 the two-penny loaf in London weighed only six ounces."—Pettegrew's *Memoirs of John Coakley Lettsom*, ii. 204.

thirty years earlier, had earned 5s. a week was now receiving, inclusive of 6s. from the parish, 15s.; but the amount of commodities represented by his original 5s. could not be purchased in 1800 for less than £1 6s. 5d. Efforts were made both by authority and precept to alleviate the distress. The corn duties were suspended; distilleries and starch-works were stopped. A proclamation was issued, and resolutions were signed, against the use of pastry and restricting individuals to one quartern loaf a week; and a saving in consumption of one-sixth is said to have been effected by an Act which forbade the sale of new bread.[1]

A much more popular remedy than these measures, prudent as they were, would have been a large grant of public money; but the ruling class had readily accepted the idea that the sufferings of the poor, like the reward of their labour, should be left under the sway of natural laws; and Wilberforce, who had "nearly resolved" to move a vote of a million, deplored the influence in this respect of the new economic doctrine. "The callousness, the narrow and foolish wisdom of servilely acquiescing in Adam Smith's general principles without allowance for a thousand circumstances which take the case out of the province of that very general principle to which they profess allegiance is producing effects as mischievous as the most determined and studied cruelty. This rather too strong, but not much." Writing in 1801 to Pitt, he forcibly expressed his fear "that a rooted disaffection to the constitution and government has made some progress among the lower orders, and even a little higher"; and declared "that in Yorkshire—in the manufacturing parts, I mean—in London and in its neighbourhood, and in parts of Essex all the lower orders are tainted." In the same year there were rumours of an "intended insurrection" at Leeds, and the authorities were much perturbed by the discovery of a seditious paper in the market-place

---

[1] Smart's *Economic Annals of Nineteenth Century*, i. 4–7.

of Manchester.[1] Nottingham, which had once rioted in
support of repression, was in 1803 rioting against it ;
and, as Cartwright remarked, the disturbances were
summarily put down " now that the popular voice is in
favour of freedom." [2]

No one did more to keep alive the spirit of liberty
in its darkest hour than the man who has just been
mentioned—Major John Cartwright,[3] known as ' The
Father of Reform ' on account of a pamphlet on this
subject which he published as early as 1776. Cartwright
had the same reverence for the early constitution as has
a Catholic for the primitive Church. He believed the
Anglo-Saxons to have been an enlightened and highly
civilised people, and was ever trying to restore the system
of government to what it had been in those remote times
when standing armies and a restricted franchise were
both, as he imagined, equally unknown, when every
freeman helped to govern and to defend his country,
when Parliaments were no less pure than democratic,
and so closely in touch with the people that a new one
was elected every year. His zeal, as one may suppose,
was not according to knowledge. Whenever he found
the word " Commonwealth " mentioned in the utterances
of a Tudor or Stewart sovereign he took this to mean
that the national polity had once been a republic ; and
he exposed himself to the raillery of the *Edinburgh
Review* by citing *Brevia Parliamentaria Rediviva*—the
title of a treatise on parliamentary writs—as " Short
Parliaments Restored." [4] The immunity he enjoyed at
a time when less conspicuous agitators could not raise

---

[1] *Life of Wilberforce*, ii. 383–387 ; iii. 6, 8, 12, 13 ; Hammond,
The Town Labourer, p. 315.   [2] *Life of Cartwright*, i. 312.

[3] Cartwright had served for twenty years in the Navy, and in
1792 was deprived of his commission in the Nottinghamshire Militia.
British soldiers are indebted to him for their greatcoats—" a comfort
which he obtained for them after repeated applications."—*Life*, i. 71.

[4] *E.R.*, xxx. 199. The Major defended himself on the plea that
he had been " too much engaged in studying English liberty to pay
attention to Roman language," and met with the happy retort " that

their heads was due no doubt to his considerable social position, to the well-known mildness and amiability of his character, and still more to the comparative harmlessness of his methods. In common with all advanced Whigs, he regarded Pitt as a traitor to the cause of reform, and was always preparing some explosion of opinion which should come " as a thunder clap to the terrified apostate " ; but the meetings and petitions he promoted were too " respectable " to be alarming ; and his old comrade, Lord Stanhope, wrote to him not unreasonably : " I must confess I have seen too much not to be thoroughly sick of the old dull road of meetings of freeholders convened by the aristocracy." Such as they were, these activities completely absorbed him, and he had little patience with other " political veterans," his equals perhaps in enthusiasm, but not in strength. Thus when Wyvil, at the same age of sixty-eight, fought shy of the chair at a public meeting, he declined to excuse him " on no better plea on your part than ' infirmities.' What so proper for age and infirmity as an arm-chair ? " [1]

The Radical victory at Westminster in 1807 attracted Cartwright to reformers of the new generation such as Francis Place, with whom he used frequently to dine, " eating some raisins he brought in his pocket and drinking weak gin and water." [2] In the company of such men the " Old Gentleman," as they called him, could not fail to see that the re-awakening he had hoped and worked for was actually in progress ; and we shall meet with him later, in 1813, no longer traversing " the old dull road of meetings of freeholders," but touring as an " itinerant apostle " through the industrial centres of the south-west, the midlands and the north of England.

To men of a liberal turn of mind who lived through

the barbarous Latin in question is only worth learning because it assists the study of English liberty."

[1] *Life of Cartwright*, i. 294, 325, 327, 381.
[2] Wallas's *Francis Place*, p. 63.

these ten years of war with Republican France, it must necessarily have seemed a time of shattered hopes and unmitigated gloom. But what was conjecture and anticipation to them is fact and retrospect to us ; and the period has a more cheerful aspect when viewed from the historical standpoint.

We have seen that the parliamentary reform movement had slowed down, if it had not come wholly to a standstill, before 1789 ; and all that can really be charged against the French Revolution is that eventually, by way of reaction, it stifled a revival which had emanated mainly from itself. It is true that the ruling classes were rendered much more suspicious of change and more determined to resist it than they would otherwise have been ; but the growth of a factory population inspired by such veteran reformers as Cartwright and Wyvil must in any case have brought them into conflict with the old demand for universal suffrage and annual parliaments ; and, if the masses were not satisfied with the results obtained in 1832, still less would they have been appeased by a reform of the legislature carried out in the latter years of the eighteenth century and directed more to the fuller representation of counties than to the enfranchisement and political reorganisation of towns. In short, one may say that the constitutional settlement had little to lose and much to gain by being deferred to a time when the consequences of the two revolutions, French and English, political and economic, could in some measure be reconciled.

In March 1802, some three months before the passing of Peel's Factory Act, the war came to an end with the Treaty of Amiens. The peace to which so many had looked forward as the fruition of their hopes lasted for little more than a year ; but the conflict in its second or Napoleonic phase, which opened in 1803, was to be waged under conditions which permitted of a more wholesome atmosphere and the prevalence of less illiberal ideas.

CHAPTER II

WE are apt to look back on our successive struggles with Revolutionary and with Napoleonic France as almost continuous, and to consider as of little moment the fourteen months of precarious peace from March 1802 to May 1803 ; and yet from the spiritual point of view the two periods of warfare are sharply defined, the keynote of the one being internal repression, of the other external defence. In the earlier period there had indeed been several threats of invasion and some actual landings, as in Wales in 1796 and in Ireland during the rebellion of 1798 ; but the impression produced by these incidents was entirely eclipsed by the excitement and alarm resulting from Bonaparte's elaborate preparations, at the renewal of the war, to transport across the Channel what he called " the Army of England." As Lord Cockburn, the well-known Scottish judge, puts the case in his " Memorials," " Instead of Jacobinism, Invasion became the word." Henceforth there was a better basis than mere coercion for the maintenance of " internal tranquillity " ; and the bonds of repression, though not removed, were unconsciously relaxed.

It was not only, however, in the spirit that it fostered but in its character that the Napoleonic differed from the Revolutionary War. Austria and Prussia may well seem to have brought on themselves the earlier conflict by their endeavours to stem the tide of revolution in France ; and, though the French, owing to their success, naturally advanced from the defensive to the aggressive, it is at least an arguable position that they had taken arms at the outset in support of their democratic constitution. But the second war, which was begun by Bonaparte as First Consul and continued by him as the Emperor Napoleon, was due wholly to his lust of conquest ; and the monarchies which withstood him could not fail in the long run to be reinforced or eliminated by the up-rising of peoples.   It was the Spaniards in this respect, after their Government had collapsed with the capture of their King, who set an example to all Europe.   The Spanish rising of 1808 was hailed with enthusiasm by both parties in Britain ; and the Whigs speedily impressed upon their opponents that they could not logically encourage a popular spirit in Spain and continue at the same time to repress it at home.   Jeffrey declared that it was " the bulk—the mass of the people—nay, the very odious, many-headed beast, the multitude—the mob itself " that had checked the conqueror's career ; and he added with natural satisfaction : " We can once more utter the words *liberty* and *people* without starting at the echo of our voices."

The *Edinburgh Review* from which these words are quoted had itself contributed largely to the diffusion of liberal ideas.   Planned in March 1802, whilst the diplo-matists were sitting in council at Amiens, by Sydney Smith, Jeffrey, Brougham and Horner, and appearing in the following October, it presented a combination, hitherto unknown, of literature and journalism, and dis-cussed politics with a " temperate air " which astonished and disappointed those who had predicted from such a source " nothing short of blood and atheism and de-mocracy."[1]   Its immediate and prodigious success was due mainly to its high literary merit ; for many—if not the large majority—of its readers, and some even of its contributors, such as Scott and Dr. Chalmers, were

[1] Horner's *Memoirs*, i. 204.

Tories ; but it rendered inestimable services to the Whigs by associating them with the supreme authority in matters of literature and taste and providing them with an organ in which, subject to no great restraint, they could express their political views. It was not till 1808, the year of the Spanish rising, that Scott had much reason to complain of " deepening Whiggery " ; and owing partly to that cause, but still more to the extreme pessimism expressed by the *Edinburgh* in regard to the war, he founded in the following year, with the aid of Canning, a rival organ, the *Quarterly Review*.

Of the movements which had collapsed under suspicion of Jacobinism, the last to succumb was the agitation against the slave trade, which had suffered merely because it pursued a legitimate object by too democratic means ; and it was naturally the first to revive. We have seen that a proposal of abolition in four years had passed the House of Commons in 1792. When this period expired in 1796, not only was no attempt made to give effect to this resolution, but a Bill for abolition in the following year was thrown out on the third reading by a majority of four [1] ; and meanwhile the Lords had rejected two subsidiary schemes—one to prohibit British merchants from supplying foreign colonies with slaves, the other to restrict the area of their operations in Africa. Wilberforce continued year after year to bring forward proposals which were now limited to gradual abolition ; and, though his stock of courage and patience was inexhaustible, it must necessarily have been replenished through the accession to the cause of his friend and future brother-in-law, James Stephen. Stephen was a member of the West Indian bar, who had returned to England for good in 1794 and then publicly avowed what he had long professed and even given effect to in private—his utter detestation of the trade. So com-

[1] " Enough at the Opera to have carried it."—*Life of Wilberforce*, ii. 142.

plete and zealous indeed was Stephen's devotion to the slaves that he found something to censure even in Wilberforce, whom he called " the Moses of these Israelites, though at the same time a courtier of Pharaoh." [1] It was not, however, from lack of zeal, but from his hope of drawing all Europe into abolition at the Peace and his desire not to prejudice this prospect by another parliamentary defeat, that Wilberforce refrained from introducing his usual motion in 1800 ; and various causes—the endeavour to prevent an extension of the trade to newly conquered colonies, such as Trinidad and Guiana, a dissolution of Parliament, illness and the preparations to resist invasion—induced him to prolong this truce for four years.

In 1804 the whole abolitionist army was once more in motion, including the London Committee, which now met regularly at Wilberforce's own house, and Clarkson as its travelling agent ; and from this point one obstacle after another was removed from its path. Success in the Commons might well seem assured now that a hundred Irish members—most of them favourable to the cause —had been added to the House. With the impeachment of Lord Melville, for which Wilberforce was held mainly responsible, having spoken " with more effect than has almost ever happened to me in the House of Commons," [2] a most formidable opponent disappeared from public life. The death of Pitt early in 1806 removed indeed a sincere friend, but brought into power a far more ardent one in Fox ; and the new Government was not only much more favourable to abolition than its predecessor, only two Cabinet Ministers being hostile, but also much less subservient to the King. George III had favoured the movement in its early days ; but, as soon as the cry of Jacobinism was raised, he opposed it with

---

[1] *Life of Wilberforce*, ii. 257. [2] *Ibid.*, iii. 225.

a bitterness and pertinacity in which with unusual filial devotion he was followed by all his sons, except the Duke of Sussex.[1]

There was little, however, at the re-opening of the campaign to foreshadow its victorious close. In 1804 it was agreed that the Lords should postpone consideration of a Bill which had been passed by large majorities in the Lower House. In 1805, as the result of over-confidence, the same measure, when brought again into the Commons, was actually thrown out. But in the following year, when Pitt's administration had been replaced by that of Lord Grenville, with Fox as Foreign Secretary, it became manifest that the fortress which Wilberforce and his friends had assailed for twenty years must soon be in their hands. The slave trade with foreign and with the newly conquered colonies was prohibited by statute ; and both Houses concurred in a resolution to put an end as soon as possible to the whole traffic. On January 2, 1807, a Bill for general and immediate abolition was brought into the Lords, and, having passed rapidly and easily through all its stages, was received by the Commons on February 10. On the 23rd it was committed by the overwhelming majority of 283 to 16 ; and one can well understand the ovation that was accorded to Wilberforce when the Solicitor-General, Sir Samuel Romilly, contrasted him as a conqueror with Napoleon, the preserver with the destroyer of human life—" such," wrote Bishop Porteus, " as was scarcely ever before given to any man sitting in his place in either House of Parliament." [2] Having been verbally amended, the Bill had again to pass the Lords ; and at noon on March 25, 1807, a few minutes before the Ministers

---

[1] On the very eve of abolition Wilberforce records " The Princes canvassing against us, alas ! "—*Life*, iii. 291. On the other hand, the Duke of Gloucester, the King's brother, was a keen abolitionist.
[2] *Life of Wilberforce*, iii. 297.

gave up their seals of office, it received the royal assent.[1]

The movement which had thus at last been crowned with success is memorable as the first attempt—outside party politics—to overthrow what would now be called a powerful vested interest.[2] Philanthropy in earlier days had had difficulties enough to contend with, but they were not of this magnitude and kind.   The slave trade was a national and colonial as well as a commercial institution ; statesmen, sailors and soldiers had all contributed to establish and extend it ; its capital value as estimated by the planters was sixty millions, whilst to Liverpool alone it brought an annual return of £300,000. It was supposed to be essential to the loyalty as well as to the prosperity of our West Indian possessions ; and in the opinion of its friends it neither should nor could be abolished because it had become an object of competition to the European Powers, and, even if all Europe should renounce it, would still be carried on in the interest of African chiefs.   That the lawyers would side with the merchants and planters in this controversy might easily have been foreseen, and in fact they were almost uniformly hostile.[3]   Burke and Lord North had both at one time or another regarded abolition as all but impossible ; and the former in 1780 had even devised a scheme for the regulation and eventual suppression of the trade which on further consideration he had thought it useless to divulge.[4]   The assumption which underlay this opinion

[1] Fox did not live to participate in this triumph. He had died in the previous September, declaring in his last moments that he longed for abolition even more than for peace. An Act making it felony to engage in the slave trade was procured by Brougham in 1811.

[2] Just as in our day " the trade " means the liquor trade, so in those days it meant the slave trade. Compare Halévy, *Histoire*, i. 431, where the section devoted to this subject is headed " L'Abolition de la Traite."

[3] " The bar were all against us. Fox could scarcely prevent Erskine from making a set speech in favour of the trade."—*Life of Wilberforce*, i. 293.   [4] Lecky, vii. 367, 373.

—that a thing really profitable in itself was to be given up merely on account of its repugnance to the moral sense—was indeed a complete illusion ; but it was specious and plausible, and could be maintained on far more honest grounds than the denial of cruelty ; and the effort to meet an opponent so well equipped with argument as well as with sophistry, mendacity and wealth proved too much, as we have seen, for Ramsay and cost the youthful and more robust Clarkson all but his life.[1] The few who could claim to be competent and disinterested judges were all at last constrained to admit that this commerce in human flesh had for many years been a losing and not a paying business ; that, far from being a nursery for seamen, it was, owing to climate, vice, hardship and ill-usage " the very grave of seamen, destroying more than all our foreign trade besides "[2]; that slave labour could be obtained from other and better sources, and in any case was at least twice as expensive as free labour ; that the only effect of abolition on the planter would be to save him from ruin ; and that, if we relinquished our share of the trade, the French were not at all likely to take it up, since they could not without our help in ships and goods carry on what they already had. The appeal to expediency, however, was or should have been superfluous and irrelevant in dealing with what Wesley had well described as " that execrable sum of all villainies " ; and the records of British philanthropy contain no more illustrious names than those of the four men—Sharp, Ramsay, Clarkson and Wilberforce—who did most to expose this iniquity to the gaze of an indignant nation.

The year 1807 is memorable for other reasons than the abolition of the slave trade. We have seen that the

---

[1] He retired from the contest, with the loss of his health and most of his small means, in 1794 and did not return to it till 1803. A private subscription to replace the £1500 he had spent was promoted by Wilberforce.

[2] Ramsay's *Objections to Abolition, with Answers*, p. 42.

enthusiasm for the Church which characterised the reigns of William and Anne had resulted in a movement for the erection of charity schools ; and the nineteenth century was to open, like its predecessor, with an endeavour to promote the education of the poor. In this case, however, it was a much controverted point whether the initiative had been taken by a Churchman or a Quaker. Joseph Lancaster, a member of the latter persuasion, began work as a schoolmaster in London in 1798. Though without private means, he resolved from the first to charge only half the usual fees ; and in 1801, relying on a subscription of £118, he opened a free school. Having this motive for economy, he employed the older boys to instruct the younger, and endeavoured to minimise, if not wholly to supersede, the use of books and stationery by hanging up cards printed in large type to teach reading, and by using slates and chalk to teach spelling, writing and arithmetic. The cost of prizes was avoided by the introduction of badges and orders of merit [1] ; and he banished the rod—which, however, he can hardly have found expensive—in favour of emblems and usages well, if not wisely, calculated to expose a pupil to the scorn or ridicule of his fellows. In virtue of his economies, he found himself within four years in a position to teach as many as seven hundred boys at a cost of no more than £260 a year ; and, having published a book in explanation of his scheme, he obtained for it royal as well as Quaker and general support, and was soon traversing the country like another Wesley, except that schools and not chapels rose behind him as the fruit of his apostolical zeal.

The sort of religious teaching which was provided in these schools—purely Biblical and unsectarian—was regarded with great disfavour by Churchmen ; and, happily for them, an Indian chaplain, Andrew Bell, had greatly developed and improved the practice of teaching

[1] Sydney Smith had seen " these ragged and interesting little nobles shining in their tin stars."—*Works*, 1859, i. 169.

by monitors—which in itself was no new institution—
in a school which was established under his auspices at
Madras as early as 1789. Bell, moreover, had borrowed
from native usage the device of sand spread over a board
to teach writing, and this at least was a novelty in Europe.
On his return to England in 1796 he anticipated Lancaster
by six years in the publication of his system ; but it
appears to have been introduced into only two schools
at a time when the rival scheme was coming into general
vogue ; and he never made any attempt to imitate the
economies which were the really novel and valuable
part of the Lancastrian method ; for, whereas in the
one case the annual cost was estimated at about £4 a
head, in the other it was no more than from 4s. to 10s.,
according to the size of the school.[1]

The controversy as to which of the two innovators
was entitled to the credit of originality was waged, after
an interchange of civilities, fiercely enough, but was soon
eclipsed in this respect by the more important question
whether "the Christian religion" or the religion of the
Church of England was to be taught in the popular
schools. The Churchmen were perhaps on the whole
the more bitter and vehement ; and conspicuous amongst
them was Robert Southey, who admitted that Lancaster
had done great good, but said that it was "pretty much
in the way that the Devil has been the cause of the
Redemption." The result was that Whigs, Quakers,
Dissenters, and even irreligious Radicals united in
forming, first the Royal Lancastrian Association, and
then the British and Foreign School Society, to propagate
the principles and methods of Lancaster, whilst Bell's
schools and most of the old charity schools were placed
under a body instituted by the Christian Knowledge
Society, the parent and guardian of the latter—the

---

[1] The average in the charity schools, where, however, the children
were always clothed and frequently boarded, was £14.—*Parl. Debates*,
ix. 540.

National Society for the Education of the Poor according to the Principles of the Established Church.   In personal character as well as in the financial aspect of their schemes the protagonists in this conflict were as complete a contrast as can well be conceived—Bell, despite the expensiveness of his system, having as wonderful a faculty for saving his own and judiciously spending other people's money as had Lancaster, despite the cheapness of *his* system, for dissipating both ; and thus, whilst the latter was soon excluded from all share in the management of what may be called his own association, the former was himself the life and soul of the National Society, received rather more than his due of academic and ecclesiastical favours, amassed a large fortune and was admitted to the posthumous honour of a tomb in Westminster Abbey.[1]

A bold but unsuccessful attempt to secure national recognition for this movement was made in 1807, when Whitbread proposed that the parochial authorities should be required to provide two years of gratuitous but compulsory education, under their own superintendence and that of the clergy, for the children of the poor between the ages of seven and fourteen.   A Bill to this effect was fully discussed in the Commons, a month after the abolition of the slave trade, on April 24.   Re-introduced after a general election in the summer had given a more Tory complexion to the House, it was amended so as to leave its adoption to be determined by a majority of the parishioners ; and, having passed in this form through the Commons, it was thrown out by the Lords, as had no doubt been foreseen, on the ground that it admitted parochial as well as clerical control.

The wonderful progress of the Scots under their system of general elementary education was naturally a theme which Whitbread and his supporters turned to

[1] *Edinburgh Review*, Nov. 1810 ; *Quarterly Review*, Oct. 1811 ; Bartley's *Schools for the People*, p. 330.

the fullest account ; and one of them declared that there were " many stations of society in this part of the Island " which none but Scotsmen were found competent to fill. It was generally agreed that the discredit accruing to England from this comparison ought in some measure to be removed ; that this could safely be done provided the poor were taught only to read ; but that to carry their education further would be to give them a distaste for manual occupations to which, as it was, they were but too little inclined. Perceval, who was to succeed the Duke of Portland as Prime Minister, remarked that Quakers were almost invariably educated, but "he never knew of an Agricultural Quaker." There were several members, however, who refused to make even this modest concession ; and conspicuous amongst them were Windham, the most scholarly of leading politicians, and Giddy, a scientist and a generous promoter of science, who twenty years later, when he had assumed the name of Gilbert, was to succeed Sir Humphry Davy as President of the Royal Society. The former made no secret from the first of his hostility to the diffusion of knowledge ; but the latter in April attacked mainly the principle of compulsion in education, a boon which, he said, " should descend like the gentle dew from Heaven "[1] ; and it was not till he found himself in the more congenial atmosphere of the new Parliament that he ventured to disclose the whole mystery of his obscurantist soul. He then said plainly that the giving of education to the labouring classes would be prejudicial to their morals and happiness—to their morals, apparently, because it would make them discontented, refractory and insolent, and to their happiness because it would enable them to read seditious, licentious and anti-Christian literature ; and he concluded by expressing his disapproval of ministering even to the material wants of the poor on

[1] Its descent from such a source ought surely to have been facilitated and not obstructed by the Church.

the ground that parish relief tended only to maintain them in habits of idleness and vice.[1]

Memorable in the annals of philanthropy, if not also in those of education, the year 1807 derives additional importance from the fact that it witnessed the rise o modern Radicalism. There was indeed no break in the personal continuity of this school, nor, at least as a latent force, had it ever become extinct; and it is remarkable how little its development had been deflected by Paine and the French republicanism he endeavoured to import. Wilkes had died in 1797; but Horne Tooke, who in 1768 had been practically his election agent for Middlesex, was still living, and so were several other men little less venerable than the " patriarch of the popular party "—Cartwright, Wyvil, Sir Philip Francis and Lord Stanhope. Tooke had the same reverence, if not quite the same enthusiasm, as Cartwright for our " glorious constitution," and was less alive to its defects, for he was no believer in universal suffrage and annual parliaments[2]; and yet it was he, and not the father—as Cartwright has been called—of personal as opposed to class representation, who was to choose a field of battle for the new Radicalism and even to present it with a leader. The ground he selected was not the historic Middlesex, but geographically was within its bounds. The City of Westminster was the most aristocratic and at the same time the least exclusive constituency represented in the unreformed Parliament. Extending from Temple Bar on the east side to Kensington Palace on the west, and from Oxford Street on the north side to the Thames on the south, it comprised the most fashionable part of London; but the population of this area—then about half built over—exceeded 150,000, and the electorate, consisting of all householders who paid " scot and lot," or in other words the local rates, numbered about 13,000.

---

[1] Hansard, ix. 537, 798, 1174.
[2] Stephens's *Horne Tooke*, ii. 41, 324.

Prior to 1780 the representation, controlled by the Dean and Chapter, had been at the disposal of the Crown ; but in that year Fox, after a struggle unprecedented for riotousness and expense, succeeded in capturing one of the two seats ; and an arrangement was then made— similar to that which prevailed in so many of the counties [1] —that the Whigs should have one seat and the Tories the other. This compromise, which extinguished for political purposes the most popular constituency in England, was challenged in 1790 and again in 1796 by Tooke, who, repudiating all corrupt influence and avowing himself equally hostile to both parties, contrived nevertheless at the second contest to poll as many as 2819 votes.[2]

In 1797 Tooke made the acquaintance of Sir Francis Burdett, and was thus enabled to render the last and not the least of his services to the liberal cause. Burdett, then in his twenty-eighth year, had just entered Parliament and had already distinguished himself by the ability and eloquence with which he attacked the repressive policy of Pitt. The two were near neighbours at Wimbledon, and the intimacy between them developed into a relation less like that of master and disciple than of father and son. Tooke was at great pains to keep so promising a politician uncontaminated by the Whigs and at the same time to counteract a tendency to Jacobinism which he had acquired from personal contact with the Revolution at Paris. In 1802 Burdett stood and was elected for Middlesex ; but the return was disputed ; and, after spending nearly £100,000 in contesting another election and three election petitions, he found himself finally unseated in 1806. The loss of so large a sum was a serious consideration even for one whose marriage into the great banking house of Coutts had made one of

[1] See p. 14.
[2] Graham Wallas's *Life of Francis Place*, p. 39 ; Stephens's *Horne Tooke*, ii. 164–227.

the wealthiest men in England ; and the defeated candidate, having better uses for his money, resolved to squander no more of it on the doorstep of the House of Commons. No departure from this resolution was involved when he allowed himself to be nominated with the famous sailor, Lord Cochrane, for the representation of Westminster ; for the reformers in that constituency, encouraged no doubt by their recollection of Tooke's comparative success, were now confident that they could overthrow the Whig and Tory coalition at no more than the necessary expense. In 1807 they triumphantly achieved their purpose and thus placed Burdett in a seat which he was to occupy without interruption for the next thirty years. This was a memorable victory, whether we look back to 1768 or forward to 1832 ; and we shall find that it has a further significance in being the first success of the political organiser, Francis Place, and— as a democratic journalist—of Cobbett. Two years later, Burdett made his first, appearance after this election as a reformer in Parliament ; and, true to the principles of his tutor, he demanded the franchise for all those, but for those only, who paid direct taxes.[1]

On the philosophical side it cannot be said that Radicalism presents the same unbroken sequence ; for Price had died in 1791, and Priestley, after living for ten years in America, in 1804 ; and Bentham, who was to take their place, was still at the later of these dates no more than a disillusioned Tory. But in this connexion the link of continuity is to be found in the first Marquis of Lansdowne, better known by his earlier title as the Earl of Shelburne, whose political career extends from 1760, when he entered the House of Commons as a satellite of Bute, to his resignation of the Premiership in 1783. It would indeed have been well for Shelburne's reputation if he had never been called upon to take an

---

[1] Halévy's *Radicalisme*, ii. 195–200 ; Stephens's *Horne Tooke*, ii. 233, 306.

active part in politics ; for an ambitious, overbearing spirit, a caustic tongue, a temper at once rash and suspicious, and "a habit of overstrained compliment "[1] combined to make him universally distrusted and disliked ; and his devotion to principles in which he anticipated and supported the French Revolution served only to increase his isolation in the midst of politicians whom Burke had taught to believe in the superiority of their traditions and instincts to science. He had indeed an abhorrence of party government, especially as practised by the Whigs, which made him on two occasions a tool of George III, and at all times a follower of Chatham ; but, whilst George and Chatham resented this merely as they would have resented any other curb on their personal ascendancy, Shelburne saw in it—what Burke also saw and exulted in seeing—an obstacle to reform in accordance with abstract ideas.[2] Pitt, who had been his Chancellor of the Exchequer, procured for him a marquisate in 1784. This was no great amends for his exclusion from office ; and Lansdowne, though he never hesitated to avow his revolutionary opinions in Parliament, spent the last thirty years of his life mainly in the seclusion of his woods and gardens, his books and statuary at Bowood in Wiltshire, studying the new political economy which he had first learned from Adam Smith during a journey from Edinburgh to London in 1761, and entertaining and corresponding with a choice company of philosophers, artists and men of letters.

Before France intervened in the American War, he had been frequently in Paris as the guest of Baron d'Holbach ; and amongst his more intimate friends were the Abbé Morellet, an economist of the school of Turgot and Smith, whom he always credited with having "liberalised his ideas " ; Dumont, the future secretary

---

[1] Sir Leslie Stephen, *The English Utilitarians*, i. 183.
[2] " Les démocrates sont des doctrinaires, et c'est pourquoi les Whigs ne sont pas des démocrates."—Halévy, *Radicalisme*, i. 269.

and confidant of Mirabeau ; Franklin, Romilly, and, for a time at least, Horne Tooke. It was he who persuaded Price to turn from theological to political speculation ; Priestley was for many years his librarian ; and in 1781 he sought out Bentham and formed with him a friendship which was the only real recognition of his first book. With men of this stamp Lansdowne was always at his best ; and Bentham, though by no means blind to the faults which had caused his failure as a politician,[1] has given us a pleasing sketch of him in the freedom and simplicity of his country home. " The master of Bowood, to judge from everything I have seen yet, is one of the pleasantest men to live with that ever God put breath into ; his whole study seems to be to make everybody about him happy—servants not excepted ; and in their countenances one may read the effects of his endeavours." And the soundness and thoroughness of his liberalism is attested by the same authority, who says that he was " really radically disposed," a sincere admirer of the French Revolution, and "the only Minister he ever heard of who did not fear the people." It was a frequent complaint of Lord Lansdowne, and one fully justified in the opinion of both Bentham and Lord Holland, that in boyhood his " education was neglected to the greatest degree " ; but, like many of his rank in what Matthew Arnold has called " the flowering time of the English aristocracy," he had a passion for intellectual pursuits, and with what result may be seen in these words written to Morellet shortly before his death in 1805 : " My mind gets every year more philosophised, and I cannot express the satisfaction it gives me to find it enlarging by dint of reflection and observation or the pleasure it gives me to see things,

---

[1] " There was a wildness about him, and he conceived groundless suspicions about nothing at all." The ambiguity so often charged against Shelburne may have been really due to a " want of clearness " in his thought and language, of which he himself was conscious.

great and small, through a just medium, unencumbered with prejudices and little passions, of which I feel I had my full share. I now look down upon them as I would upon a fog in a valley." [1]

The political philosophy of Bentham was a deduction —and a very belated one—from a principle which he had established at the outset of his juridical studies ; and it will suffice here to indicate how the thread of philosophical Radicalism was severed by him in his twenty-eighth year and left, as it were, a loose end till he himself returned in his old age to continue it in a new and permanent form. As early as 1776, the year in which were issued the American Declaration of Independence and Adam Smith's "Wealth of Nations," he had laid the foundation of modern political science by showing that in every organised community there is a sovereign power which, whoever its holder or holders and whatever the conditions of its exercise, is in itself unlimited, and the decrees of which are to be obeyed, so long as order is preferred to revolution; on their own authority and without reference to any question of origin or natural right. The "Fragment on Government" was no less fatal to the fiction of a social compact than to that of a division of powers in the British constitution as expounded by Blackstone, which was the immediate object of its attack ; but from the Utilitarian standpoint, which was common to both Priestley and Bentham, it would seem merely to have diverted the advance of Radicalism from one path to another ; for, if men are born neither free nor equal, but with a natural propensity to seek happiness and avoid pain, the power to coerce them ought surely to be lodged where, if abused, it will injure as few persons as possible. Bentham, however, was insensible to the democratic tendency of his argument and confessed long afterwards that he was

---

[1] Fitzmaurice's *Life of Shelburne*, 3 vols., *passim* ; Holland's *Memoirs of the Whig Party*, i. 39–43 ; Stephens's *Horne Tooke*, i. 159, 433 ; Halévy's *Radicalisme*, i. 268–270 ; Lecky, v. 132–139.

unable to see it for more than forty years. The politics
of his family had been Jacobite and were now Tory ; and
a Tory of the school of Hume and Gibbon, valuing
intellectual but not political freedom, he himself continued to be. Following the trend of French liberalism
before the Revolution, with which he had come into
personal contact at Paris, he relied on an enlightened
public opinion, operating through a free press, as sufficient
for the restraint and guidance of absolute rule ; and
he lived in daily expectation that one or another of the
benevolent despots who then abounded in Europe would
invite his assistance in drawing up a legal code. Indeed,
he offered two schemes of this kind to the new rulers of
France when they were contemplating or framing a
constitution. His inclusion in the gift of French citizenship was due to this cause.as well as to his friendship with
Brissot, president of the committee which selected the
names ; but the honour, such as it was—and Bentham,
like Wilberforce, regarded it as a very dubious compliment—would not have been bestowed, had it been
generally known that he was then at work on his
" Anarchical Fallacies "—a short treatise, not published
till 1816, in which he demolished the Declaration of
the Rights of Man.[1]

A series of disappointments as author, law-reformer
and philanthropist had no doubt its share in the political
development of Bentham. The " Fragment on Government," which was published anonymously, made so
favourable an impression that it was ascribed to several
eminent lawyers, including one so eminent as Lord
Mansfield ; but interest in it declined with the discovery
of the author ; and a much larger and more ambitious
work, " An Introduction to the Principles of Morals and
Legislation," which appeared in 1789, did not obtain even
this transient recognition. Meanwhile in the obscurity of
his chambers in Lincoln's Inn he had traversed almost

[1] Halévy's *Radicalisme*, i. 275 ; ii. 37.

the whole field of civil and criminal jurisprudence, exploding fictions, working out general principles, bringing everything to the touchstone of utility, and accumulating manuscript at the rate of twelve to fifteen folio pages a day.   His intimacy with Shelburne and his long and frequent visits to Bowood must have made him known to many distinguished people ; but for anything like general recognition he had to wait till 1802, when Dumont published in French at Paris a selection from his printed and unprinted works ; and even then he met with more appreciation in Russia, Spain and South America than in Britain, so that Hazlitt, some twenty years later, could say of him : " His reputation lies at the circumference, and the lights of his understanding are reflected with increasing lustre on the other side of the globe." [1]   Curiously enough, we are told that, having had mainly a continental reputation during his life, he has had only an insular one since his death.[2]

The practical English mind was better fitted to comprehend the philanthropist than the jurist ; and Bentham in this capacity had certainly gained a reputation, but one in which pity was mingled with respect. He had known Howard and was trying as a prison-reformer to carry on his work.   For nearly sixty years before the colonial revolt, the British Government had disposed of its convicts by transporting them to the tobacco plantations of North America and especially of Maryland.   The system had worked well for the criminals, whom it was frequently the means of reclaiming to an honest and industrious life, and not less well for the planters who found white labour of this kind so profitable that latterly they had agreed to defray the cost of its passage.   But this outlet for social wastage was closed by the opening of hostilities in 1775 ; and, the prisons having consequently become more over-crowded and

---

[1] *The Spirit of the Age*, p. 3.
[2] Sir Frederick Pollock's *History of the Science of Politics*, p. 104.

pestilential than ever, two Acts were passed—one in 1776 for the institution of convict ships or "hulks" and the other in 1779 for the erection of a penitentiary in which criminals were, if possible, to be reformed under a system of isolation and hard labour.   The latter scheme had been suggested by the success of a prison built on Howard's principles and with his advice by the Duke of Richmond at Horsham [1] ; and Howard himself, Eden and Blackstone were appointed "supervisors" to carry out the Act. They failed, however, to agree in the selection of a site ; Howard resigned ; and, though new supervisors not only found a site but were preparing plans, the scheme was abandoned in favour of transportation, which had again become possible owing to the discoveries of Captain Cook in the southern Pacific.   In 1784 Parliament sanctioned the despatch of criminals to New South Wales under the old system of indentured labour ; and in 1786 a penal settlement was founded at Botany Bay.[2]

Bentham did not approve of "hard labour," that is, of labour exacted as a punishment and not as an occupation ; and in 1791 he published a scheme for bringing to bear on a criminal during his detention every species of good influence—industrial, educational and moral. The local habitation of this ideal was to be a "circular building, an iron cage glazed, a glass lantern as large as Ranelagh," which he called the "Panopticon or Inspection House," because in the centre was an apartment from which the governor, whilst himself unseen, could look into "every cell and every part of a cell," so that "a sentiment of a sort of invisible omnipresence" should pervade the whole prison.[3]   Next year the death of his father, a wealthy solicitor, put him in possession of the funds required for prosecuting this inquisitorial, if not

[1] Lord Mansfield remarked in 1788 that the number of prisoners presented for trial from this district had been reduced by one-half.

[2] Lecky, vii. 325, 326, 335 ; Griffiths's *Memorials of Millbank,* 2nd edition, pp. 7–11.

[3] Davidson's *Political Thought,* pp. 107–113.

eerie, project ; and he at once approached the Government with a proposal that he should be empowered to erect and to manage an institution for the treatment on his own principles of a thousand convicts. Dundas, the Home Secretary, warmly welcomed his suggestion, and so apparently did Pitt ; but it was not till 1794 that he obtained the sanction of Parliament, and five years more were consumed in fruitless endeavours to acquire a suitable and available site. At last in 1799, after spending great part of his means in premature contracts, he succeeded in purchasing the lands at Pimlico—then a marshy tract known as Tothill Fields—on which Millbank Penitentiary now stands ; but only to this small extent is the present building associated with Bentham. The " Panopticon " continued for a dozen years longer to be a subject of doubt and hesitation to the official mind ; but in 1811, on the adverse report of a committee, it was finally dismissed, and in 1813 an Act was passed under which the inventor was awarded as compensation a sum of · £23,000. The same Act provided for the erection at Millbank of a penitentiary, which was at once begun on a plan furnished by open competition, was partially opened in 1816, and completed at a cost of £450,000 in 1822.[1] Wilberforce, at this time an intimate friend of Bentham, had endeavoured to assist him in the prosecution of his claims and witnessed with keen resentment the indignities to which he was exposed. " I have seen the tears run down the cheeks of that strong-minded man through vexation at the pressing importunities of creditors and the insolence of official underlings when day after day he was begging at the Treasury for what was indeed a mere matter of right." [2]

Bentham had once said of the British constitution that it " stood perhaps at no great distance from the

---

[1] Griffiths's *Memorials of Millbank*, pp. 8-22.
[2] *Life of Wilberforce*, ii. 171. One is reminded of Daniel Doyce and the Circumlocution Office.

summit of perfection." After such an experience, he must necessarily have judged more soberly of its merits ; and Wilberforce may have been right in assuming that many of the "harsh opinions" he subsequently adopted were "the fruit of this ill-treatment." But another and more direct influence was at work to produce a change in his political views. From 1788 to the end of the century his attention had been engrossed mainly by the "Panopticon" and the French Revolution. In 1802 he returned to the study of jurisprudence, and to that branch of it—the theory of evidence—in which the common law was most in need of reform. Whilst carefully analysing the value of evidence, he was disposed as a Utilitarian to insist that the more one can get of it the better. He found, however, that English judges in the course of their decisions had built up a most intricate system of rules for delaying, excluding and attenuating evidence ; and this led him to denounce "judge-made law" as scarcely less mischievous than "priest-made religion," and its predominance as a tyranny "the most all-comprehensive, most grinding and most crying of all grievances."[1] As the constitution, like the law, of England, was based on precedent rather than on statute, and as the two systems were in practice inextricably intertwined, Bentham could not disparage the one without reflecting on the other. Now at last, as one of his critics has remarked, he was fairly on the road to Radicalism[2] ; and the final stage of his journey was accomplished under the guidance of James Mill, who was to be his chief interpreter to English readers, whilst Dumont discharged the same function to a more numerous circle abroad. It was in 1808 that he made the acquaintance of Mill, and next year we find him writing a "Catechism of Reform."

[1] Sir Leslie Stephen, *The English Utilitarians*, i. 276–279.
[2] " Parti du toryisme et dès maintenant en route vers le radicalisme."—Halévy, ii. 200.

That it should have taken sixty years to make a democrat of one whose maxim was " the greatest happiness of the greatest number " is an intelligible, though surprising, fact ; but the explanation given by the philosopher himself of this phenomenon may well be the " perfect riddle " to us that it was to a writer in the *Edinburgh Review*. Bentham says that for long it never occurred to him to doubt that, if the ruling class could be made to see what was for the good of the community, they would at once do it, but that at last it dawned upon him that government in every form has " had for its object the greatest happiness, not of those *over* whom, but of those *by* whom it has been exercised " ; and as late as 1822, when he was seventy-four years of age, we find him still gloating over the discovery of this by no means recondite truth : " A clue to the interior of the labyrinth has been found ; it is the principle of self-preference. If self-preference has place in every human breast, then if rulers are men, so must it have in every ruling breast." [1]

Whilst Bentham was studying the theory of jurisprudence, attempts were being made to repeal some of the statutes which were most opposed to the principles of that science. The English criminal code, though unsullied by torture or arbitrary imprisonment, was the most sanguinary in Europe, and—what is more surprising—its severity was the outcome of modern and even recent times. Treason, rape and the burning of a dwelling-house are said to have been the only capital offences under the old common law.[2] As late as 1688, after all the ferocities of Tudor and Stewart legislation, the number of such offences did not exceed fifty [3] ; but from this period or a little later Parliament developed quite a passion for confronting wrong-doers with the gallows ; and the growth of crime, which was the pretext

[1] *Edinburgh Review,* lxxviii. 494.
[2] *Parl. Hist.,* xix. 240.   [3] Lecky, vii. 316.

I

for this legislation, must no doubt be ascribed to the industrial movement which, as we have seen, accompanied the Revolution, to the consequent expansion of towns, and above all to the substitution as the popular beverage of gin for beer. London had probably never been in a position to guarantee to its citizens the safety of their goods and persons ; but under the influence of gin-drinking its situation in this respect became unspeakably worse. Smollett, referring to 1730, said that "thieves and robbers were now become more desperate and savage than they had ever appeared since mankind were civilised." The magistrates in 1744 declared that the abuse of spirituous liquors was responsible for "the cruelties which are now exercised on the persons robbed, which before the excessive use of these liquors were unknown in this nation"; and Horace Walpole wrote in 1751, "One is forced to travel, even at noon, as if one were going to battle." No considerable mitigation of the evil seems to have been effected, despite a great improvement in the lighting of the streets, till a more efficient police was organised in 1753.[1] During the kingship of George II, from 1727 to 1760, capital offences were created at the rate of one for every year of the reign [2]; and this record was surpassed under his successor, no fewer than sixty-three such statutes being passed in the first fifty years.[3] On the other hand, whilst the number of persons sentenced to death increased with the growing severity of the law, the ratio of executions to convictions fell during this period, 1760–1810, from much more than a half to little more than an eighth [4]; and it was no doubt the discretion exercised by the Crown in Middlesex, and by the judges on circuit, which caused death penalties to be multiplied in so reckless and light-hearted a fashion. Burke once observed that,

[1] Lecky, ii. 107–111.   [2] *Parl. Hist.*, xix. 240.
[3] Erskine May's *Constitutional History*, ii. 595.
[4] Romilly's *Observations on the Criminal Law*, 1810, pp. 8, 9.

if a country gentleman could obtain nothing else from Government, " he was sure to be accommodated with a new felony without benefit of clergy "[1]; and the highest authority on this subject puts the case thus : "Agreeably to the genius of modern politics, which estimate property far above life, though scarce a tax bill escapes solemn and repeated discussions in Parliament, yet every novice in politics is permitted without opposition to try his talents for legislation by dealing out death among his fellow creatures; and laws of this kind commonly pass as of course without observation or debate."[2]

In 1764 the Italian philosopher, Beccaria, published his famous " Essay on Crimes and Punishments," in which he argued that " public utility," and not the degree of guilt, is the sole foundation of human as distinguished from divine justice ; that men have no right and no need " to cut the throats of their fellow creatures " ; and that penalties ought to be certain and immediate rather than severe, and " so contrived as to have the greatest possible effect on others with the least possible pain to the delinquent." The work was received with great favour in Italy, six editions being called for within a year and a half ; and in a French translation published by Morellet it was adopted as their text-book by all the sovereigns and statesmen who were then using absolutism as a means of reform.[3] An English translation appeared in 1767 ; but its only practical result appears to have been the appointment by the Commons in 1770, on the motion of Sir William Meredith, of a Committee " on so much of the criminal laws as relates to capital offences." The Committee recommended that several statutes, including two against gipsies, should be repealed ; but a proroga-

---

[1] Erskine May, ii. 596.

[2] Romilly's reply to Madan's *Thoughts on Executive Justice*, p. 43.

[3] " How happy were mankind if laws were now to be first formed ; now that we see on the thrones of Europe benevolent monarchs, friends to the virtues of peace, to the arts and sciences, fathers of their people."—Beccaria's *Essay*, 4th English edition, p. 116.

tion of Parliament put an end to this suggestion as well as to a similar one carried through the Commons by Sir Charles Bunbury in 1772 ; and Meredith, who returned to the subject in 1777, commented to no purpose on the injustice and impolicy of a system which prescribed the same penalty of death for pocket-picking as for murder, and which, owing to the natural humanity of judges and juries, was so uncertain in its operation that not one capital sentence in twenty was put into force.[1]

The latter defect in the code, which most people regarded as its only redeeming feature, was denounced as a mere abuse by Martin Madan, a cousin of the poet Cowper, who had deserted the Bar to become an Evangelical preacher and had been very popular in that capacity till a plea for polygamy published in 1780 compelled him to resign his charge. Madan accused the judges of having assumed a dispensing power similar to that for which James II was deposed. He said that they had " for many years been preferring their own feelings as men to their official duty," and that punishment had been " rendered so uncertain, or rather the suspension of it so certain, as to prevent the operation of the laws." [2] His pamphlet went into a second edition and was blamed for " the sacrifice of many lives " ; for, whereas in 1783, the year before its publication, there were fifty-one executions in London, in 1785 there were no fewer than ninety-seven.[3]

It was reserved for Paley, the preacher of contentment to the poor, to justify the English criminal law both in its principles and in its practical application. In his " Moral and Political Philosophy," published in 1785, he maintained that crimes ought to be punished, not in proportion to their guilt, which could be known only to

---

[1] *Parl. Hist.*, xvi. 1125 ; xvii. 448 ; xix. 234.
[2] *Thoughts on Executive Justice*, pp. 13, 36, 49.
[3] *Memoirs of Romilly*, i. 89. In Scotland from January 1768 to May 1782 only 76 persons were condemned to death and 54 executed.— Lecky, vii. 319.

God—and so far he was in agreement with Beccaria—but " in proportion to the difficulty and the necessity of preventing them " ; and on this ground he did not scruple to defend the death penalty in cases of sheep-stealing, horse-stealing and the theft of clothes from a bleaching green, not because those crimes were " more heinous than many which were punished merely by imprisonment," but because the property, being more exposed, required the terror of capital punishment to protect it. He also argued that justice must be administered in one or other of two ways—either by making few offences capital and treating them invariably as such or by making many offences capital and exempting in practice all but a few ; and the second or English method he regarded as much the wiser and more humane, because " few actually suffer death, whilst the dread and danger of it hang over the crimes of many." Even Paley, however, was constrained to admit that pocket-picking could not justly be made liable to this terror.[1]

A revision of the penal code had been suggested by Meredith and Bunbury, and was no doubt hoped for by Bentham when he published his " Principles of Penal Law " ; but the times were adverse to any such drastic change, and no reformer could expect to succeed who did not apply himself to some particular Act. This was the task undertaken by Sir Samuel Romilly, the most liberal, and with Francis Horner, the most entirely virtuous, of the Whigs. Romilly was the grandson of a Huguenot refugee ; he had been frequently in Paris and was in full sympathy with the humanitarian movement which preceded, and to a great extent with the democratic movement which followed, the French Revolution. As early as 1786, three years after he was called to the Bar, he published a reply to Madan, which, though favourably reviewed, had a much smaller circulation than the pamphlet it criticised, only a hundred copies being

[1] *Works*, 1844, pp. 225-227.

sold.[1]   In 1806 he entered Parliament as Solicitor-General in the Ministry of all the Talents ; and, having been unable during his brief tenure of office to raise the question of judicial reform, he did so as a private member in 1808.

The statute he selected as the object of his first attack was the Elizabethan Act which made pocket-picking capital if the sum " privily " stolen was not less than twelve pence.   This was one of several old laws which had acquired a much wider range with the fall in the purchasing power of money, so that, as both Romilly and Horner remarked, whilst everything else was rising in price, the life of man was daily growing cheaper.   The Act had rarely, if ever, been enforced within living memory—largely owing to the liberal and humane interpretation of the word " privily," which was held to exclude all cases in which the person who had lost his watch or purse was conscious of being robbed.[2]   The Pocket-Picking Bill, introduced in 1808, met with little opposition in the Commons and was accepted in silence by the Lords ; but all the efforts of its promoter were insufficient to procure the repeal of the Act of William and Mary which made it a capital offence to steal as much as five shillings privately in a shop.   The Bill passed the Commons in 1810, but was rejected by thirty-one to eleven in the Lords ; and amongst the majority were the Archbishop of Canterbury, the Bishop of London and five other prelates.   The measure was re-introduced—only to meet the same fate —in 1813, 1816 and 1818.   Two other Acts of the same nature were unsuccessfully attacked ; but the Pocket-Picking Bill was not the only breach which Romilly contrived to make in the penal code.   In 1811, supported by petitions from the linen manufacturers of Belfast and the calico printers of London, who said that the death penalty discouraged prosecution, he carried the repeal of that penalty in cases of stealing from bleach-yards ;

---

[1] *Memoirs of Romilly*, i. 89.
[2] *Parl. Hist.*, xi. 397, 883, 884.

and next year he exempted from capital punishment soldiers and sailors who were found begging.[1]

Romilly's efforts, more persistent than successful, to mitigate the temper of criminal legislation were highly characteristic of a period which, on the whole, was one of promise rather than fruition ; but when we turn from practical life to the academic sphere, which was then confined to Oxford and Cambridge, we find that substantial progress was already being made. The modern method of teaching at Oxford appears to have originated in 1636 under the chancellorship of Archbishop Laud, when courses of lectures and studies, extending respectively over four and three years, were prescribed for the B.A. and M.A. degrees, and when also disputations as a test of merit were practically superseded by oral examinations. Comprehensive, if not thorough, as these examinations were, they were to be conducted by all the masters in turn ; and we are told that, if the curriculum was not beyond the average capacity of students "the race of passmen in the seventeenth century must have been cast in a heroic mould." The Laudian system, in so far as it was ever enforced, survived for more than a century and a half ; but long before the end of that period it had sunk into complete decay. Adam Smith concluded his career, or rather his residence, at Oxford in 1746, and might have said then what he said thirty years later, that the majority of the professors had "given up altogether even the pretence of teaching."[2] Gibbon, who had only one lesson from his tutor in the course of fourteen months, found that " public exercises and examinations were totally unknown " ; and in 1770 John Scott, the future Lord Eldon, obtained his bachelor's

[1] *Memoirs of Romilly*, ii. 252, 317, 325, 365 : iii. 19, 95, 242, 331. Romilly was not prepared to advocate the abolition of capital punishment.—*Ibid.* i. 278. His friend, William Allen, the Quaker philanthropist, formed a society for this purpose in 1808.—*Life of William Allen*, i. 104.

[2] Rae's *Adam Smith*, pp. 20–24.

degree in Hebrew and history on the strength of his knowledge that Golgotha was the Hebrew word for "the place of a skull" and that King Alfred was the reputed founder of University College.[1]   There were of course facilities for private study—not to mention a superabundance of leisure ; but many days passed between 1730 and 1740 without the Bodleian Library attracting a single student, and the day was a marked one which included the handling of more than two books. The Jacobite spirit of Oxford was no doubt responsible to some extent for its decline as an educational centre ; but the process continued long after that spirit had been replaced by equal devotion to the reigning house.   Thus from 1736 to 1810 the annual number of admissions never rose to a hundred—a total which had frequently been exceeded in the reigns of Anne and George I.   " Except praying and drinking," wrote Jeffrey in 1792, " I see nothing else that it is possible to acquire in this place." [2]

With the dawn of a new century Oxford awoke somewhat suddenly from its long sleep.   In 1800 steps were taken to institute an Honours Degree ; and the Honours list was not only to be divided into a higher and a lower grade, but the names in each were to be arranged in order of merit.   During the Napoleonic War a further incentive to competition was introduced in the shape of teaching in classes.[3]   When Peel went to Oxford in 1805, an Honours school had been established in Mathematics as well as in Classics, and he himself was the first student to obtain the highest distinction in both.[4]   Ward, afterwards the first Earl of Dudley, had graduated, shortly before the new regulations came into force, in 1802 ; and, on re-visiting the University ten years later, he was astonished to find that it had become " a place

---

[1] Campbell's *Lives of the Lord Chancellors*, ix. 120.
[2] Brodrick's *History of Oxford University*, passim ;   Cockburn's *Life of Lord Jeffrey*, i. 40.
[3] Brodrick's *Oxford University*, pp. 189, 191, 192.
[4] Parker's *Sir Robert Peel*, i. 21.

of education," in which it was "much more *the thing* to read than to let it alone "—a change which he regarded " as one of the most important national improvements " of his time. There were from seven to eight hundred students, including many of the highest rank ; and " you may easily imagine," he wrote, "what an effect must be produced upon the whole state of society, and that within no very long time, by their being made to do a great deal, instead of encouraged to do nothing at all— which is the real difference between the old and the new system." [1]

The University of Cambridge had been conspicuous in almost every intellectual movement from the Reformation to the reign of Charles II, when it produced the famous philosophical school known as the " Cambridge Platonists." In the early part of the eighteenth century it appears to have participated to a considerable extent in the Oxonian torpor ; but the institution of the Mathematical Tripos about 1750 raised it to the pre-eminence in that science which it has ever since retained.[2] Writing in the year after the close of the Napoleonic struggle, Coleridge asserted that the war had had " its golden side " ; and it is remarkable that he cited as the first, if not the strongest, proof of this assertion " the late and present condition of manners and intellect among the young men of Oxford and Cambridge, the manly sobriety of demeanour, the submission to the routine of study in almost all, and the zeal in the pursuit of knowledge and academic distinction in a large and increasing number." [3]

Meanwhile the Evangelical revival, which had a powerful representative at Cambridge in Charles Simeon, was entering on its final and most expansive phase. We have seen that this movement had originated in the

[1] *Letters to " Ivy,"* pp. 182, 183.
[2] Mullinger's *History of Cambridge University*, pp. 168, 174.
[3] *Church and State*, 1839, p. 354, note.

lower—one might almost say the lowest—class, that it had gradually worked its way through the middle class, but that the upper class, the least susceptible to what has been termed the " herd instinct," had long presented to it an almost unbroken front ; and, when we consider the temper of the aristocracy in those days, its resistance to such a force will cause no surprise. " The governing class," it has been admirably said, " consisted of gentlemen who were not mere politicians and sportsmen. No stories of their dissipations can obscure the truth that they were essentially scholars, men of taste and refinement, who enjoyed nothing more than talking about literature, the meaning of words, the ideas of writers, or history, or pictures, or travel. They were at least as happy in a library as they were in the saddle or round the card table. They knew what they liked, they were at ease about their taste, they could act as patrons of art and letters with the security of persons trusting their own judgment, rather than the nervous eagerness of persons following anybody's judgment in preference to their own." [1] Wilberforce, the first really important convert to be made by Evangelicalism in this circle, was no stranger to its intellectual life. His Diary, even at times when he was " working like a negro " for the abolition of the slave trade, contains such entries as these : " Epictetus twice, Horace by heart " ; " I propose to read at least a hundred lines of Virgil daily—often more " ; and, though he never attained to the high level of scholarship which was the daily walk of Fox and Windham, his colloquial powers, aided by buoyancy of spirit, grace and geniality of manner and a finely toned voice, can have been little, if at all, inferior to those of the latter, whom he himself pronounced to be *facile princeps* in conversation—" decidedly the most agreeable scholar-like gentleman or gentleman-like scholar I ever remember to have seen." " Wilberforce," wrote

[1] Hammond, *The Town Labourer*, p. 274.

Henry Thornton to Hannah More, " has bought a house near Bath, which I a little lament on the ground of the bad economy of it, for he is a man who, were he in Norway or Siberia, would find himself infested by company, since he would even produce a population for the sake of his society in the regions of the earth where it is least." This was the testimony of a devoted friend ; but Madame de Staël described him to Sir James Mackintosh as " the best converser I have met with in this country. I have always heard that he was the most religious, but I now find that he is the wittiest man in England." [1]

Wilberforce's " Practical View of Christianity," which Burke commended on his death-bed,[2] was published in 1797 ; and the growth of Evangelicalism which this essay did much to promote may be traced in what was its most prominent external feature—the observance of Sunday. This institution had never lost the importance secured for it by the Puritans in our social life, and it was not till after the middle of the eighteenth century that even the upper classes ventured openly to throw off its restraint. As early as 1693 indeed one-fourth of the hackney coaches in London were licensed to offer themselves for hire on Sunday ; and Defoe, who denounced this permission as " the worst blemish " of William's reign, lamented that it had been extended to the whole number before the death of Queen Anne. But the highways continued for the next forty or fifty years to be unfrequented on that day by stage coaches and wagons ; and as late as 1744 a lady who entertained her guests with a Sunday evening concert did so only

---

[1] *Life of Wilberforce*, i. 302 ; ii. 95, 143, 350 ; iii. 447 ; iv. 167. Burke, it may be noted, did not belong by birth to the ruling class and, despite his learning and eloquence, never had much affinity with its æsthetic spirit. It has been well said of him by one of his warmest admirers : " If any one has imbued himself with that exacting love of delicacy, measure and taste in expression which was until our own day a sacred tradition of the French, then he will not like Burke."—Morley's *Burke* (" English Men of Letters "), p. 212.

[2] *Life of Wilberforce*, ii. 208.

"at the risk of her windows." In 1765 it was complained that "on no other day do so many coaches with coronets pass through the country towns and villages," and that, whilst the long-distance traveller was not allowed to begin or continue his journey on Sunday, the coaches within a radius of ten or twelve miles of London, which were used mainly by excursionists, plied as regularly on Sundays as on week days. From this period, or a little earlier, the Sabbatarian tradition was treated with less and less respect. Fashionable people—the men especially —almost ceased to go to church, at all events when in town, and, if they did go, behaved with little reverence or decorum. Cabinet meetings and dinners, Court levees and card-parties, were frequently held on Sunday ; and in 1778 was started the first Sunday newspaper.[1] "What must the lower kind of people think," wrote Madan in 1785, "when they see coachfuls of the nobility and gentry either purposely travelling the roads on Sunday or whirling about from one assembly to another, thus making it a time of amusement and recreation ? "[2]

The noble and the wealthy had long been of opinion that religion—especially in the form superintended and largely manned by members of their own class—was a soporific essential, if not to the contentment, at least to the resignation, of the poor. Horace Walpole, for example, in 1765 complained of a dinner party in Paris that "the conversation was much more unrestrained, even on the Old Testament, than I would suffer at my own table in England if a single footman was present." Dread of the French Revolution did much to strengthen this feeling ; but the religious developed much more slowly than the political reaction, and was not fully established till after the conclusion of peace in 1815. Seven years after the fall of the Bastille, we find Wilber-

---

[1] Lecky, iii. 15–17, 476 ; vi. 12.
[2] *Thoughts on Executive Justice,* p. 197.

force lamenting that in Manchester "the church attendance of the better kind of people had much diminished of late," and that the merchants, in order to economise time, made a practice of travelling on Sunday ; but in 1802 he had the satisfaction of recording in his Diary, "Many young rising legal men religious—Sunday consultations becoming far rarer—lawyers attending public worship." In 1798 it was noted in the *Annual Register* as "a wonder to the lower orders throughout all parts of England to see the avenues to the churches filled with carriages "[1]; and about the same time a similar phenomenon was to be seen in Scotland : "Individuals of great political importance, who for many years had never entered a church door, ostentatiously walking up and down the High Street of Edinburgh with Bibles in their hands to attend public worship."[2] Not only the writings of Wilberforce but his personal exertions contributed largely to bring about a stricter observance of Sunday. Resolutions to respect the sacred character of the day were circulated under his auspices and signed by "many amongst the highest ranks." It was due mainly to him that the Speaker, after standing out for three years, consented in 1801 to hold his levees on Saturday, instead of Sunday, evening. In 1805 Wilberforce prevailed upon Parliament to withdraw the sanction it had given to Sunday drilling—a practice which had been countermanded in deference to the Dissenters when the militia was instituted or revived in 1757.[3] Perceval, who became Premier in 1809, some three years after the death of Pitt, was our first really devout Prime Minister, and the last till Gladstone assumed the office in 1868 ; and Wilberforce had little difficulty in inducing him to forego the summoning of Parliament on Monday, in order to save members from the temptation to travel on

[1] Hammond, *The Town Labourer*, p. 235.
[2] George Combe's *American Notes*, p. 163.
[3] Lecky, iii. 16.

the previous day. With a similar object he laboured to abolish the Monday market at Smithfield.[1]

It was inevitable that the growth of pietism which found expression in this Sabbatarian movement should also express itself as a demand for ecclesiastical reform, and the more so, as most of the abuses which prevailed in the Church were indefensible from the legal as well as from the Evangelical standpoint. As early as 1534— the year in which Henry VIII renounced the authority of the Pope—an Act had been passed to ensure that the clergy should apply themselves exclusively and fully to their pastoral duties. They were expected of course to cultivate their glebes and, if there was a surplus, might dispose of it at a profit ; but they were not to become farmers or stock-breeders, and in particular they were to live at their cures under a penalty for non-residence of £10 a month, or £120 a year—a sum which has been reckoned at about ten times the value of the average benefice. The Act had " almost slept for ages "— almost but not quite ; for the modern depreciation of money had made it less unreasonably severe, and it had occasionally, though very rarely, been used as the instrument of parochial exasperation or personal malice.[2] Non-residence, hitherto regarded as a mere technical offence, assumed a sinful as well as an illegal aspect now that earnestness and a sense of responsibility had revived in the Church ; but Parliament, which was little susceptible to this spirit, would hardly have bestirred itself in the matter if the clergy had not claimed its protection against persons who as extortionists or

---

[1] *Life of Wilberforce*, ii. 163 ; iii. 7, 46, 265, 364, 397. Some readers of Jane Austen may have noticed that in *Persuasion*, written in 1816 and her last work, one of Anne Elliot's objections to her father's heir is that with him " Sunday travelling had been a common thing." There is little of such pietism in the earlier novels. When Catherine Morland is ejected from Northanger Abbey, it does not appear to have added to her distress that she had to travel home on Sunday.

[2] *Edinburgh Review*, v. 301.

informers were calling them to account for their disregard or ignorance of the law. These "pests of society," the freebooters of Evangelicalism, are said to have become active about 1798 [1]; and, in order, if not to prohibit, at least to restrict their operations, a measure was introduced in 1801 and in 1802 by Sir William Scott, brother of Lord Eldon and afterwards Lord Stowell, and carried by him in 1803. We find it referred to some years later in the House of Lords as " the Act for the protection of non-residence," and by the same speaker as intended to encourage residence [2]; and the apparent contradiction is easily explained. On the one hand, an incumbent, who was absent from his cure, without being resident at another, for three months in one year, was to forfeit a third of its annual value; " monitions " were to be issued which, if not attended to, might involve a sequestration of income; and, in order to make residence more attractive, the clergy were permitted to engage in the usual agricultural pursuits. On the other hand, non-residence was for the first time legally recognised, the bishops being empowered to grant licences for this purpose in specified cases, and the archbishops with consent of the Privy Council in all cases recommended to them by a bishop.[3]

This measure was less distasteful to the Tories, who almost engrossed what little of Evangelicalism had yet found its way into politics, than to the Whigs; and it was strongly opposed by Sir Francis Burdett on the ground that it would extend the political influence of the bishops, and consequently of the Government, by placing the clergy under their " absolute control." He suggested with good reason that the bishops, instead of being called upon to develop a sense of duty in others, should have been admonished by Parliament to cultivate

[1] *Parl. Debates*, xxxv. 1551 ; xxxvi. 1514.
[2] *Ibid.* xvii. 764.
[3] 43 Geo. III, c. 84.

it in themselves [1] ; for in the matter of plurality and non-residence they were the worst and least excusable offenders, and had taken care to see that they were expressly exempted from the operation of the Act. Few, if any, of the bishops were content to enjoy only the revenues of their sees. Three of them are said to have held in succession one of the best endowed rectories— that of Stanhope. Bishop Watson, the amiable and truly liberal scholar whom we have met with as the defender of Christianity against Gibbon and Paine,[2] pursued his studies at Windermere on the income derived from the see of Llandaff, which he visited every three years, a professorship at Cambridge, two rectories and a prebend's stall. Pretyman—in 1803 he assumed the name of Tomline—was for more than thirty years Bishop of Lincoln and Dean of St. Paul's ; we read of a Bishop of Exeter who had the nominal oversight of St. George's, Hanover Square—a parish of 40,000 inhabitants ; and even Porteus, the nearest approach to an Evangelical prelate, held at one time two rectories, and was praised for keeping only one—the rich living of Hunton in Kent —when he became Bishop of Chester.[3]

Benefices such as Stanhope and Hunton were not so numerous that their retention by men who had become bishops could fail at this period to provoke comment ; but there was an order of clergy below that of incumbents to which Sir William Scott's Act was calculated to attract attention ; for Parliament, in so far as it encouraged residence, would supplant a curate, and, in so far as it dispensed with residence, had incurred an obligation to see that the deputy was adequately paid. Something, but very little, had been done, not indeed to maintain, but to retrieve the position of curates since, with other ecclesiastical grievances, it had been remedied in the

---

[1] *Parl. Debates*, xxxvi. 1516.   [2] See p. 73.
[3] Overton's *English Church in the Nineteenth Century*, 1800–1833, p. 7.

days of Queen Anne. An Act of 1714 had provided that a bishop before licensing any curate to serve in place of a rector or vicar should secure for him a stipend of not less than £20 or more than £50, and, on complaint of curates already licensed, might appoint for them a similar provision. At the end of the eighteenth century it was computed that the purchasing power of money had fallen during that period by at least two-thirds, so that £20 in 1714 was equivalent to £60 in 1800, and £50 to £150; but in 1796, when the curates at last succeeded in obtaining the intervention of Parliament, the maximum salary was raised only to £75, whilst the minimum was left nominally at £20, in reality at less than £7.[1] In other words, the curate could at the best be only half as well off as he had been in Anne's reign, and at the worst might be, and frequently was, thrice as poor. In the latter case he naturally sought permission to serve more than one parish—a feat which he accomplished by " riding with indecent haste from church to church "; and an instance was cited and reluctantly admitted in Parliament, in which a farmer's wife had compelled the curate to return to the reading desk because he had left out several of the prayers.[2]

Sydney Smith sought to combat the scandal arising from this state of things by pointing out that there were two classes of curates—independent young gentlemen, fresh from the Universities and secure of promotion to higher posts, who assumed the office for practice and not for profit, and youths of very humble rank who were content with less than the wages of a common labourer in consideration of having to do only a fraction of his work.[3] The argument, however, most frequently put forward by apologists was that curacies were ill-paid

[1] 36 Geo. III, c. 83. In Wales even the nominal minimum was no more than £7 till Horsley, when Bishop of St. Davids, 1788–1793, succeeded in raising it to £15.—Overton's *English Church*, 1800–1833, p. 20.

[2] *Parl. Debates*, xxv. 210. [3] *Works*, i. 256.

because the poverty of the livings would not permit of their being paid well. The livings in general were indeed poor, 4000 of them being under £150 a year and 800 under £50 [1]; but it appeared from statistics which were available when the Residence Act had been several years in operation that the difference between the average salary paid where the living was under £150 and where it exceeded—and in many cases far exceeded—that level was only £10—the difference between £35 and £45.[2]

Sir William Scott was thus fully justified in following up what he had done to reform and indulge the beneficed clergy with a Bill for the better payment of curates ; but this measure, being wholly adverse to the interest of incumbents, and not as in the former case at least half in their favour, was far more strongly opposed. Part of it was indeed carried—a grant of £8000 for the relief of such curates as should be deprived in consequence of the Residence Act [3]; but Scott, after the failure of a second attempt, desisted from his main purpose in 1804. The task was then taken up by Perceval, first as Attorney-General and then as Chancellor of the Exchequer ; but in 1808 he also had to abandon his design ; and the measure was not carried till 1813 under the auspices of Lord Harrowby, who delivered and published in its support a powerful and luminous speech. The Bill of 1808 appears to have been framed by Bishop Porteus,[4] who died in that year ; but the prelates, one or two excepted, persisted to the last in opposition, headed by the Archbishop of' Canterbury and the Bishop of London—a phenomenon which painfully surprised even so Tory an organ as the *Quarterly Review*. Lord Harrowby's Act provided that every non-resident should forfeit his legal

---

[1] *Parl. Debates*, xvii. 753 ; xxvi. 296.

[2] *Quarterly Review*, xix. 45.

[3] 44 Geo. III; c. 2. Not many curates can have been entitled to this relief ; for, seven years later, out of about 11,000 incumbents, only 4412 were legally resident.—*Parl. Debates*, xvii. 764.

[4] *Life of Wilberforce*, iii. 364.

position as such who did not, on the removal or death of a curate, nominate another to be licensed by the Bishop. The latter was to see that he had a salary assigned to him of not less than £80 or the whole value of the living. If there were 300 parishioners, the salary was to be £100 ; if there were 500, it was to be £120 ; and if there were 1000, it was to be £150. Where the value of the living was more than £400, a salary was to be awarded irrespective of population, but not exceeding £200. A significant clause in the Act was that no curate should be licensed to serve more than two churches in one day.[1]

A plea that did good service on behalf of the curates was the growth of Dissent and the necessity, in view of this danger, that parishioners should know something more of their clergyman than his features and "the sound of his voice." There were said to be 12,000 chapels throughout the country and little more than 11,000 churches, whilst of the latter over 1000 had no parsonage house or none that was habitable.[2] The Nonconformists who caused most uneasiness to the authorities, ecclesiastical and civil, were not, however, the pastors, more or less permanent, of chapels, but the Wesleyan itinerants, who were permitted by their sect, without any inquiry as to age or fitness, to become preachers, and whose claim to be licensed as such under the Toleration Act the Justices of the Peace seldom ventured to refuse, though it entailed certain privileges and notably till 1802 that of exemption from military service.[3] Lord Eldon informed the House of Lords that when he was a young man and liable to the Militia ballot, he had been advised

---

[1] 53 Geo. III, c. 149. In 1817 the various Acts relating to incumbents and curates were consolidated as one statute—57 Geo. III, c. 99. Few modern writers have dealt with this subject, which is not even mentioned in the eighth volume (Warre Cornish) of the *History of the English Church*. Canon Overton's allusions to it in his *English Church*, 1800–1833, are meagre and inaccurate.

[2] *Parl. Debates*, xvii. 762, 765, 769, 1098.

[3] *Ibid.* xix. 1130.

to get himself exempted by paying sixpence for a licence to preach. Some of the preachers were mere boys, backward in education but prematurely inspired, and many were more or less illiterate, as was proved by the misspellings in their forms of application and by the fact that they sometimes picked up the wrong licences from inability to read their own names.[1] Churchmen and leading Dissenters seem to have been agreed that this abuse ought not to continue unchecked ; for Lord Sidmouth was acting with the concurrence of Dr. Coke, head of the Wesleyan Methodists, and of Dr. Adam Clarke when in 1811 he proposed to enact that no one should be entitled to a licence who was not either the pastor of a registered chapel or a preacher whose qualifications were attested by a certain number of householders.[2] We have seen that Pitt had been dissuaded only at the last moment from bringing in a similar proposal in 1799[3]; and, the Toleration Act being " the palladium of religious liberty," Dissenters of all denominations united at once in its defence. We are told by Lord Holland, one of the Whig leaders who had assisted to stir up this commotion, that " for some days no places were to be had on the stage coaches and diligences of the kingdom ; all were occupied with petitions to Parliament against the measure "; and that when it came up in the Lords for the second reading, " not only the table was filled but the House was filled with parchment." The private remonstrances of Wilberforce, Perceval and Clarke can hardly have been needed to convince Lord Sidmouth that it was hopeless to proceed with so unpopular a measure ; and he consented " with a bad grace " to withdraw his Bill.[4]

Itineracy was too recent a development of Dissent to

---

[1] Twiss's *Life of Lord Eldon*, ii. 172.
[2] The Bill is printed *verbatim* in *Parl. Debates*, xix. 1133.
[3] See p. 83.
[4] Pellew's *Lord Sidmouth*, iii. 38–66.

have been within the view of those who framed the statutory Toleration of 1689. The Justices of the Peace, or those of them who had been in sympathy with Sidmouth, now put a more literal construction on the Act by refusing to license preachers who had not undertaken a particular charge ; and their decision was upheld on appeal by the Court of King's Bench. Hence arose a new agitation to which the Government yielded in 1812 by passing what came to be known as the New Toleration Act.[1] Meetings and meeting-houses were still to be registered ; but the number of persons, exclusive of the family, who might assemble for worship in a private dwelling without complying with this regulation was raised from five—the number prescribed in the more or less obsolete Conventicle Act of Charles II—to twenty. Preachers were to take the oath of allegiance only if required to do so by a magistrate—not necessarily as a qualification for licence ; but the Lords had succeeded in restricting exemption from the Militia ballot to those who were preachers by profession or who had no other occupation than that of a schoolmaster. Methodism, though far from respecting an indolent and non-resident clergy, had more affinity with the Church than with Dissent, and could justly claim to have fostered " a spirit of subordination and a zeal for work in the lower classes " ; but the Act of 1812, however it came to be passed by a Tory Government, was hailed with some reason as " a favourable omen of the increasing liberality of the present times." [2]

Meanwhile an economic situation was developing which threatened to raise far wider issues than those of ecclesiastical reform. We have seen that the war now in progress was a struggle of peoples and nations to repel or shake off the domination of Napoleon, and consequently

[1] 52 Geo. III, c. 155.
[2] *Parl. Debates*, xxiii. 995, 1105. On the whole subject see Halévy, *Histoire*, i. 404–409, whose narrative is a good illustration of his minute and exhaustive research.

was much less unfavourable to internal freedom than had been the war with Republican France. As time went on, its character in this respect throughout Europe became constantly more marked ; but in Great Britain there was less need for national cohesion after the victory of Trafalgar in 1805 ; and the result of this battle, though it secured the country from invasion, was to inaugurate a period of commercial strain and acute social distress. Unable any longer to contest our supremacy at sea, Napoleon endeavoured to undermine it by a universal proscription of our commerce, which from the place of its origin was known as the Berlin Decree. In answer to this edict, and mainly with a view to extorting its recall, the British Government issued a series of Orders in Council. In January 1807 they announced their intention to stop all trade between ports under French control—in other words, the coasting trade of France and her allies ; and, this measure having failed entirely to effect its purpose, they proceeded in November, not indeed to interdict the commerce of neutrals with France, but to make it less profitable to the enemy by requiring it to pass through British ports where it was to be regulated and in certain cases taxed.[1] With the minor exception of Sweden, the only neutral country was the United States. Napoleon's complete blockade of Great Britain did not affect the Americans because, though nominally a maritime blockade, it could be enforced only on the shores of the Continent, and hence was known as the " Continental System " ; but our restricted blockade of France, with a powerful fleet to make it effective, was a heavy blow to their trade ; and at the end of the year, irritated still further by the search of their ships for British naval deserters, they expelled foreign vessels, recalled

---

[1] The earlier of these Orders was issued by the Ministry of all the Talents, the later by the Tory Government of Perceval. The chief prompter in both cases was supposed to be Wilberforce's brother-in-law, Stephen.—Lord Holland's *Further Memories*, p. 159.

their own, and withdrew from all intercourse with Europe.[1]

Neutral trade meant so much more to France—which indeed had no other [2]—than to us that the Orders may have been a good instrument of war ; but as a means of commercial redress they had signally failed ; and loud and persistent was the demand for their recall. It was hoped that the closing of markets in one quarter of the New World might be recompensed by the opening of markets in another ; but the trade with South America, which was the reward of our efforts on behalf of Portugal and Spain in the Peninsular War, was prosecuted in a spirit of wild speculation which brought many, if not most, of those who embarked in it to ruin. We are told, indeed, that more Manchester goods were sent out to Rio Janeiro in a few weeks than had been consumed there during the previous twenty years.[3]

Whatever may have been the military value of the Orders in Council, it was obtained during the five years of their continuance at a heavy and increasing cost. In 1809 the diminution in imports and exports was estimated at eleven millions sterling. In place of thirty-two million lbs. of raw cotton formerly imported from the United States, only five million lbs. could be procured from Asia and the Portuguese colonies of South America. The poor rates in Manchester had risen from £24,000 to at least £40,000 ; and of the thirty-eight mills in that town, only six were at work. In 1810 the Brazilian speculation and the seizure by Napoleon of British goods in the Baltic produced a commercial crisis which began in London and soon spread throughout the country. " In Manchester and other places," it was reported, "houses stop not only every day but every hour." This year, contrary to expec-

---

[1] Smart's *Economic Annals*, vol. i. chap. x.
[2] France opened the trade with her colonies to neutrals in time of war, when she could not carry it on herself, and closed it in time of peace.	[3] Smart, i. 184.

tation, there was an abundant harvest ; but the winter of 1810–1811 was exceptionally severe. A fine, though belated, spring was followed by a summer of scorching heat ; and the harvest of 1811 was deficient all over Europe. In some parts of England it was said to be the worst since 1800, and wheat at all events was little more than half the average crop. Meanwhile the commercial and industrial depression was going from bad to worse. The *Annual Register* for 1811 refers to " frightful lists of bankruptcies in every gazette, amounting to an aggregate to which no former year exhibits a parallel." The cotton workers of Manchester represented to Parliament that most of them were not employed more than three days a week ; and at Glasgow the handloom weavers, who in 1806 had considered themselves underpaid at 17s. 6d. weekly, were now earning only 7s. 6d. During the latter half of this year the price of wheat rose from 86s. to 106s.; and in certain districts where there was local as well as general privation the impatience of the people could no longer be restrained.[1]

The opening of South America to British trade had caused a good deal of capital to be invested—much of it by outsiders—in the manufacture of hosiery at Nottingham, where the artisans worked in their homes for masters who supplied them with frames. The frame itself was by no means a recent invention ; but in 1809 the introduction of an improved frame conspired with the collapse in exports to cause both a displacement and a depreciation of labour[2] ; and the distress culminated, after the bad harvest of 1811, in an epidemic of frame-breaking which was known, for no very intelligible reason,[3] as "the Luddite riots." The disturbances began on a Monday in

[1] Smart, i. 192, 227, 271, 272, 275 ; Harriet Martineau's *History of England,* 1800–1815, pp. 387, 388.

[2] Smart, i. 273.

[3] Said to be from Ned Ludd, an imbecile who in a fit of exasperation caused by his village tormentors destroyed a couple of stocking frames about 1779.

November and continued for a whole week, during which many frames—on one day "nearly a villageful"—were wrecked. Before the end of the year the disorder had spread into Derbyshire and Leicestershire. The Government acted with great vigour, as many as 2000 cavalry and infantry being despatched to Nottingham in three weeks; but the rioters soon became so expert at their work that they could destroy a frame almost noiselessly in one minute; and, protected by sentinels and the sympathy of their fellow workmen, they seldom failed to escape detection. Neither winter nor spring saw the last or even the worst of these outrages, which extended in a few months from stocking-frames to machinery in general. At least one factory was burnt at Manchester; and in the West Riding of Yorkshire, which latterly was the chief scene of depredation, cloth-mills were entered and gutted night after night. · Horsfall, a leading manufacturer of Huddersfield, was waylaid and murdered in daylight by three men who had been deputed to take his life [1]; and, though the commission of such a crime can hardly have come within the normal purpose of an organisation which was believed to have spread its net from Glasgow to London, it was bold enough to compass nocturnal drilling and the raiding of militia depots for arms. In February 1812 frame-breaking, which had hitherto been punished only with transportation, was made a capital offence. Nottingham does not seem to have suffered under this Act; but eight Luddites were executed at Manchester and fourteen at York.[2]

The Orders in Council were rescinded in June of this year—too late to avert war with the United States and consequently to relieve the industrial distress. Perceval, the author of the Orders in so far at least as they affected

---

[1] " It was said that at the time the fatal shot was fired, there was a general shout of triumph from the tops of houses, hay-stacks and other elevated situations."—*Life of Wilberforce*, v. 35.

[2] Martineau, pp. 392–398 ; Pellew's *Viscount Sidmouth*, iii. 80–97 ; Smart, i. 273.

the American trade, had perished by the hand of a private and insane assassin in the previous month ; and his death was hailed in the manufacturing districts with indecent demonstrations of joy.[1]   A fact of more importance to disturbers of the peace was that Sidmouth at this time became Home Secretary—an office which he was to hold for the next ten years.   A month or two before the York executions in January 1813, for which he was responsible, order had been fully restored.

Wilberforce was one of a Committee appointed by the Commons to investigate the Luddite disturbances ; and he complains in his Diary that he could get none of his colleagues—not even so decided a Tory as Lord Castlereagh—to agree with him that "the disease was of a political nature."[2]   Except for some tincture of politics at Manchester, it was indeed wholly economic ; and no suspicion is thrown on its character in this respect from the fact that in 1811, shortly before the outbreak, a society had been established in the interest of reform, and another projected, though it was not constituted till the following year—the Reform Union and the Hampden Club.   Major Cartwright was in both cases the dominant spirit.   These societies, though they advocated annual Parliaments, were so moderate in their idea of representation that they demanded it only for those who paid direct taxes ; the members were almost all men of wealth and social position ; and some of them evinced great astonishment and displeasure when they heard that Cartwright, who had already visited some of the disturbed districts with a view to "turning the discontents into a legal channel favourable to Parliamentary Reform," was about to undertake with the same object a much more comprehensive tour.   No man, it was thought, with any pretensions to be a gentleman could undertake such a part as that of " travelling reformist " or " itinerant apostle," especially when the people to be converted were riotous or at least

---

[1] *Life of Wilberforce*, iv. 29.   [2] *Ibid*. p. 36.

discontented mechanics.   Cartwright was deaf to all such remonstrances, even when addressed to him by his old comrade, Wyvil ; and in January 1813 he started on a month's hard travelling which was to carry him from Newcastle in the north to Bristol and Reading in the south—a circuit of nine hundred miles.   Up to this point only two petitions for reform had been framed—one at Manchester, the other at Halifax, and " through fear of persecution " many of the signatures to the former had been torn off ; but the " Father of Reform," then in his seventy-third year, communicated an enthusiasm which carried away both the timid and the indifferent ; and soon after his return to London he had received 292 petitions, signed by about 199,000 persons, and the promise of many more.   Owing to the reluctance of members to present them, few if any of these ever found their way to the House of Commons ;   but the spirit they expressed was to assert itself at the next economic crisis ; and the two societies which Cartwright represented were adopted as models for imitation in towns and villages throughout the country.[1]

The diffusion of a democratic spirit, which made its first advance in 1800, had thus been carried a stage forward ; but it was the outcome of social discontent and was now to be held in check for a time by an improvement in industrial conditions.   At the end of 1812 Napoleon re-crossed the Niemen with little more than a tenth of the great army he had raised for the invasion of Russia.   In March 1813 he was confronted with a league rather of peoples than of sovereigns for the liberation of Europe ; and, even before the battle of Leipzic in October had reduced him to the defence of his own frontier, almost the whole Continent had been re-opened to British trade. The mere prospect of such a change had been enough to give a stimulus to production which increased as antici-

---

[1] *Life of Cartwright*, ii. 31–64 ; Veitch's *Genesis of Parliamentary Reform*, pp. 343–345.

pations were realised ; employment, long scarce and precarious, became plentiful and well-paid ; and wages rose rapidly in actual as well as nominal value.   The harvest of 1813 was one of the largest and finest on record ; and we are told that, what with good wages and cheaper food, " the manufacturing population were in a more satisfactory state than they had been during any part of the twenty years preceding." [1]   In April 1814 the Allies entered Paris ; Napoleon abdicated ; and the war which had lasted with one brief interlude from 1792 was brought to a triumphant and what then seemed a conclusive issue.

[1] Tooke's *History of Prices*, ii. 6.

CHAPTER III

DISILLUSIONS OF PEACE, 1814–1820

THE Peace of 1814 was to prove in some respects even more disappointing than that of 1802. Its interruption in the following year, caused by the escape of Napoleon from Elba, comprised indeed no more than a hundred days, and it was then permanently established; but, whilst the war which re-opened in 1803 was on the whole favourable to liberal ideas, one cannot say as much for the Peace which Wellington wrung from France in 1815 on the field of Waterloo. We have seen that the over-throw of Napoleon was accomplished rather by the peoples of Europe than by their rulers; and it seemed natural, if not inevitable, that the former should be admitted, in reward of their exertions, to a share of political power. Most of the Allied sovereigns did in fact promise con-stitutions to their subjects; but these were either never established or soon recalled; and the adjustment of States and boundaries made at the Congress of Vienna was so little in harmony with national aspirations that it could not fail in the long run to excite revolt. No two States were so much indebted to the patriotic effort of their peoples as Prussia and Spain; but in Prussia a pamphleteer who had sought to prove that the country did not owe its salvation to popular enthusiasm was honoured by the King, and in Spain the cause of con-stitutional monarchy was from the first discountenanced by the Allied Courts, and finally, with their sanction and the aid of France, was summarily suppressed. Austria was the only Great Power which had never stooped to flatter or conciliate the democratic spirit ; and for the next thirty years the Austrian Minister, Metternich, was the dominant personality in European politics.

Neither absolutism nor the acquisition of alien populations was an object of policy to British statesmen ; but they could not be wholly unaffected by the political atmosphere of Europe ; and in this country economic forces were more than sufficient to create antagonism between Government and people. However the war may have affected other industries, it had certainly stimulated agriculture ; but much of the development that had taken place was unequal and unsound. The growth of manufactures must in any case have increased the demand for food ; and the war, in so far as it restricted importation or made it more precarious or costly, had diminished the supply. This process was pure gain to the landowners, whose rents rose in some cases fivefold and on the average were doubled,[1] as cultivation was forced down to inferior soils ; and the high prices required to make the tillage of such soils remunerative gave of course a premium to all farmers who had an advantage in the quality of their land or in their personal skill. The profits of the farmer were, however, very far from stable at a time when his operations were exposed to the vicissitudes of war as well as of weather ; and we have seen that anything the labourer gained as a producer of wheat was much more than counterbalanced by the hardship and uncertainty of his position as a consumer.[2] The longer the war continued, the more difficult it became for the two favoured classes to realise that their gains were ephemeral and abnormal. Agricultural improvements, such as enclosing, were prosecuted at no small expense by the best landlords[3] ; and the more improvident

[1] Nicholson's *History of the English Corn Laws*, p. 96.
[2] See p. 86.
[3] Cunningham's *Growth of English Industry and Commerce*, iii. 728.

set a bad example to their tenants, many of whom were making speculative purchases of land, and many more were straining both their means and credit to maintain themselves and their families as gentlemen farmers. As was said in Parliament—doubtless with a touch of aristocratic scorn—they were drinking wine instead of ale ; their sons were following the hounds instead of the plough ; and their daughters were " strumming on the harpsichord " instead of milking the cows.[1]

If this prosperity, such as it was, had continued till the Peace, attempts would still have been made—for they were mooted as early as March 1813—to ensure to the landed interest a continuance of its gains ; but peace came in the wake of a harvest so abundant that the price of wheat fell in six months from 121s. a quarter to 75s. ; the next harvest—that of 1814—was almost equally good ; and what this meant to an inflated agriculture may be gauged from the fact that in the three years 1814–1816 nearly a third of the country banks—and there were 700 of them—failed.[2] Hitherto nobody had been either enriched or impoverished by the Corn Laws which, even as revised in 1804, put no bar in the way of importation so long as the home grower could get 63s. for his wheat ; and prices since then had never even approximated to so low a level. Something like con-sternation prevailed among the middle and lower classes when they learned that Government meant to inaugurate the peace by withholding the long-expected boon of cheap bread. The number of petitions presented against the measure was the greatest, according to Lord Grey, " that had ever perhaps been known in the history of Parliament.'' Liverpool, Bristol, Leeds, Manchester and Glasgow were conspicuous in the movement ; 40,000 signatures are said to have been obtained in London on a single Saturday ; and in several Scottish towns as well as at Westminster there were serious riots. The main contention of Ministers

[1] Smart, i. 455.   [2] Martineau, p. 398.

was the rather singular one that if the largest possible home crop could be wrung from a reluctant soil, bread, however dear now, would eventually become cheap ; but they adhered to it in the face of all protests ; and in 1815 the Corn Bill which prohibited importation till the price had risen to 80s. became law.[1]

The poor at least had no reason to be alarmed when they heard farmers complaining that they could not pay rent and landlords that they could not let farms ; and we have seen that cheap food was not the only advantage enjoyed by the manufacturing population at the close of the war.   Large profits and high wages were then being earned under the influence of a vast mercantile speculation, which differed only in point of magnitude from that which had terminated so disastrously in 1810.[2]   Just as British merchants had exploited to the utmost their admission to the markets of Argentina and Brazil, so in 1813, at the first indication of a general peace, they had purchased all that was available of home and colonial produce, and next year were despatching their argosies to continental ports.   " Everything,". said Brougham, " that could be shipped was sent off ; all the capital that could be laid hold of was embarked " ; and he mentioned that " the frenzy " extended far beyond the regular traders and included " not only clerks and labourers but menial servants."   It soon appeared that continental consumers, much as they may have coveted British goods, were no more able to pay for them, after some twenty years of exhaustive warfare, than had been the Spanish and Portuguese colonists.   " Either no returns whatever were received or pounds came back for thousands that had gone forth " ; and unfortunately, just before the collapse of this speculation, another had been launched—rather premature than improvident—in view of peace with the United States.[3]

[1] Smart, i. 447, 450 ; Meikle, p. 220.
[2] See p. 135.   [3] Smart, i. 526–530

Meanwhile peace itself was found to be a rather questionable boon. The Napoleonic struggle was no exception to the rule that war at the best is a mere destruction of wealth ; but Great Britain, which was always outside the actual scene of hostilities, could not fail to gain in industrial activity from the paralysis of its neighbours ; and Napoleon had no sooner issued the Berlin Decree than he was forced to suspend it in order to procure clothing from Yorkshire for his troops. In fact, so far as Europe was concerned, the two opposing blockades, continental and maritime, did little more than convert British commerce from a legitimate into a contraband traffic. ʼ Peace reduced and then extinguished this monopoly ; and the revival of industry abroad was accompanied by all the derangement inseparable from its readjustment at home. Not only the armament makers, but all who were concerned in the production and carriage of food and clothing, had to reckon with the cessation of large Government orders ; and unemployment was aggravated by the discharge of some 300,000 soldiers and sailors.[1]

The distress of 1811 had been acute and widespread, but, according to Brougham, it might almost be described as prosperity in comparison with that which now prevailed.[2] Superabundance and scarcity—much to sell and a low price, little to sell and a high price—were equally supposed to be the ruin of agriculture ; and at the close of 1815, after three successive good harvests, inferior farms all over the country were lying untilled. Many of them could not be let even when offered rent-free. Throughout the next year the general condition of industry was at its worst. There was a diminution of nearly 20 per cent. in the import trade, of 16 per cent. in the export trade ; and no use could be found for about 5000 vessels. Every month on an average 170 merchants and manufacturers became bankrupt. The price of iron had fallen from

[1] Smart, i. 539.   [2] *Ibid.* p. 595.

L

£20 a ton to £8 ; and the stoppage of blast-furnaces caused great suffering not only amongst the men directly affected but amongst the miners who had supplied them with coal. In Birmingham, the chief seat of the iron manufacture, one-third of the male operatives, in addition to all women and children, were idle, and the rest could obtain at most only half-a-day's work. The state of the cloth manu-facture was better only in this respect, that half-time was not so general amongst those who were still employed. Amongst the cotton-weavers (who were the greatest sufferers of all from the substitution of machinery for hand labour) the average rate of wages had fallen from nearly 14s. a week in 1802 to the "fearful point" of 4s. 3½d.; and even from that they had to deduct about a shilling for the rent of their looms. The one thing that alleviated an all but intolerable situation was the cheapness of bread ; but this advantage disappeared as early as May 1816 in anticipation of a harvest—imperilled by a late spring and incessant summer rains—which proved to be "one of the worst harvests ever known." The price of wheat, which was 52s. at the beginning of the year, had risen to 103s. before its close.

The people seem to have borne their sufferings with great patience and self-control till cheap bread began to fail them in the spring ; but from this point disorder was little less general, and naturally much more con-spicuous, than distress. In the fen country round about Ely much land had been reclaimed from the marshes, hurriedly and wastefully cropped, and on the decline of prices allowed to fall out of tillage ; and here towards the end of May there was an orgy of violence and looting on the part of unemployed peasants, with the result that thirty-four of them were sentenced to death and five were hanged. Meanwhile incendiarism—the firing of ricks, barns and thrashing machines—had become rife in Suffolk ; in July Luddism re-asserted itself with all its old fury and precision—this time at the expense of lace-frames in Leicestershire ; and in October miners were rioting—not in Staffordshire where their condition was the most pitiable—but in South Wales. Towards the end of that month there was a riot in Birmingham ; and Lord Sidmouth informed one of his correspondents that " the neighbourhood of Manchester was very bad, and Nottingham hopeless."[1]

We have seen that Cobbett had been at work as a Radical journalist since 1807. His *Weekly Political Register*, " loaded with more than half its amount in stamp," was published at a shilling and a halfpenny, and at this price could be known to most working-men only in so far as it was read aloud at their meetings. He now resolved to issue a supplementary edition which should contain no news, and consequently, being a pamphlet and not a newspaper, could be sold stamp-free at twopence. The success of this expedient, which he adopted for the first time on November 2, 1816, was instantaneous and complete. The circulation of the paper in its cheap form went up at a bound from 750 copies to 40,000 or 50,000 a week ; it was read " on nearly every cottage hearth " throughout the manufacturing districts ; and, as Cobbett at this period discouraged machine-breaking and strove to divert the people from aimless violence to constitutional agitation, one may accept the statement of one of his most judicious admirers : " Riots soon became scarce, and from that time they have never obtained their ancient vogue with the labourers of this country."[2]

The new departure in journalism was discredited exactly a month later by a miniature insurrection in London, and on January 28, 1817, by what could be described as an attempt to shoot the Prince Regent, the window of his carriage being " perforated by two

[1] Smart, i. 489, 490, 594, 595 ; Walpole, i. 402, 417, 422, 423 ; Pellew's *Sidmouth*, iii. 145–156 ; Martineau's *History of the Peace*, i. 64–66.   [2] Carlyle's *William Cobbett*, pp. 189–195.

stones or bullets from an air gun." [1]   A similar outrage had occurred in 1795, and it now led in Parliament to the same results.   Secret committees were appointed in both Houses to investigate the state of the country, and these soon convinced themselves that a vast conspiracy to subvert the constitution was being carried on through a network of Hampden Clubs.   In March, when over 500 petitions in favour of reform had been presented and repelled—mostly on the ground that they were printed—the Habeas Corpus Suspension Act of 1794, the Sedition and Treason Acts of 1795, and an Act of 1797 to prevent the seduction from their allegiance of sailors and soldiers were all literally or virtually re-enacted.   If these measures had been extravagant or superfluous twenty years earlier, much more were they so now when the country was at peace, when the ancient monarchy had been restored on a limited basis in France, and when the prophet of so-called sedition was not the republican and cosmopolitan Paine but the Radical and typically English Cobbett.   In one respect, however, the state of affairs really was more critical from the official point of view than it had been in 1795.   Cartwright and Cobbett, the organiser and the journalist, had   accomplished   their   work.   The   disease   which Wilberforce as late as 1812 had prematurely diagnosed as political was now actually of that nature, and, though still acute only under certain economic conditions, was soon to become chronic.   The Sedition and Treason Acts, which had once served only to augment the popularity of "Billy Pitt," were felt by hundreds of thousands as a galling restraint on their freedom ; and Sidmouth and Castlereagh, the reputed authors of this legislation, were detested and abhorred.

The *Political Register* was suspended for over three months owing to its author having sought refuge in

[1] Pellew's *Sidmouth*, iii. 168.

America ; and, when it re-appeared on July 12, 1817, readers who exulted in its thunder had necessarily to be content with distant and belated peals. Cobbett was independent, uncorrupt, and, so far, had discouraged violence ; but probably no English agitator for whom so much can be said has ever equalled him in inconsistency and habitual intemperance of speech. If he had any definite opinion, it was that the country was being ruined by its financial system—its taxes, its paper money and its debt. There were few public men of his time except Windham—and even with Windham he quarrelled—who did not experience both the fulsomeness of his praise and the fury of his abuse. The *Register* had been established as an organ of ultra-Toryism in 1802, and when, about four years later, it had gone over to the opposite extreme, many of its political judgments had of course to be reversed ; but Cobbett's treatment of his fellow Radicals, Burdett, Hunt and O'Connell, is not covered by this plea, nor indeed is his attitude towards the Catholics. Beginning as a keen opponent of their claim to eligibility for Parliament, he ended by supporting it and by writing a history of the Reformation even more antipathetic than that of Lingard, which, " able and good as I think it (as far as I have read), will never until the last page shall have been destroyed by the hand of time produce a thousandth part of the effect that mine will produce in the space of three years." Always at the mercy of emotions which his power and popularity as a writer gave him no inducement to restrain, he so delighted in combat that, like Wesley, he could look back at the last on a supremely happy life. Almost all sections of the community were within the circuit of his lash— Jews, Scotsmen, Quakers, Evangelicals, Dissenters, Whigs, financiers, landlords and farmers ; and the landlords were not specially unfortunate when he described them as " the most base of all the creatures that God ever suffered to disgrace the human shape."[1]   We shall find that many of the peasantry suffered imprisonment, transportation and even death on account of agrarian disturbances in 1830, and that Cobbett was accused, not without reason, of having incited to incendiarism, which was then a capital offence.   Nor was his influence in other respects inconsistent with this charge.   He himself said in effect that he would rather see the people well fed and clothed than enlightened ; and he was certainly less successful in achieving the former result than in frustrating the latter.   One can understand his denunciation of the potato—for introducing which Sir Walter Raleigh was "one of the greatest villains upon earth "—because, being cheaper than bread, it was "the suitable companion of misery and filth " ; but he defended the ruinous Poor Law and such brutal pastimes as bull-baiting and cock-fighting, ridiculed Savings Banks, the Useful Knowledge Society and Mechanics' Institutes, derided the demand for popular education as "despicable cant and nonsense," and sought to diffuse his own distaste —which he shared with Bentham—for imaginative literature, including the works of Sheridan, Fielding, Milton and "the punning and smutty Shakespeare."[2] Democracy and illiteracy were in his opinion quite compatible terms.

Cobbett returned from America in November 1819, bringing with him the bones of Thomas Paine, whom he now revered but had once denounced as "the greatest disgrace of mankind."   By this time another economic crisis had developed, and the working classes were engaged in their first serious attempt to obtain political power.

The industrial depression which had caused so much

---

[1] The indifference to truth involved in all this swearing at large was no doubt mainly unconscious ; but Cobbett could on occasion be a shameless liar.—Carlyle's *Cobbett*, pp. 213, 214, 220.   Cartwright, the soul of simplicity and honour, was too guileless and unpractical to vie with him as an agitator.

[2] Kent's *English Radicals*, pp. 290–305.

distress and disorder in 1816 was followed about the middle of the next year by a great revival of trade. In September 1817 the ironmasters were said to be so busy with the home market that they could not execute their foreign orders ; and in December Walter Scott wrote : "Trade of every kind is recovering and not a loom is idle in Glasgow." In 1818 as compared with 1816 there was a threefold increase in the importation of wool and linseed, and the total value of the imports was more than doubled. Incomparably the largest of these was cotton ; and a month before the end of the year Liverpool alone had imported as much cotton as had come into the whole kingdom in 1817. This prosperity, which was supposed to be the natural, though belated, result of peace, had really originated in a shortage of supplies caused by the previous depression ; and, as in the Brazilian speculation of 1810 and the Continental speculation of 1813, so now the importers had much overestimated the deficiency they were called upon to make good. Early in 1819 the symptoms of a disastrous general speculation began to appear in their invariable order—commercial bankruptcies, rising in six months to twice the average ; a contraction first of credit and then of manufacture, and finally unemployment and a fall in wages. In April 1819 the Lancashire cotton-mills were almost idle, whilst large cargoes of the raw material still continued to arrive ; at the same time in Yorkshire there was "an alarming decrease" in the production of cloth ; and in summer the condition of industry and the consequent distress were reported from all quarters to be even worse than they had been in 1816.[1]

An economic crisis much less acute than this would have sufficed to rekindle the political agitation, which had never wholly died down ; and rekindled it was on a quite unprecedented scale. Not only was there the old network of societies petitioning and corresponding

[1] Smart, i. 654, 655, 689 ; Tooke, ii. 24–27, 61 ; Walpole, i. 448.

with a view to parliamentary reform, but huge open-air meetings were held—a practice which had not hitherto been generally adopted.   Women as well as men attended these meetings ; and the *Annual Register* records as " an entirely novel and truly portentous circumstance " that a Female Reform Society had been instituted at Bolton.   A circumstance more ominous and quite as novel was that the Radicals— openly it is true and without arms—were undergoing drill.   They themselves represented this practice as intended merely to facilitate the marshalling of their processions and also as a healthful exercise for sedentary weavers and spinners ; but in official quarters this new-born zeal for order and hygiene was naturally regarded with suspicion.   The earliest meetings were occupied mainly with devising remedies for ,the prevailing distress ; but the political interest rapidly became dominant ; and in July 1819, at the second of two great demonstrations, the people of Birmingham took the bold step of claiming, or rather asserting, representation in Parliament.   Their original intention had been to choose four " members " for the town ; but at the suggestion of Cartwright—still as active as ever in his eighty-first year—they adopted the more modest plan of commissioning a " legislatorial attorney " to present a letter to the Speaker—a mode of application which Cartwright called " sending a petition in form of a living man instead of one on parchment or paper." [1] Their choice fell on Sir Charles Wolseley, a Staffordshire baronet, who, as he informed his audience, had taken part in the storming of the Bastille.   Next month a meeting was held with a similar object at Manchester, but proved to be of far greater moment ; for it was dispersed by the military at no small sacrifice of life and limb, and was long remembered with execration by both Whigs and Radicals as " the Manchester massacre."

The Government did not on this occasion, as in 1817,

[1] *Life of Cartwright,* ii. 165.

ask Parliament to suspend the Habeas Corpus Act ; but late in 1819 they passed a series of measures, aimed chiefly at unauthorised arming and drilling and seditious meetings and literature, which are known as the Six Acts. One of these enactments, which subjected all pamphlets below a certain size to the stamp duty on newspapers, put an end to the cheap edition of Cobbett's *Political Register*, nicknamed the " Twopenny Trash " ; and the effect of the whole series was to crush, though not to extirpate, the zeal for reform. At Glasgow indeed there was an outbreak, which involved some actual fighting, as late as April of this year ; but the popular discontent found no further expression till it was appeased by the return of prosperity in 1821.

At this point our attention must be diverted to a theme which, though of a different character, is not unconnected with the social and political unrest. We have seen that the church-building project of 1712 was the only item in the Anglican revival of that age which had not been resuscitated under Evangelical auspices before the French Revolution[1] ; and the war, which postponed its adoption on the ground of expense, had the more serious result of infecting it with the anti-Jacobin spirit. Reference has been made to the ecclesiastical theatres suggested as an addition to the Establishment by Arthur Young in 1798. Perceval, just before his assassination in 1810, informed the Archbishop of Canterbury that he had been looking into the demand for more churches, and in five days would be in a position " to take some active step." Earl Grosvenor, a prominent Whig peer, did take such a step —apparently without success—in 1813. And now in 1818, during the first transient gleam of prosperity which had yet shone on the Peace, Parliament was easily induced to vote a million towards the erection of churches in the more populous parishes. With the aid of private

[1] See p. 43.

subscriptions, which already amounted to £50,000,[1] it was estimated that from 150 to 200 of these could be built.[2]

Whatever exception might be taken to the motive and the source of this grant, the need for it could not be questioned—so great in some districts had become the pressure of population on the rule that all religious ceremonies conferring a civil status must be performed in a parish church. The town of Norwich indeed had thirty-six churches, or nearly one for every thousand of its people ; but in the crowded dioceses of London and Chester, if all the inhabitants had presented themselves simultaneously at the church doors, about a million of them in either case must have been shut out. The result was that the rites of baptism, marriage and burial, owing to their " perpetual and almost ceaseless repetition," could not be celebrated with decency—not to say solemnity—or even with the care sufficient to guard against mistakes or frauds.[3]   In the parish church of Manchester there were from forty to fifty christenings every Sunday afternoon, besides those on week days, whilst on Christmas Day, Easter Sunday and Whitsunday the number rose to an average of 140 to 200. Mr. Wray, one of the two incumbents, declared in " A Statement of Facts "[4] that on a recent first of January he himself had christened ninety-three children ; that on the following sixth of February twenty-nine couples were married ; and that the banns of marriage published every Sunday morning—all for the first, second and third time—were seldom less than 120, and once lately had been 156.

This state of things was referred to by Vansittart, who as Chancellor of the Exchequer brought the Bill

[1] Warre-Cornish's *English Church*, p. 79.
[2] Hansard, xxxviii. 712, 717, 833.
[3] *Ibid.*, xxxvii. 1120, 1121, 1130.
[4] Printed in appendix to Yates's *The Basis of National Prosperity*, 1817, p. 354.

into Parliament ; but neither he nor the Prime Minister, Lord Liverpool, had it mainly or at all in view when they dilated on the enormous importance of the measure —the latter describing it as " the most important " he had ever introduced. Liverpool frankly acknowledged, or rather hastened to explain, that its object was to promote the public security by making the poor more contented, more meek and submissive, and also to counteract the influence of Dissent, especially as a means, and, as Lord Harrowby admitted, the only considerable means, of instruction for the young. That the national Church should be extended at the cost of the national exchequer was accepted on all hands as beyond dispute— indeed Sir William Scott affirmed that so august an institution should not condescend to accept the voluntary contributions of its members. Lord Holland ventured only to suggest that some canonries or prebends might be temporarily suppressed in order to raise funds, and— in his capacity of spokesman for the Nonconformists— to point out that they bore the expense of their own chapels and ministers and also paid tithes. At a time when the Church insisted on baptising, marrying and burying Dissenters, it may logically have been entitled to their support ; but it was surely somewhat incongruous that they should contribute with other tax-payers to a scheme which was designed, in the words of the Premier, " to remove Dissent." [1]

The Evangelicals, whether Methodists or Churchmen, had never any difficulty in inculcating what Arthur Young called "that truly excellent religion which exhorts to content and to submission to the higher powers."

[1] Hansard, xxxvii. 428 ; xxxviii. 709, 712, 718. In 1824, when a further grant of half a million was voted, it appeared that 98 churches had been built. Bennet said that the new churches in London " seemed to vie with each other in deformity " ; and, with regard to the edifice in Langham Place, he proposed that it should be pulled down and offered " to subscribe a fair proportion of the expense."—Hansard, N.S., xi. 35.

Wesley himself had been as good a Tory as a Churchman, and his followers were more faithful to his political than to his ecclesiastical principles. Cobbett, in his wild way, said that " the bitterest foes of freedom in England have been and are the Methodists."[1]   In 1811, when it was proposed to abridge the freedom enjoyed under the Toleration Act, they issued a manifesto setting forth the favourable influence they had exercised for fifty years '' on the promotion of loyalty in the middle class, of the spirit of subordination and of willingness to work in the lower class."[2]   So, too, during the democratic agitation of 1819 a conference of Methodist ministers at Bristol addressed an appeal to the members of their sect, exhorting them to avoid '' political parties and associations '' and to ''remember that you belong to a Religious Society which has from the beginning explicitly recognised as high and essential parts of Christian duty to fear God and honour the King, to submit to magistrates for conscience sake and not to speak evil of dignities."[3]   Evangelicalism was naturally repelled by the connexion which had been established by the French Revolution, or even earlier by the writings of Priestley, between democratic and irreligious opinions ;   and it continued to wage the anti-Jacobin warfare initiated by Hannah More in her penny tracts.   Wilberforce, though he favoured Catholic Emancipation and retained some sort of allegiance to Pitt's latest and mildest scheme of parliamentary reform, made himself conspicuous on every possible occasion as an enemy of personal freedom and freedom of the press, and consequently was characterised by Place as ''an ugly epitome of the devil."[4]   Cobbett was neither a free-thinker nor a Dissenter but a good

---

[1] Hammond, *The Town Labourer*, p. 281.   The victims of Cobbett's abuse were seldom without companions in misfortune.   In this case the Methodists were bracketed with the farmers—'' the loudest, the most hardened and the most brutal of all the enemies of freedom in England.''—Kent, p. 299.   [2] Halévy, *Histoire*, i. 407.
    [3] Hammond, p. 281.   [4] Wallas's *Place*, p. 147.

Churchman ; yet Wilberforce considered him the worst demagogue—"the most pernicious of all"; and what Cobbett thought of Wilberforce may be inferred from the place he assigned to him in a list of undesirable persons who were not to be met with in America : "No Cannings, Liverpools, Castlereaghs, Eldons, Ellenboroughs or Sidmouths. No Bankers, no squeaking Wynnes, no Wilberforces. Think of *that !* No Wilberforces ! "[1] Pietists of a coarser grain than Wilberforce were naturally even more disposed to magnify the importance of religion as an adjunct to the police force ; and this idea was very bluntly expressed by a clergyman named Yates, who published an appeal for church-building and based it largely on the ground of "daily increasing insubordination" and the danger of an "assault upon the enviable possessions of those now distinguished by wealth and power." "No laws, no civil police, no military power, no political wisdom can be sufficient for the defence of existing possessions and authorities if unaided and unsupported by the sanctions of religion."[2]

As it was thought desirable to build churches with a view to diffusing a pious and presumably submissive spirit, one might suppose that from a similar motive there would be equal zeal to establish schools. But here, as we have seen, the question had been raised whether the ignorance which led to violence was not a lesser evil than the enlightenment which prompted to drastic reform. This obstacle, though somewhat weakened owing to the decline of Anti-Jacobinism, still remained, and had recently been reinforced by another, arising out of the rivalry in the manufacturing districts between Church and Dissent.

England and Wales at this period were unquestionably the least and worst educated countries in Protestant Europe ; and Brougham, who had taken the place of

[1] Hammond, p. 238.
[2] *The Basis of National Welfare*, pp. 17, 61.

Whitbread as the advocate of popular education, procured in 1816 the appointment of a Select Committee to inquire into the means of instruction provided for the poor. The investigation, with its promoter as chairman, was at first confined to London,[1] but was soon extended to the whole of South Britain; and Parliament could have had no sounder or more ample basis for legislation than was contained in the parochial returns which were presented and summarised by Brougham.

We have seen that the first modern attempt to educate the poor was the institution of charity schools during and after the reign of Queen Anne. These still existed, and in one respect may be said to have flourished; for the Committee found that their number in London " exceeded anything that could have been previously believed," and that the annual voluntary contributions were well maintained. But, though presentable enough in form, they had sadly degenerated in spirit. A century of alms-giving had enabled them to accumulate funds which were applied, not in clothing and educating as many children as possible, but in providing for a few— most of them boarders—at unnecessary expense. The mastership in too many cases had become a sinecure, the duties of which were discharged by an incompetent and ill-paid deputy; and the whole system had fallen into the rut of a narrow and lifeless routine. Of a similar grade but of recent origin were the Bell and Lancaster schools—the former, as well as many of the charity schools, managed in the interest of the Church by the National Society, and the latter, on an undenominational basis, by the British and Foreign Schools Society. In a much lower category were the " dame schools " or " threepenny schools," in which some

---

[1] The number of illiterate children in London was found to be 120,000; and about 3000 of their parents objected to send them to school because they wished to " let them out " to common beggars.— Hansard, xxxiv. 1230.

50,000 children were looked after, and presumably taught to read, by old women at a charge of threepence a day. These were found to be more valuable from a moral than from an educational standpoint, the children being usually sent too young, and taken away when just old enough, to learn ; and whatever access of intelligence as well as of piety may have accrued from the Sunday schools can hardly be reckoned here, as many of their pupils were also week-day scholars. The average ratio of children between seven and thirteen years to the whole population was reckoned as one-tenth, and this was actually the proportion attending school in Scotland and Holland and in the four northern counties of England ; but for the whole of England, even if we include the dame schools, the proportion was barely one-fifteenth, whilst in Middlesex—as in Wales—it fell to one-twentieth and in Lancashire to one-twenty-fourth. Of about 12,000 parishes or chapelries there were 3500 without " the vestige of a school " ; and in Manchester and Salford during a recent period nearly 10,000 marriages had been recorded in which neither of the parties could sign their names.[1]

The Select Committee was dissolved in 1818, and

[1] Hansard, xxxiv. 636, 1232 ; N.S., ii. 61–63 ; Brougham's *Speeches*, iii. 231 ; Halévy, *Histoire*, i. 501. In Switzerland only one person in sixty was unable to read and write. Scotland must have been handicapped in these comparisons by the prevalence of illiteracy in parts of the Highlands—a Celtic district which had not the statistical independence of Wales. Alexander Somerville, a private in the Scots Greys, was of opinion that the reputation gained by Scottish Regiments during the Napoleonic War was largely due to the fact that the men, unlike the great majority of English and Irish soldiers, were able to write home to their friends. " It was the writing quite as much as the fighting of the Scots regiments which distinguished them."—*Autobiography of a Working Man*, p. 188. Sir James Mackintosh, referring to his experience in India, said that morality was best preserved amongst those of our soldiers and sailors abroad who, like the Scots, were able to keep in touch with their relatives. Those who could write " carried their homes with them wherever they went."—Hansard, N.S., ii. 91. Many of the Highland soldiers must, however, have been illiterate. See Colonel Stewart's *Sketches of the Highlanders*, 2nd edition, i. 102, and Appendix XXXI.

two years later Brougham brought forward its natural sequel—a Bill for the education of the poor. His scheme provided that any two Justices of the Peace, the parish clergyman or any five resident householders might apply to Quarter Sessions for the establishment of a school, the cost of which, if not exceeding £200, was to be advanced by the treasurer of the county and paid out of the Exchequer. The capital charge devolving on Parliament would be about half a million.[1] The current expense would be borne by the landowners, and would cost them at most only a pound a head. The master, who must be a Churchman, was to be elected at a meeting of householders; but the resident parson was to have a veto on their choice, and the school was to be managed as well as founded under ecclesiastical control. On the other hand, no religious book but the Bible was to be taught—the Church Catechism being relegated to a meeting on Sunday evenings which the children of Dissenters need attend only if their parents did not object; and no form of worship was to be used but the Lord's Prayer. Whitbread's Bill of 1807 had been wrecked by the bishops; but this scheme displeased the Nonconformists without conciliating the Church, and Brougham soon withdrew it, chiefly owing to the perturbation it had caused amongst Dissenters and Catholics. "The House," he said, "would hardly believe the extent to which this alarm had gone."[2]

Meanwhile, as a topic of secular interest, this question had been quite eclipsed by another which in the course of its investigation had unexpectedly emerged. The Select Committee of 1816 had been appointed to inquire into the education of "the lower classes" in London;

[1] A smaller sum, according to Brougham, than had been given for the building of six churches, but this is nonsense. Probably he said sixteen, which would be little over the rate of extravagance in church-building. One must remember that there were great complaints at this period of inaccurate reporting.

[2] Hansard, N.S., ii. 68–91.

and so very humble was the rank specifically mentioned for inspection that it included children belonging to, or accompanying, persons found begging. The Committee, however, soon convinced themselves that, before they could ask Parliament for a grant in aid of popular education, they must know what funds were already available for this purpose; and accordingly they extended their investigation to the schools of Christ's Hospital, Charterhouse, Westminster and St. Paul's. In 1817 their work was suspended owing to the illness of their chairman; but next year they not only horrified the *Quarterly Review* by calling before them the heads of Eton and Winchester, but procured a Bill for the appointment of a Commission to inquire into the application of charitable endowments. So far Ministers had professed to favour the design, but they now became directly hostile. The Bill was returned from the Lords in a mutilated and impotent condition, and when the list of Commissioners appeared, the promoter of the whole movement was found to be not of their number. "A Letter to Sir Samuel Romilly," in which Brougham gave vent to his very natural indignation, went through eight editions in a month; and a controversy ensued which "agitated all men all over the country" and "for months raged with unabated fury both within the walls of the Universities and without."[1] The Government could not long withstand the storm it had raised; and in 1819 a Commission was appointed of which Brougham was a member and which conformed on the whole to the original scheme—a scheme which not five weeks earlier was still being fiercely assailed in the Ministerial press.[2]

The Commissioners, even under the new Act, were hampered by the exclusion from their survey of schools which had "Special Visitors" appointed by their founders; but, divided as they were into five itinerant

[1] Brougham's *Speeches*, iii. 15, 220.
[2] *Edinburgh Review*, xxxii. 90.

boards which might and did appear simultaneously in different parts of the country, they caused much wholesome alarm amongst all who were conscious of having neglected or misapplied educational funds. And there were many such ; for obsolete ideals and the decay of once prosperous towns had reduced the ancient grammar schools—which we should now call secondary schools— to a condition which was thus described by Chief Justice Kenyon, himself an old pupil, in 1795 : "Empty walls without scholars, and everything neglected but the receipt of the salaries and emoluments." These schools had originated at a time when Latin was the universal language of religious, professional and official life, and when also the parochial clergy were recruited mainly from men of humble rank. Many of them, it is true, were founded or remodelled after the Reformation ;[1] but that movement, an offspring of the Renaissance, did little more from the educational standpoint than divert the popular aspiration from mediæval to classical Latin, whilst adding Greek and even Hebrew as indispensable to the Scriptural defence of Protestantism ; and indeed it was in the Puritan epoch, with its fine maxim, "Better unborn than untaught," that the grammar schools appear to have been at their best. After 1660 they declined in proportion to the growth of an industrial spirit which made it seem more important that the mass of the poor should be taught to read and write than that the path of scholarship should be opened to a gifted few. In 1680 a French religious order, Les Frères des Ignorants, was founded for the promotion of elementary teaching, and no doubt contributed to the rise of the English charity schools. As fewer and fewer of the "town boys" presented themselves for gratuitous instruction in Latin, and as the master was

[1] " The schools to which Edward VI gave his name were not one of them originally of his foundation. They were mostly very old schools refounded with poorer endowments."—Gairdner's *English Church in the Sixteenth Century*, p. 314.

not obliged or disposed to teach anything else,[1] the school either developed into a boarding establishment for private pupils or practically—it might be even actually—ceased to exist. In the former case the trustees spent the income at their disposal in repairing and enlarging " a vast house." In the latter case what they did with the funds was too often a mystery to all but themselves. In Berkshire the income from endowments was £20,000, but only a quarter of this sum was legitimately applied.[2] Much the most common form of abuse was that in which the lands constituting the endowment were let by the trustees to personal or municipal friends, and this method was quite openly practised as a means of corrupt influence by the Corporation of Huntingdon ; but a City Company was found to be appropriating several thousands a year from a foundation at Trowbridge in Kent ; Lord Lonsdale, under a will which his father had no right to make, was in the same relation to a charity at St. Bees ; and at Pocklington in Yorkshire, where there was only one pupil and the lower schoolroom had been turned into a carpenter's workshop, an absentee master and a deaf usher divided between them an income of at least £900 a year. In some cases nothing was left to mark the disappearance of a school—not even an idle and highly paid master ; in others there was no master because there never had been a school ; and in view of such facts even so rigid a Tory as Lord Ellenborough was constrained to admit the existence of " enormous frauds."[3]

---

[1] It has been suggested that, where the endowment included an usher, he was intended to teach reading and writing ; and this was the duty assigned to him in the statutes of St. Bees school, Cumberland.—Nicholas Carlisle's *Concise Description of the Endowed Grammar Schools*, 1818, i. 157. [2] Hansard, xxxviii. 339 ; N.S., ii. 57.

[3] Foster Watson's *The Old Grammar Schools*, 1916—an admirable sketch ; *Edinburgh Review*, vols. 31–33. Under an Elizabethan statute many previous attempts had been made—nearly all before 1746—to remedy " charitable abuses."—Hansard, xxxviii. 606 ; and this effort, though by far the most thorough, was no more successful.

If the State could not provide such elementary instruction for the children of the poor as was proposed in Brougham's Bill without offending either the Church or Dissent, there was no such dilemma in the way of its protecting them from industrial ill-usage or over-work.   But we have seen that economic doctrine was almost as great an obstacle in the one case as religious doctrine in the other.   Though Parliament had not yet begun to follow Adam Smith in the direction of free trade, it was dominated, if not obsessed, by his opinion that any attempt to interfere with the natural course of industry must do more harm than good. Something had been done or at least enacted in 1802 for the safeguarding of pauper children sent down from London to work in the Lancashire cotton mills.[1]   In their case the public responsibility could not be denied ; but Sir Robert Peel, the author of this legislation, had for several years been endeavouring to extend it to children who were at least nominally free.   Now that water-power was being supplanted by steam, factories were no longer built in isolated valleys, but in towns where child workers could be obtained from the sur-rounding population ; and these, owing to the poverty of their parents, especially among the handloom weavers, began work very early in life, and had to submit to whatever daily duration of labour the employer might exact.   About a sixth or even a fifth of them are said to have been under nine years of age and a considerable proportion under seven ; and they usually worked for fourteen or fifteen hours every day but Sunday, with intervals of half an hour for breakfast and an hour for dinner.   Evidence, even medical evidence, seems to have been as easily procurable in support of this system as it had been in favour of the slave trade ; and just as the West Indian planters had asserted that their negroes, after a comfortable, if not luxurious, voyage

[1] See p. 82.

across the Atlantic, were well housed and fed and were worked just hard enough to keep them in good condition, so the manufacturers drew a most alluring picture of child life in a cotton mill. Mr. Peel, son and heir of Sir Robert, after listening to some of their speeches in the House of Commons, remarked that, if all they said was true, Parliament ought to be petitioned to erect such mills as hygienic institutions. In one Scottish factory the annual death-rate amongst the children was stated in evidence as only one in 445 ; and Peel, quoting the inquiry of a poet in reference to the Goddess of Health :

> In what dim and dark retreat
> The coy Nymph fix'd her fav'rite seat ?

said it would certainly have been surprising if the reply had been " in the cotton mill of Messrs. Finlay and Co. at Glasgow." [1] Sir Robert's Bill was introduced in 1815 and passed four years later. It prohibited juvenile labour under the age of nine and forbade all persons under the age of sixteen to be employed more than twelve hours a day, exclusive of meal-times ; but the whole Act—which affected only the cotton manufacture —was nullified by its enforcement being left to the Justices of the Peace—many of them manufacturers— under whose supervision the Act of 1802 had so signally failed to achieve its purpose.[2]

One can easily understand the repulse of philanthropy when it came into conflict with such powerful interests as were entrenched in the factory and the school ; but how are we to explain its failure for more than fifty years to put down so defenceless as well as so indefensible a practice as the employment of children in sweeping chimneys ? None of the familiar arguments could be used in support of this abuse, which was recent in origin

---

[1] Hansard, xxxviii. 358.
[2] Hutchins and Harrison, *Factory Legislation*, p. 21.

and insular, if not even local, in range. In no country but our own was there such a phenomenon as a " climbing boy." Even here he had appeared in England only within the previous century—being coeval, one supposes, with the sort of chimney required for a modern grate—and was unknown in Scotland till 1788 ; and, whilst London had five hundred of this " helpless and infantine race," there were not as many more in the whole of England. The child who was forced, kidnapped or sold into this trade had to serve a novitiate, first of terror, and then—owing to the bruising of his elbows and knees—of acute physical pain. Chimneys a foot in diameter could, it was said, be climbed with ease by a boy of seven ; but there were a good many chimneys which even a younger child could not climb with anything approaching to ease, being in fact only seven inches square ; and these he had to sweep naked, as otherwise he was liable to be jammed by the mere rumpling of his shirt.

The revolt against this distinctive barbarity of our social life takes us back to the days of Jonas Hanway, who sought with some success to alleviate it by articles of apprenticeship which should be signed by the master in presence of a Justice of the Peace.[1] A Bill promoted by Hanway, but which he did not live to see enacted, was passed in 1788. It provided that a boy must not be apprenticed before he was eight years old, should be thoroughly washed at least once a week, and should not be compelled—as was then and long afterwards a common practice—to go up an ignited chimney in order to extinguish the fire. Only the more prosperous masters—20 out of 200 in London—paid any attention to this Act ; and nothing further was done till a Society for Superseding Climbing Boys was formed in London in 1803. In that year the best of several sweeping machines was produced by an inventor named Smart, and proved successful in all but a very few cases—

---

[1] Pugh's *Hanway*, p. 200.

these being flues tortuous, in parts even horizontal, which were found mainly in aristocratic mansions. The London Society and at least two others which had been formed in Sheffield and Leeds did their best to bring this machine into general use ; and in 1817 the cause was taken up in Parliament by Henry Grey Bennet, a younger son of the fourth Earl of Tankerville, who had the support of Wilberforce and of public meetings in all the large towns. Bennet endeavoured to prohibit chimney-climbing, and—when that attempt failed—to minimise its hardships and dangers ; but the two Bills he succeeded in sending up to the Lords were both rejected, mainly through the influence of those who owned narrow and tortuous chimneys and " could well afford to alter them if they pleased."

Two points may be noted in this connexion as throwing a sinister light on the temper of the age. One is the fact that in or about the year 1818 chimneys seven inches square, which only a child of four or five could sweep, were still being built ; and the other is the attitude of Sydney Smith, writing—of course anonymously—in the *Edinburgh Review*. Smith begins his article on " climbing boys " by remarking that without the evidence brought before Parliament " the miseries of these poor wretches " could hardly have been conceived, and concludes thus : " After all we must own that it was quite right to throw out the Bill for prohibiting the sweeping of chimneys by boys, because humanity is a modern invention ; and there are many chimneys in old houses which cannot possibly be swept in any other manner." Well might Bennet say of such an argument as frankly stated in Parliament that it was " sacrificing the children of the poor in order to preserve the chimneys of the rich." [1]

[1] Smith's *Works*, ii. 82. A full and excellent account of the whole subject is given by Mr. and Mrs. Hammond in *The Town Labourer*, pp. 177–193. Chimney-climbing by children was not fully suppressed till 1840.

If the preservation of their chimneys was an object of selfish concern to the rich, still more, in so far as they were landlords, was the preservation of their game ; and the means employed in both cases, if not equally cruel, were at least equally unique, the man-trap, or at least the spring-gun, being as exclusively national an institution as the "climbing boy."[1] By the common law, as generally construed, the landowner, great or small, had a proprietary interest in his game ; but this usage had been overridden since the Restoration by a series of statutes intended to increase the importance of the squirearchy and to secure it against the predominance of personal wealth.[2]

Under these statutes the right of sporting was confined practically to landowners of at least £100 annual value, and certain penalties were annexed to both the buying and the selling of game. The prohibition to purchase seems never to have been enforced ; and, whilst the poulterer was seldom prosecuted for selling game at the instance of his rich but landless customers, the marauding peasant who furnished most of the supplies, in proportion as he waxed bolder and more ferocious, was shot, trapped and mercilessly punished. The development of this illicit market gave a great impetus to poaching, especially during the distress which followed the Peace. One whole village is said to have been engaged in it, including the principal shopkeepers and even the parish constable. In 1817 twelve hundred persons were imprisoned for this offence, in addition to those who had fled to avoid arrest ; and the House of Lords was informed by one of its members that in the small county of Bedford the number of committals for poaching had risen from

---

[1] Romilly, iii. 284.

[2] The Act—always evaded or ignored—which established a landed property qualification for the House of Commons was passed in 1712. Swift wrote about this period : " Power, which, according to an old maxim, was used to follow land, is now gone over to money."—Lecky, i. 250.

thirteen in 1814 to twenty-four in 1815, thirty-three in 1816, sixty-one in 1817 and eighty in 1818. An Act was passed in 1816—which Romilly declared to be unexampled in any other country—providing that any person found in an enclosure at night with a gun or any device for killing game might be transported for seven years at the discretion of two magistrates. Next year it was re-enacted in a form applicable only to armed persons; but, even as thus modified, it merely strengthened the desire to avoid capture and led to more frequent and violent affrays between poachers and keepers. Less mischievous, but equally ineffective, was a revival of the prohibition to purchase game. The great argument for the Game Laws was that without the assured gratification of their sporting tastes proprietors would not reside on their estates. Sydney Smith thought that this benefit might be assured on less inequitable terms, and said, pertinently enough, "If gentlemen cannot breathe fresh air without injustice, let them putrefy in Cranbourne Alley." [1]

An increase of pauperism as well as of poaching was a natural result of the rural distress; and, as the Poor Law system was now forcing itself on the notice of Parliament, it will be well to review here its origin and development and first, by way of contrast, to glance at the condition of pauperism in Scotland.

The Scottish Poor Law was more than twenty years older than the English, having been established in 1579. Its administration was soon transferred from the justices and magistrates to the kirk sessions; and the method of compulsory assessment, which was authorised but not prescribed in the initiating Act, was so far from commending itself to these bodies that only eight of them had adopted it before 1740. A century later, it had been extended to nearly half the population; but this half was

[1] Smith's *Works*, ii. 54, 333, 335, 337; Hansard, xxxv. 338, 837; xl. 374.

concentrated in little more than a third of the parishes ; and the average rate of assistance over the whole country was only £1 13s. 6½d. a year, or ninepence a week. Great credit was claimed for this system on account of its cheapness, the private liberality, the habits of industry and self-reliance which it was assumed to promote ; but those who exulted in the fact that Scotland had relatively only half the pauperism which existed in England and maintained it at a quarter of the cost were at little pains to analyse their boast. Only outdoor relief was given ; and as a matter of right, if not wholly of custom, it was confined to the disabled poor whose names could be entered on what was called the " permanent roll." It had long been established that the heritors or landowners could be assessed only for the support of this class ; and throughout the whole north of Scotland, where the average annual allowance was only 9s. 4d., or at all events in the Highlands, even this exiguous burden on land was evaded or repelled. Dr. Alison, who was mainly instrumental in procuring the new Scottish Poor Law of 1841, ascribed the high death-rate from fever in the towns to a mass of destitution wholly unrelieved ; and the town council of St. Andrews were not at all singular in their experience of parish relief as "nothing else than a system of protracted starvation." Indeed, but for the prevalence of begging, which made it " difficult to reside in the country districts with peace and safety, not to speak of enjoyment," starvation, not protracted but rapid, would have been its inevitable result.[1]

In contrast with this provision for the poor, of which extreme parsimony was at all times the distinguishing feature, we have now to consider one which was long firmly, if not sternly, administered, but which culminated in a carnival of lavishness and indiscriminate abuse. The Elizabethan Act of 1601, which founded or consolidated the English Poor Law, ordained the compulsory

---

[1] *Church and Reform in Scotland,* 1797–1843, pp. 246–254.

assessment which the Scottish statute had merely authorised ; and for this purpose it required overseers to be
appointed in every parish who should tax the inhabitants
in order to provide funds, not only for relieving the lame,
the blind, the aged and infirm, but for purchasing materials on which the able-bodied should be set to work.
Some attempt had already been made to establish a
workhouse or " house of correction " in each county, and
this scheme was further developed in the following reign ;
but no important addition was made to the Poor Law
till the Settlement Act was passed in 1662. The object
of this ambiguous and ill-drafted measure[1] has been much
discussed. It originated not with the county members
but with the representatives of London and Westminster ;
and, as the rate of tenancy which exempted from its
provisions far exceeded that of the peasant's cottage, it
has been suggested that its main object was to check what
was then regarded as the alarming growth of population in
the large towns ; for, though the migration of labour from
one rural parish to another is mentioned in the preamble,
the persons there indicated are so abnormally nomadic
that they " at last become rogues and vagabonds." But,
whatever may have been the purpose of the Act, it declares
plainly enough that, where a person had come into a
parish and was living in a house of less than £10 annual
value, he might within forty days be removed if he were
deemed likely to require relief. Before the end of the
century this rule had been in some respects stiffened, in
others relaxed. On the one hand, the immigrant must
give notice of his arrival, and the forty days were to be
reckoned from the reading of this notice in church. On
the other hand, if he brought with him a certificate from
his former parish, he could not be removed till he had

---

[1] The first and principal clause is a mixture of preamble and legislation ; and Eden said of it that it " has occasioned more doubts and
difficulties in Westminster Hall and has perhaps been more profitable
to the profession of the law than any other point in English jurisprudence."—*State of the Poor*, 1797, i. 175.

become actually chargeable. At the same time various new qualifications for settlement were recognised, such as contracts of apprenticeship and hiring and the discharge of an annual office ; but this singular law became more obscure and disputable with every extension of its scope [1] ; and the ratepayers were overburdened by the growth at their expense of a litigious spirit. The general result was that the labourer was discouraged from going further afield than his own parish in quest of employment or with a view to bettering his condition ; and in later days, when the industrial revolution had begun and a large supply of cheap labour was as much coveted as it had once been dreaded, the peasant might easily enough settle in such places as Sheffield, Nottingham or Leeds, but, being almost invariably refused a certificate, could leave it only at great risk.[2]

So far, and for many years later, the tendency of the Poor Law was to greater rigour. Thus in 1696 the pauper and all his family were required to wear on the right shoulder " a large Roman P and the first letter of the name of the parish cut either in red or blue cloth." In 1722 Justices of the Peace were forbidden to order relief without consulting the overseers ; and by the same Act it was provided that the overseers might purchase or hire a house for the maintenance and employment of the poor, that several parishes might combine for this purpose, that a parish possessing a workhouse might offer to receive the poor of another parish, and that, wherever such an institution was available, the names of the poor who refused to enter it should be struck off the roll. Many workhouses were established in consequence of this Act, and, ten years later, there were said to be about fifty in London and sixty throughout the country.[3]

[1] See Sydney Smith's summary of the " afflicting questions " that might arise on the hiring of a ploughman for a year.—*Works*, ii. 135.

[2] Sir George Nicholls's *History of the English Poor Law*, i. 194, 234, 239, 293, 341; Hammond, *The Village Labourer*, pp. 112–120.

[3] Nicholls, i. 359; ii. 14–18; Hammond, *The Village Labourer*, p. 146

It may be well to remind ourselves at this point that the industrial revolution comprised agriculture as well as manufactures and that its effect was in some respects more severely felt in the country than in the towns ; for, whilst the introduction of machinery brought impoverishment or ruin to the village artisan, the progress of enclosure was at the same time cutting off his auxiliary means. The conversion of common fields and pasture into private farms had been going on in England at various periods and within certain limits since the time of the Tudors, but in the latter half of the eighteenth century it was prosecuted on a quite unprecedented scale. It has been estimated that some 240,000 acres were enclosed before 1760 [1] and 2,400,000 between 1761 and 1801. The two classes which stood to lose and not to gain from this movement were the open-field farmers and the cottagers. The minority who were owners received allotments ; but these had to bear the cost of fencing and were usually too small to provide in themselves the means of livelihood ; and the cottagers had certain rights, such as those of pasturing cows, gleaning, and the cutting of turf and wood, for the loss of which no compensation was given. Consequently the farmer was reduced to the position of a hired labourer ; and the labourer, who had been able to supplement his earnings as farm-worker or mechanic, became a wage-earner only.[2]

It was probably to meet the demands of this social crisis that the Poor Law was for the first time seriously relaxed. The Act of 1782, commonly known as Gilbert's Act, was applicable only to parishes in which a two-thirds majority of the rate-payers should adopt its provisions ; and such parishes were permitted to group themselves

[1] The small total is probably explained by the fact that enclosing had hitherto been confined mainly to the demesne lands of the proprietor.

[2] *Quarterly Review*, April 1912 ; Hammond, *The Village Labourer*, pp. 41, 106 and *passim* ; Gonner's *Common Land and Inclosure*, p. vii.

within a radius of ten miles from a common poorhouse. The preamble commented severely on the harshness and incompetence of overseers ; and in the " Gilbert incorporations " these functionaries were restricted to collecting the rates, whilst the whole management of the poor was entrusted to a salaried guardian for each parish and a visitor for each group, appointed by the Justices of the Peace, and in the latter case presumably one of themselves or of the same social rank.   The poorhouse was to be reserved for those who were unable to work ; and the guardian was to find employment as near their own homes as possible for the able-bodied paupers, to arrange, to receive, and, if necessary, to supplement their wages.[1]

In view of what seems to have given rise to this Act, one might suppose that the tendency it embodied would soon have been checked ; for the growth of a large manufacturing population was already making itself felt, and, eleven years later, the nation was involved in its long struggle with France.   Under these new conditions enclosing, which had hitherto been carried out for the purpose of converting arable land into pasture and consequently had diminished employment, was now directed to the improvement and extension of tillage [2] ; but the labourer suffered far more as a consumer of wheat from war prices than he gained as a producer from war profits ; and when scarcity was added to war, the Poor Law as it stood before 1834 entered on its final and disastrous phase.   A local indiscretion precipitated, and was to give a name to, this change.   On May 6, 1795, in the interval between two bad harvests, the Justices of the Peace for Berkshire met at Speenhamland.   The meeting had been called with the object of reviving the Elizabethan statute for the regulation of wages [3] and of fixing them at a level which should make the labourer independent of the

---

[1] Nicholls, ii. 89.
[2] *Quarterly Review*, April 1912, p. 454.   [3] See page 75.

parish ; but the policy adopted was just the reverse of this—the issuing of a " bread-scale," according to which the labourer and each of his family were to receive assistance in a proportion determined by the price of bread. The supplementing of wages from the rates had long prevailed, as we have seen, in the "Gilbert incorporations," and it had given rise elsewhere to the practice of sending the able-bodied pauper " on the rounds " in quest of work, whence he was called a " roundsman "; but the Speenhamland scheme furnished a standard of relief no less convenient than novel ; and all objection to it on the score of legality was removed a few months later when the Workhouse Act of George I prohibiting outdoor relief was repealed as "injurious to the comfort and domestic situation and happiness " of the poor, and the Justices recovered their power to grant assistance without consulting the overseers. Meanwhile an Act had been passed which, whilst it annulled some of the facilities for gaining a settlement, made the need for one less urgent. Under this statute the labourer could not be removed from a parish till he had become actually chargeable ; and he had thus an incentive—which was soon very much needed—to maintain his independence.[1]

It is obvious enough now, and was even then foreseen, that the adoption of the allowance system in preference to that of a minimum wage could not fail to foster pauperism, because it would demoralise the labourer by effacing in his mind the fundamental distinction between wages and alms, and would assure him of the same measure of support whatever the character or the responsibilities of his private life. But the arguments which prevailed on this occasion are easily understood. In those days of industrial expansion and war a large population was deemed essential to both national welfare and national power. High rates, being a public charge, were accepted as a plea for reduction of rent, but not high wages, which

[1] Nicholls, ii. 118–120, 122, 124, 137 ; Hansard, N.S., ix. 697.

were supposed to be a matter of individual discretion ;
and the farmer had good reason to favour a system which
rendered labour plentiful and cheap, and, whilst leaving
him the sole gainer, made the whole parish contribute to
its cost. Moreover, it was to his interest that wages
should be stable as well as low, a rise granted in time of
dearth being always difficult to withdraw ; and there
were even attempts to throw a sort of glamour over the
Poor Law by presenting it to the peasantry " as an institution for their advantage peculiar to this country," and
one by means of which " their own share in the property
of the kingdom was recognised." This delusion, propa-
gated from no disinterested motive, was accepted in all
innocence by Cobbett, who quite exulted in the Poor Law
and denounced Malthus, its first fully competent critic, as
a " monster," a " shallow and savage fellow," a " hard-
hearted misanthropic economist." During the last dis-
tressful years of the eighteenth century the Speenhamland
or allowance system was fully established in the south of
England and to a great extent in the Midlands ; but
it never made much impression on the hardier spirit of
the north ; and in two counties, Northumberland and
Durham, it was always wholly unknown.[1]

Whitbread in 1807 had endeavoured to grapple with
pauperism as well as with the need for education ; and
at the Peace of 1815 the evil had grown to such dimensions
that Parliament was forced to attempt its abatement,
if not its cure. In 1775, when the industrial revolution
had just begun, the total amount expended in relief of
the poor was one and a half millions. In 1815 it was
about six millions ; and for the year ending March 25,
1818, it reached the high-water mark of seven and three-
quarter millions. Rates of nineteen and twenty-one
shillings in the pound were not uncommon. In one parish
all but sixpence of the daily wage was being paid out of

[1] *Poor Law Report*, 1834, pp. 60, 121–132 ; Hammond, *The Village
Labourer*, pp. 161–170 ; Kent's *English Radicals*, p. 305.

the rates, and in some districts the great majority of the peasants were paupers. A few years earlier, the ratio of illegitimate births to population had been one in twenty-eight. Now it had doubled, being one in fourteen. As the burden of pauperism increased, the keener became the desire of parishes to evade its weight. In 1776 the sum spent in litigation and in the removal of paupers was £35,000. In 1803 it was £190,000, and in 1815 it was £287,000.[1]

It has been suggested that the landlords, who were making more than they cared to admit out of both the industrial revolution and the war, adopted the allowance system as a means of bribing the farmers and of enervating as well as conciliating the peasants. That the system was sanctioned and to some extent introduced as early as 1782 is unfavourable to such a view ; but it was certainly in this apprehensive spirit that the problem was approached by Parliament in 1817. In that year a committee to consider the Poor Laws was appointed by the Commons and another by the Lords ; and the former presented a long, elaborate and inconclusive report. The attitude they would have liked to adopt towards the poor was one which they could not " so well express as in the emphatic language of Mr. Burke : ' Patience, labour, frugality, sobriety and religion should be recommended to them ; all the rest is downright fraud.' " [2] Distracted, however, between their consternation at the increase of the rates and their dread of the consequences if they should

---

[1] Porter's *Progress of the Nation*, i. 78–84 ; Smart, i. 577, 705 ; *Annual Register*, 1817, p. 298. The worst feature of the Poor Law was, of course, the local severity of its pressure. In proportion to population, the increase in the rates from 1801 to 1831 is said to have been 7¼ per cent., and no doubt it was much more than covered by the increase of wealth.

[2] Compare with this utterance that of Dr. Chalmers, the Scottish ecclesiastical Burke : " When the people [*i.e.* the poor] are not misled, they do not move. If they are not previously set agog, they give little or no disturbance."—*Church and Reform in Scotland*, 1797–1843, p. 252.

deal drastically with a system which had " become inter-
woven with the habits and very existence of a large class
of the community," they ventured only to recommend
the expediency of " providing such a check as may lay
the foundation for a better system." Scotland, where the
" protracted starvation " of paupers had been carried to as
high a pitch as their indulgence in England, was supposed
to furnish in this matter as bright an example as it certainly did in education. Some twenty years later, Dr.
Alison was to say of the Scottish upper classes that they
were doing much less for the relief of the poor than those
of any other civilised state in Europe [1]; but the heritors
who dominated the kirk sessions, little as they paid into
the poor-box, did as a rule assist in distributing its con-
tents ; and, as a safeguard against extravagance, the
Committee were anxious that the wealthier parishioners
should undertake this function in England.[2] Hence the
Parish Vestry Act of 1818, which provided that every
person rated at £50 and upwards should have one vote
for every £25 of assessment up to the limit of six, and the
Select Vestry Act of 1819, providing that vestries might
elect a sort of executive committee, and that the unpaid
overseers holding office for one year might be assisted,
as in the " Gilbert incorporations," by a salaried and
permanent official.[3] As the poor rates seem rather to
have diminished per head of the population from this
date to 1834, we may assume that these measures were
as effectual as could be expected from their very limited
range.

Huskisson in 1817 described the Poor Law as "a
bounty on improvidence "; and, whatever may have been

---

[1] *Church and Reform in Scotland*, 1797-1843, p. 253. In Edinburgh
an exemption enjoyed by lawyers reduced the rental liable to assess.
ment by about a fifth. In the assessed parishes the obligation o-
the landowners was limited, as we have seen, to the disabled poorf
In the non-assessed parishes they were not obliged and frequently
refused to contribute at all.—*Ibid.*, p. 249.

[2] *Annual Register*, 1817, pp. 266, 274, 290.

[3] Nicholls, ii. 192-200 ; Porter, i. 81.

the effect of the Vestry Act and the Select Vestry Act, it must have been powerfully assisted by a movement which was then sanctioned by Parliament for the encouragement of thrift. It was hard enough for the labourer or artisan to save money, and he could not be expected to do so till he had the same inducement as his superiors in social rank —a place, and a safe place, in which his savings could fructify as well as accumulate and an assurance that he should be able to use them for his sole benefit when and how he pleased. None of these advantages could accrue to him as a member of one of the Benefit Clubs or Friendly Societies which are said to have originated in Spitalfields amongst the Huguenot refugees and were then in the heyday of their reputation, their number having increased between 1802 and 1820 from about ten thousand to fifty thousand. As the rate of contribution was usually the same for all ages, these associations ceased to attract the young as soon as the original members began to grow old and infirm ; and, as they could be broken up at any time on a vote of two-thirds, they were in a constant state of dissolution and renewal. This lack of permanence must in itself have frustrated their success when they endeavoured—as most of them did—to furnish a provision for old age in addition to their customary benefits—sick pay and burial money ; and, moreover, in nine cases out of ten they met at a public-house, where the need for thrift was brought into perilous competition with the temptation to waste.

What was obviously required was an extension of banking facilities to the poor on a scale proportionate to their small means ; and, though several attempts in this direction were made before and after the beginning of the nineteenth century, the first that really succeeded and became a model for imitation was " The Parish Bank Friendly Society of Ruthwell " in Dumfriesshire, established by Henry Duncan, an able and versatile minister of the Scottish Church, in 1810. Duncan was no less successful in the advocacy than in the execution of his scheme, which was adopted first at Kelso and then in many English and Scottish towns ; but the Edinburgh Bank, one of the earliest and most influential, introduced a variation of method, which soon became the rule—that the business should be conducted by unpaid Trustees and Managers in whose election the depositors had no voice. In 1817 the Government was empowered to receive deposits from such Trustees and to pay interest at the rate of threepence per cent. a day or £4 11s. 3d. a year. This Act came into force on August 6, 1817.   From that date to January 5, 1818, nearly £330,000 was received, and in the course of that year more than a million and a half.[1]   Cobbett, with his usual perversity, attacked what he called " the bubble of Savings Banks " as all but " the most ridiculous project that ever entered into the mind of man " ; but only in Lancashire was this senseless raving attended with transient success, echoed though it was by the Friendly Societies and gravely countenanced by the *Times*.[2]

If the increase of pauperism was causing apprehension at this period, so also was the increase of crime ; and the tragic death of Sir Samuel Romilly [3] on November 2, 1818, did not arrest the movement he had initiated for a reform of the penal code.   Romilly was a political philosopher rather than a politician ; but, realising that any general indictment of English criminal legislation would only excite alarm, he had thrown his whole energy into a detailed and consequently uncongenial attack.   He lived,

---

[1] Porter, iii. 143.

[2] Brabrook's *Provident Societies* and Lewins's *Banks for Savings, passim* ; *Quarterly Review*, October 1816.   The *Times* had reached the remarkable conclusion that, the more working-men saved, the more likely were they to become paupers.   " With the habit of parsimony the mind becomes degraded, and the workhouse or an application to the dispensers of parochial relief lose (*sic*) their horrors."—Lewins, pp. 81, 84.

[3] Died by his own hand.   A similar fate had befallen Whitbread and awaited Castlereagh.

however, just long enough to see his favourite maxim, that excess of severity does not prevent crime, which had been struck out of one of his three successful Bills, accepted in another[1]; and the foundation of a triumph for his successor had thus been laid.

On March 2, 1819, Sir James Mackintosh proposed the appointment of a Select Committee to consider as much of the criminal law as related to capital punishment. Wilberforce declared that in all his long experience of the House of Commons he had never heard " a more able address, a more splendid display of profound knowledge of the subject with such forcible reasoning from the facts,'' as that in which Mackintosh supported his motion. Less eloquent, but no less weighty, was the speech of Fowell Buxton, the brother-in-law of Elizabeth Fry ; and a memory so revered as that of Romilly gave a subdued lustre, a tone of elevation and dignity, to the whole debate.[2] " The sacred fabric reared by our ancestors " to protect the lives and property of Englishmen was now at last thoroughly exposed as a recent and disreputable invention which the hostility of public opinion had converted into a positive inducement to the perpetration of crime. Injured persons would not prosecute ; judges laboured to procure an acquittal ; juries perjured themselves rather than convict. Of 223 capital offences then on the statute book, two-thirds had been created since 1714 and one-third in the current reign ; and only twenty-five had been punished as such within the last seventy years. It was a capital offence for a bankrupt to conceal any of his assets ; and yet, though fraudulent bankruptcy was of almost daily occurrence, not one person in seven years had been arrested on this charge. In 1817 no fewer than 31,180 forged notes[3] were presented for pay-

[1] Hansard, xxxix. 839.

[2] Said Buxton, quoting the epitaph on Hannibal : " We lament him at all times, but most vehemently do we desire him in the day of battle.''

[3] So in Hansard, but hardly credible.

ment at the Bank of England ; but only 142 persons were prosecuted, 62 convicted, and 14 executed. One instance was cited in which a person had destroyed a bill of exchange for over £100 rather than appear against a forger ; and another instance mentioned by Romilly was recalled, in which a jury had declared, " as they hope for salvation, so help them God," that bills and notes for the same sum were worth only thirty-nine shillings—theft from a dwelling-house to the amount of £2 being capital. No longer prepared to deny the necessity for a revision of the penal code, the Government proposed to refer this task to a Committee on Gaols which had been appointed on the previous night—a committee already so over-burdened with functions that a member who had announced his conversion to reform described it as " *de omnibus rebus et de quibusdam aliis.*" But the House was not to be imposed upon by any such device ; and Mackintosh carried his motion by 147 votes to 128—a result which was hailed with " repeated cheers." [1]

Wilberforce summed up the pleasure he had derived from the debate by saying that prejudice had " faded before truth like the dusk before the more perfect light of day " ; but rarely indeed was such a phenomenon to be seen in the House of Lords ; and Mackintosh, though he met with less resistance than Romilly, had great difficulty in carrying the measures recommended by his Committee through the Upper House. He succeeded indeed in 1820 in removing about thirty felonies from the capital list, including fraudulent bankruptcy and the theft of five shillings from a shop ; but Lord Eldon fully justified his reputation as an obstacle to reform, refusing all concessions to forgers, raising the death level in shop-lifting to only ten pounds, and insisting that the extreme penalty should be retained in the case of persons con-victed of such offences as stealing £2 from a dwelling-house, maiming cattle, damaging embankments, cutting

[1] Hansard, xxxix. 787, 808, 809, 814, 817, 820, 827, 828, 839.

down trees and going about at night with "blacked faces." [1]

Various attempts were made to explain the increase of crime—predatory rather than violent—which had recently taken place. According to Mackintosh, it was not till 1808 that the growth of crime had seriously outstripped that of population ; and he ascribed this result to the enormous issue then made of inconvertible notes, which had reduced the purchasing power of the sovereign from twenty to fourteen shillings. Castlereagh sought to prove that the prevalence of such offences as house-breaking and highway robbery was due to the great numbers of men who had been dismissed without means of livelihood from the army and navy ; but Alderman Wood declared that, whilst discharged soldiers and sailors had frequently come before him as paupers, only in one case out of eighty had they appeared as law-breakers. He also mentioned that, of 350 male prisoners then in Newgate, there were but twelve who had served in the navy ; and one may safely agree with this enlightened London magistrate when he attributed the evils complained of to " the congregated state of our prisons," and the want of any general attempt to classify or find work for their inmates. " There are in every county in England," wrote Sydney Smith in 1821, "large public schools maintained at the expense of the county for the encouragement of profligacy and vice and for providing a proper succession of housebreakers, profligates and thieves. . . . The moment any young person evinces the slightest propensity for these pursuits he is provided with food, clothing and lodging, and put to his studies

---

[1] The statute of George I, known on account of this clause as the " Black Act," had made over twenty offences capital. One of these was that of being found disguised on a highroad, " so that," said Mackintosh, " if a gentleman is going to a masquerade and is obliged to pass along a highway, he is liable, if detected, to be hanged." —Hansard, xxxix. 791 ; N.S., i. 227 ; ii. 137, 492, 524 ; *Memoirs of Sir James Mackintosh*, ii. 382–392.

under the most accomplished thieves and cut-throats the county can supply."[1]

The carrying of Mackintosh's proposal for a revision of the penal code on March 2, 1819, has been described as " the first great victory which the reformers achieved "[2]; and it is all the more memorable in view of the similar success of Brougham on the question of charitable endowments.[3] The liberal spirit, the revival and growth of which we have traced during the Napoleonic War, was now diffusing on all hands an atmosphere less unfavourable to reform ; and a serious obstacle to its progress was removed by the suppression in this year of the Radical unrest. " Do you not think," wrote Peel to a fellow Tory in 1820, " that the tone of England—of that great compound of folly, weakness, prejudice, wrong feeling, right feeling, obstinacy and newspaper paragraphs which is called public opinion—is more liberal, to use an odious but intelligible phrase, than the policy of the Government ? Do you not think that there is a feeling becoming daily more general and more confirmed in favour of some undefined change in the mode of governing the country ? "[4] Of this feeling, in so far as it proceeded from more general causes than revolutionary doctrine or social injustice, Whigs and not Radicals were the natural exponents ; and we have now to trace the movement which under Whig auspices was to culminate in the Reform Bill of 1832.

[1] Smith's *Works*, ii. 202 ; Hansard, xxxix. 745, 758, 786, 843. Despite the labours of Howard and Neild and the personal ascendancy acquired by Elizabeth Fry about 1818 over the female inmates of Newgate, nothing effective was done in the way of prison reform till Pentonville, the first jail to be constructed on the principle of separate confinement, was opened in 1843.

[2] Walpole's *History*, ii. 66.

[3] See p. 161.   [4] *Croker Papers*, i. 170.

CHAPTER IV

THE LIBERAL SPIRIT, 1820–1828

SINCE the triumph of democracy in France in 1789 there had been two agitations to introduce that form of government into Great Britain, and both had failed, the suppression of Radicalism by the Six Acts in 1819 being no less complete than the suppression of Jacobinism by the Sedition and Treason Acts in 1795. But much had happened in the course of these twenty-five years to promote a more enlightened and tolerant spirit. Popular opinion, which had welcomed the Sedition and Treason Acts, was entirely adverse to the Six Acts ; and, whilst the former had inaugurated a period of repression and stagnation, the latter were actually of advantage to liberalism, since they dissociated it from the propagation of revolutionary ideas. Consequently, as we have seen the future lay with the Whigs ; but the Whigs, though an aristocratic party, could not dispense with popular support, and, in order to obtain it, must either supplant the Radicals or, better still, convert them to their own political views.

Not till the period we have reached did such a development seem at all probable ; and even now there were not a few Whigs who, like William Lamb, the future Lord Melbourne, were "against reform altogether." Anti-reformers indeed affected to regard the two classes of their opponents with equal alarm ; for both wished to introduce a uniform electoral system, and so to do away with those diversities of the borough franchise which were supposed to make Parliament a faithful, though un-sightly, reflection of the national life.   But the Radicals demanded universal suffrage, whilst the Whigs, aiming at collective rather than personal representation, asked only for household suffrage.   " The question between us and Mr. Bentham "—to quote the *Edinburgh Review* of 1818—" is whether all interests will be best protected where the representatives are chosen by all men or where they are elected by considerable proportions only of all classes of men."   And, whereas the Radicals were theorists dominated for the most part by the idea of natural rights, the Whigs were so far disciples of Burke that they refused to condemn any political institution, however anomalous, so long as it answered in practice.   Introducing a Reform Bill in 1797, Charles, afterwards Earl, Grey, based it entirely on the corruption and inefficiency of Parliament, and said it was nothing to his purpose that Cornwall returned almost as many members as Scotland and that the smallest of the small boroughs was as fully represented as Yorkshire.[1]   Even this argument for reform would hardly have been endorsed by Horner, who not only saw " a great deal of practical benefit result, even to the interests of liberty and popular rights, from the most rotten parts of the constituent body," but maintained that Parliament had never been long out of sympathy with the people.[2]

Whigs and Radicals were, however, entirely at one in their repugnance to the suppression of opinion, and the effect of this common interest became manifest in the early years of peace.   With the Whigs had long been associated a small section of half-converted Tories headed by Lord Grenville, who had combined with Fox in 1806 to form the Ministry of all the Talents.   There was a good deal of liberalism in Grenville, but it was confined to his advocacy of less restricted commerce, the abolition of the Slave Trade and Catholic Emancipation ; and he

[1] *Parl. Hist.*, xxxiii. 645, 680.   .   [2] *Memoirs*, i. 462.

it was who, as Pitt's lieutenant in the Lords, had introduced the Sedition and Treason Bills. In March 1817 he
supported what Bentham called the "liberticide Acts";
and an alliance which had discredited the popular pretensions of the Whigs then came to an end.[1] On January
25, 1817, appeared the first number of the *Scotsman*,
which was speedily recognised as the most powerful
provincial newspaper, and, whilst repudiating the demand
for universal suffrage, maintained that it was social, not
political, in origin and would disappear as soon as the
upper classes sought to conciliate and not to beat down
the poor. A great public meeting in support of the
Opposition was held at Edinburgh on December 16, 1820.
Jeffrey, who was the principal speaker, commented on
the want of sympathy between the upper and lower
classes, and said : " It is to fill up this chasm, to occupy
a middle ground, and to show how large a proportion of
the people are attached to the constitution, whilst they
lament its abuses, that such meetings as this should be
assembled." The policy set forth in this speech gave
great offence to the Tories, and one of their journals
described it happily enough as " Mr. Jeffrey's plan for
the regeneration of the Radicals by their passage through
the purgatory of Whiggism." [2]

Nor were signs wanting that the Radicals were becoming conscious of their inability to stand alone. Whilst
Cobbett continued to villify the " dirty sneaking Whigs,"
Cartwright advocated a " union with the Radicals of
the better men among the Whigs." [3] Bentham was of
opinion that " man must change his nature " before
there could be any real sympathy between the Whigs
and the people, unless indeed the former should dismiss
as hopeless the prospect of their return to power. But,
whilst friendship was impossible, he thought that much

[1] *Life and Opinions of Charles, Second Earl Grey*, p. iv.
[2] *Church and Reform in Scotland*, 1797–1843, pp. 166–169.
[3] *Life of Cartwright*, ii.

might be gained from co-operation.   No abuse could ever be eradicated in this way, but " even by such hands there is scarce an abuse but may be clipped."[1]   In 1820 Wade published his "Black Book or Corruption Unmasked." One of his chapters is devoted to the abuse of charitable endowments;   and in this section he condemns the " criminal neutrality " of the middle classes and seeks to dispel their alarm.   " What interest in common have the agricultural, the commercial and manufacturing classes with the privileged orders that they should be the dupes of their selfish fears and misrepresentations ? How could their interests be endangered—nay, would they not be infinitely bettered—by a Radical Reform ? "[2]

As this was the last sort of reform that the middle classes desired, their " criminal neutrality " was likely to continue so long as the Radicals refused to moderate their demands ; and just at this juncture, when both sides had become alive to their mutual need, an incident occurred which led to a violent quarrel.   For eleven years after the memorable election of 1807 there had been no contest at Westminster ; but at the general election of June 1818 one of the two seats was vacant owing to the absence of Cochrane in South America, and the Radicals had consequently to find a new colleague for Sir Francis Burdett.   They chose Douglas Kinnaird, but soon withdrew him in order to give Burdett their whole strength ; and the result justified their caution ; for, though Burdett was returned, he was placed second to Romilly, one of the most advanced Whigs.   Throughout the country the Whigs gained thirty-two seats ; and this success was extolled in the *Edinburgh Review* as showing that the people were " no longer under the guidance of shallow pretenders to constitutional learning[3] or base dealers in vulgar sedition," but were returning to their " natural leaders."

[1] *Reform Catechism*, pp. cccxxvii–ix.
[2] *Black Book*, pp. 143, 144.
[3] This was aimed at Cartwright.

A few months later occurred the suicide of Romilly, due to the death of his wife. The Westminster Radicals, smarting under their recent defeat, had now an opportunity for revenge. In February 1819 Place presented a paper to the electors, in which he attacked the Whigs as " a corrupt and profligate faction " and their leader, Lord Grey, who had been one of the Friends of the People, as having belied his pledges to the cause of reform. The Whigs had not intended to oppose Hobhouse, the Radical candidate ; but, on his refusal to dissociate himself from Place's report, they put forward George, brother of William, Lamb. Amongst Lamb's canvassers are said to have been " the young gentlemen of almost all the Club Houses," and he was returned, beating Hobhouse by 600 votes. Lord Erskine published a vindication of the Whigs from the aspersions cast upon them during the election ; and Place in his reply declared that the only difference between the Tories and the Whigs was that the one sought to exalt the Crown at the expense of the aristocracy and the people, and that the other wished to subject both the people and the Crown to their own oligarchical rule. No less exasperated were the Whigs. Grey wrote to a friend in reference to Burdett and Hobhouse that he must " avoid even the intercourse of private society with them whom I consider as having degraded themselves from the character of gentlemen." At the meeting of Parliament on November 23 he said he regarded " radical reform " as nothing less than " radical subversion " ; and Tierney, the Whig leader in the Commons, in moving an amendment to the address, said he desired it to be known that he was " as much an enemy as any man to the Radical leaders," and wished " to mark in the strongest terms his contempt of their understanding, his disgust at their proceedings and his jealousy of their objects." [1]

[1] Wallas's *Place*, pp. 128–139 ; Butler, *The Passing of the Great Reform Bill*, p. 34 ; Hansard, xli. 9, 73.

The lamentable occurrence at Manchester in the previous summer had not assuaged—as might well have been expected—the bitterness of this feud ; but it went far to convince the people that the Radicals were not their only friends. The Manchester magistrates may have been guilty only of an error in judgment when they attempted to arrest Hunt at the very moment when he was addressing a vast open-air meeting ; but of greater political importance was the indiscretion of the Cabinet when, without waiting for any report but that of the magistrates themselves, it advised the Prince Regent to express his "approbation and high commendation " of their conduct. This was too much for one of the most amiable and illiberal of the Whigs. Earl Fitzwilliam, nephew and heir of Lord Rockingham, was at this time Lord Lieutenant of the West Riding of Yorkshire, having been appointed in succession to the Duke of Norfolk, who had been dismissed in 1798 for a seditious toast. He was one of the alarmists inspired by Burke who had joined Pitt's Ministry during the French Revolutionary War, had opposed the abolition of the slave trade, had always favoured repression and steadily discountenanced reform. Yet he promoted and attended a meeting at York to demand an inquiry into the proceedings at Manchester, and in consequence was summarily deprived of his post. The Duke of Hamilton testified in another way his sympathy with the Manchester victims ; for he sent £100 for their relief, accompanied by a letter which was believed in some quarters to have enlightened thousands of those who had regarded "rank and wealth as united in a conspiracy against the people."[1] Lord Grey's followers were much divided in opinion as to the seriousness of the popular agitation ; and he himself, writing to General Sir Robert Wilson, one of the most forward group, did not conceal his apprehension that their dissensions on this point might "leave no possibility of public union."

[1] *Church and Reform in Scotland*, 1797–1843, p. 167.

Grey's own view was pessimistic in the extreme ; for in this letter he warned Wilson that, if the men who were exploiting rather than following Burdett should succeed in exciting a revolt, "I shall not precede you many months on the scaffold." [1] The Whigs, however, were almost unanimous in their opposition to the six repressive measures which were hurried through Parliament in a late autumn session ; and they were soon enabled to rise still higher in popular esteem. In 1820, when the Prince Regent had succeeded his father, as George IV, a storm of indignation was aroused by the trial of Queen Caroline ; and the Whigs—aided by some of the Tories—had not only the credit of having defeated the Bill of Pains and Penalties, but derived a reflected lustre from Brougham, who conducted the Queen's defence and on this account attained to a popularity unparalleled since the days of Wilkes.

It may be well at this stage to glance at the old representative system and at the efforts which had been, and were still being, made to arrest its degeneration and abuse. The only sound part of this system was the county franchise which, dependent since 1430 on a forty shilling freehold and, expanding with the fall in the purchasing power of money, had come to include almost all the absolute owners of land [2] ; but this franchise was, as we have seen, [3] of little use in a large majority of the counties, where the voice of the freeholders was either stifled by aristocratic or Government influence or was nullified by an agreement amongst the magnates that one seat should be Tory and the other Whig. There were in any case only forty counties in England, whilst the number of represented boroughs was 203, each returning two members, except Abingdon, Banbury, Bewdley, Higham Ferrers and Monmouth which returned one, and the City of London which returned four. Voting quali-

---

[1] Butler's *Great Reform Bill*, pp. 34, 35.
[2] Copyholders were excluded till 1832.   [3] See p. 14.

fications were extremely diverse ; but, over and above the varieties of local usage, there were certain broad distinctions which enable us to distinguish two classes of constituencies and several subordinate groups. Fifty-nine boroughs had retained, formally at least, a popular franchise ; and these may be subdivided into the " scot and lot " boroughs, in which all resident ratepayers were entitled to vote, and the " potwalloper " boroughs in which every head of a family was qualified who provided his own victuals.[1] In all other boroughs the common law right of election belonging to householders had been restricted by local custom or had wholly disappeared. In thirty-nine boroughs it depended on the holding by burgage tenure of ancient tenements ; in forty-three it had been engrossed by the corporation ; and in sixty-two, including London, Liverpool and Bristol, it was the privilege of a freeman, or in other words was restricted to the trade guilds.

Some of the strangest anomalies in representation belonged to the first of these groups.   In some cases the tenements which conferred the vote had to be occupied ; and, where no term of residence was prescribed, they might be untenanted till within a few days of the poll. The existence of a chimney was the usual evidence of occupation insisted on in the case of these " vote-houses," which were commonly mere hovels. Frequently, however, the franchise was dependent, not on an actual dwelling, but on ownership of a particular site ; and the title-deeds were known as " snatch papers," from the celerity with which they passed from hand to hand before an election. The notorious Old Sarum in Wiltshire, the site of a vanished town, consisted of ploughed fields. A tent had to be erected within the burgage area for the

---

[1] A potwalloper was defined as " an inhabitant in the borough who had a family and boiled a pot there " ; and the name had originated in days when freemen occasionally took their meals in public in order to show that they were not serfs and owed their subsistence to no lord.—Porritt, *The Unreformed House of Commons,* i. 31.

official who recorded the five votes; and close at hand was a cottage in which refreshments were supplied to visitors whose curiosity had been excited by this, " the rottenest borough on the list." The members for Droitwich were elected by the reputed owners of a salt-spring which in 1832 had been dried up for a century and a quarter; and a burgage qualification might be under water, as at Downton, or a coal-house or a pig-sty, as at Richmond.[1]

No great significance, however, attaches to the classification of boroughs; for in most cases the effect of a popular franchise was counterbalanced by aristocratic influence or the paucity of electors. Gatton and St. Michael were " scot and lot " boroughs; but in both cases there were only seven electors, whilst at Rye, the smallest freeman borough, there were but six. The small urban constituencies were commonly known as " rotten " or decayed boroughs; but most of them had always been mere villages, having been enfranchised by the Crown in its own interest before the Revolution of 1689, when it had the power of creating and suppressing parliamentary boroughs—a prerogative used to some purpose in Cornwall, which returned forty-four members —only one fewer than the whole of Scotland. In such boroughs territorial and Treasury influence was of course paramount. Not a few of them were available for purchase; and an independent man, like Romilly, at a time when he had no chance of popular election, considered this the least objectionable way of entering the House. But the majority of patrons gave their nomination to relatives and friends whom they could trust to further their political views. The Duke of Norfolk had eleven seats at his disposal; Lord Lonsdale nine; Lord Fitzwilliam eight; Lord Darlington seven; the Duke of Rutland, the Marquess of Buckingham and Lord Carrington had each six. England and Wales were repre-

[1] Porritt, *The Unreformed House of Commons*, vol. i., *passim*.

sented in the Unreformed Parliament by 513 members. Of these, according to a computation published in 1810, 371 owed their seats practically to nomination—218 being returned by 87 peers, 137 by 90 commoners, and 16 by the Government.[1]

Electors had been bribed and their rights perverted and manipulated ever since service in Parliament—once regarded as a thankless duty—had come to be an object of ambition ; but in the latter half of the eighteenth century, when wealth was rapidly increasing and the autocratic designs of George III had embittered political strife, these evils had increased to such an extent that they could no longer be overlooked. In 1763 a successful candidate for Durham was unseated, in whose favour 215 honorary freemen, mostly non-resident, had been admitted after the issue of the writ ; and an Act ·was then passed which debarred voters of this class from the hustings if they had obtained their freedom within the previous twelve months. But ordinary freemen, that is, persons qualified by birth or apprenticeship, could still be admitted as the prospects or exigencies of polling might suggest. In 1812 at Bristol 1720 ordinary freemen were admitted a month or two before an election, and a thousand at Malden in 1826,[2] when an election was actually in progress. The worst type of freemen had no means of livelihood more respectable than their votes and were sometimes conveyed to the hustings from jail, which indeed is said to have been their usual abode. In earlier times a freeman forfeited the franchise if he had been absent from the borough for a full year ; but this

---

[1] May's *Constitutional History*, edition 1912, i. 223, 224, 232, 243 ; *Croker Papers*, ii. 52.

[2] The general election of this year was held during one of the hottest summers ever known in England. " Hard-working people sat up all night to watch the springs—some to carry home drink to their children—others to have a commodity of cold water to sell in the morning. In some high-lying towns the richest people made presents to one another of little pitchers of fresh water."—Harriet Martineau's *History of the Peace*, Bohn's edition, ii. 29.

usage was generally obsolete ; and one of the heaviest expenses incident to an election in some of the large towns was that of importing and entertaining a host of non-resident freemen. Lord Penryn in 1790 spent nearly £30,000 in an unsuccessful canvass of Liverpool.[1]

Customs and excise officers were, as we have seen, disfranchised in 1782 ; and, as seventy elections were believed to depend on their votes, the influence of Government was seriously curtailed. We are told that in one Cornish borough only one elector survived. In 1809 an Act was passed—with little practical effect—to prevent the sale of seats. At the general election of 1818 Sir Manasseh Lopez[2] was one of six successful candidates who were unseated for bribery. In this there was nothing unusual ; but a new and serious complexion was given to the case when Lopez was tried and convicted at Exeter and sentenced to a fine of £10,000 and imprisonment for two years. When a borough was found to be incurably corrupt, the usual remedy was to enlarge the electorate by permitting the freeholders of the district in which it was situated to vote for the borough as well as for the shire. This was done in the case of New Shoreham in 1770, of Cricklade in 1782 and of Aylesbury in 1804. But in 1821, when Grampound, a freeman borough in Cornwall, had been disfranchised, Lord John Russell proposed to transfer its two representatives to the populous town of Leeds.[3] A Bill to this effect passed the Commons ; and, though the Lords insisted on the two members being assigned to Yorkshire, the occurrence is nevertheless memorable as the sole change made in the representation prior to 1832.

[1] Porritt, i. 58, 65, 66, 76.
[2] For some account of this converted Jew, see Picciotto's *Sketches of Anglo-Jewish History*, p. 305.
[3] Why Leeds was thus favoured is not clear, its population in 1819 being 54,000, whilst that of Manchester was 112,000 and that of Birmingham 97,000. Sheffield with 52,000 came next to Leeds.— *Croker Papers*, i. 136.

The growth of a spirit favourable to reform may be traced to advantage in the early career of the statesman who has just been mentioned. Born in 1792 and the son of a Duke of Bedford who had been one of the Friends of the People, Lord John Russell would no doubt have attained sooner to the full stature of a reformer if the effect of his upbringing had not been counteracted by the reactionary temper which prevailed during his youth. His first notable speech in Parliament was made in 1817 against the Habeas Corpus suspension ; and he appears to have taken Mackintosh severely to task for his qualified and half-hearted opposition to the Six Acts. But Lord Holland had early impressed upon him that all that was required of a " good Whig " was " a certain disposition to reform of Parliament and no alarm at it if the present mode be found to be inadequate to ensure the confidence and enforce the will of the people "[1]; and his first appearances in the cause were not inconsistent with this cautious advice. Thus in July 1819, when Burdett proposed that early in the next session there should be an inquiry into the lack of popular representation, Russell declared himself in favour of triennial parliaments, but said he could not go the length of supporting " an inquiry into the general state of the representation, because such an inquiry was calculated to throw a slur upon the representation of the country and to fill the minds of the people with vague and indefinite alarms." A few months later, when the Six Acts were passing through Parliament, he proposed that boroughs which had been convicted of bribery should be disfranchised and their members transferred to towns of not less than 15,000 inhabitants or to some of the largest counties, and also that means should be taken " to detect and prevent corruption in the election of members of Parliament." At the same time he said he thought the present moment unfavourable even for " a proposal of moderate reform," and declared

[1] *Early Correspondence of Lord John Russell*, i. 137–210.

that " the principles of the constitution of this House are pure and worthy." In 1822, after another attempt to purify the franchise, he complained that the House had agreed only to punish corruption when brought to its notice and compared its attitude to that of a magistrate who should avow his readiness to convict offenders, but should refuse to " send out a single officer of police to apprehend and detect them." Consequently he proposed —what he had hitherto deprecated—an inquiry into the general state of the representation, and outlined a scheme which was certainly much in advance of anything he had yet suggested. One hundred of the small boroughs were to lose one member each ; and, of the vacant seats, sixty were to be given to counties and forty to towns. The House was not called upon to express its opinion of this scheme ; but it rejected the motion for an inquiry by 269 votes to 164.[1]

Nine years later, Lord John Russell was to take a leading part in remodelling the House of Commons ; but now as always he was out-distanced as a reformer by one of the three statesmen who were to be associated with him in that task. John George Lambton, a land-owner of great antiquity and wealth, was born in the same year as Russell and inherited the same liberal bias, his father, like the Duke of Bedford, having been one of the Friends of the People. Russell's health was not good, but Lambton's was wretched [2] ; and the impetuous and irascible temper for which he was notorious in the counsels of his party must be ascribed mainly to this cause. In such a man moderation was rather to be desired than expected ; and, his personality being as popular as his politics, he was known amongst the miners on his estate as " Radical Jack." Entering Parliament in 1813, he

[1] Hansard, xl. 1496 ; xli. 1093, 1105, 1106 ; N.S., vii. 51, 78, 79, 139.
[2] He said to Creevey that he thought it " damned hard that a man with £80,000 a year can't sleep."—*Creevey Papers*, ii. 49.

represented his native county of Durham for fifteen years and took from it his title when he accepted a peerage in 1828. In December 1819 he gave notice of his intention to bring forward a measure of reform, and declared to Grey, with his usual vehemence, that he would never forgive Lord Holland for having privately expressed his opinion that " if carried, it would be as bad as a revolution."[1] The scheme was introduced in April 1821— having been delayed on account of the proceedings against the Queen—and went much further than that which Russell was to propose twelve months later. Parliaments were to be triennial ; the country was to be divided into electoral districts, each of 25,000 inhabitants and returning one member, and the franchise was to be extended to all householders who paid direct taxes.[2]

In 1816 Lambton had married as his second wife the eldest daughter of Earl Grey ; and the acquisition of such a son-in-law, however little it may have deflected the Whig leader from his habitual caution, did not contribute to his peace of mind. In 1797 Grey had scandalised Pitt by avowing in Parliament that, though he did not approve of universal suffrage, he would prefer it to the present system[3] ; but now, as we have seen, he denounced Radical reform as " nothing less than radical subversion " ; and towards the end of his long life he remarked to his son that one word from Fox " would have kept me out of all the mess of the Friends of the People, but he never spoke it."[4] Many of the borough-owners who followed Grey would, however, have been most disagreeably surprised by a revival of his zeal ; and he could not more effectually have secured the ultimate triumph of reform than by discouraging extremists and adopting as his main object " the preservation of the Whig party in Parliament."[5]

[1] Reid's *Lord Durham*, i. 131.   [2] Hansard, N.S., v. 367, 376.
[3] *Parl. Hist.*, xxx. 808 ; xxxiii. 680.
[4] *Life and Opinions*, p. 11.   [5] Reid's *Lord Durham*, i. 129.

Writing to Lambton on January 3, 1820, Grey admitted that public opinion in favour of reform had " greatly increased," but expressed grave doubt whether it had increased enough, at all events in the most influential quarters, " to afford any reasonable hope of its being carried during my ,life or even during yours "[1]—and Lambton was twenty-eight years his junior. That public opinion was becoming more favourable to reform even during the panic of the Six Acts was indeed a highly significant fact ; and, to judge from his pessimism at this period, Grey must have been astonished at the progress made by the movement during the next few years. Even the more enlightened Tories were still opposed on principle to anything like a remodelling of the House of Commons ; but on that very account they were the more anxious to purify the old system and adapt it to new conditions. " Burn Grampound to the ground," wrote Croker, " rather than undertake its defence or leave it to the enemy as a cover whence to assault us " ; and as early as 1820 he had urged upon Lord Liverpool that the franchises of Grampound and three other delinquent boroughs should be transferred to Manchester, Birmingham, Leeds and Sheffield. In 1822 he wrote to Peel that " almost the whole press and all public meetings are loud for reform," and that " at tables where, ten years ago, you would have no more heard reform advocated than treason you will now find half the company reformers."[2] The Whig nobles who had hitherto denied or ignored the need for reform were now rapidly giving way. " We are getting very much into the Reform line,

---

[1] Reid's *Lord Durham*, i. 129.

[2] *Croker Papers*, ii. 52, 54, 137. Edinburgh had always been the citadel of Scottish Toryism ; but a petition in favour of reform was resolved upon at a great meeting held there in 1823. It was confined to householders who paid the police assessment, and the number of signatures was found to be only 700 less than the total number of those who under such an extension of the franchise would have been entitled to vote.—*Church and Reform in Scotland*, 1797–1843, p. 191.

I assure you," wrote Creevey in 1821. " The Duke of Devonshire has declared for Reform." [1] And in the following year Lord Fitzwilliam, whose " determined hostility to Reform " had roused the wrath of Lambton, and also Lord Darlington, the future Duke of Cleveland, announced their conversion. [2] In 1824 Lord Redesdale, a rigid Tory, complained that " liberality is the word of the day " [3]; and in the first number of the *Westminster Review*, which was issued in that year, we find it stated that " there is an obvious deference for the people," and that statesmen, divines, authors and journalists " all seem impressed with the rise of a new power and, blessing or cursing, they pay to it a certain degree of homage."

The change in the public attitude towards reform was due much less to political propagandism than to the action of forces economic and social. Radicalism of the militant type had always been the outcome of industrial distress, and the effect of the repressive measures adopted at the close of 1819 was aided by a general revival of trade. As early as the spring of 1821 the textile workers were said to be fully employed, and their wages good— in some cases even doubled. [4] In February 1822 Lord Liverpool informed the Upper House that he had been at some pains to ascertain the state of the working classes in London and could say with confidence that they had never been " in a better condition than they are at the present moment." Next autumn the country was enjoying its fifth successive good harvest, and the average annual price of wheat, which since the Peace had never been lower than 71s., and had usually been much higher, was then 53s.—the lowest price since 1798. [5] These prosperous conditions had naturally a quieting effect on the populace of the towns whose demand for universal

---

[1] *Creevey Papers*, ii. 6.
[2] *Croker Papers*, ii. 52 ; Reid's *Lord Durham*, i. 131.
[3] Quoted by Smart, *Economic Annals*, ii. 234.
[4] Smart, ii. 20.   [5] Tooke, ii. 104 note, 389.

suffrage had been a serious obstacle to reform ; but they had quite a different influence in the rural districts, not on the peasantry—always more interested in the consumption than in the production of corn—but on the landowners and farmers. Now as in 1815 there was acute agricultural depression ; for tillage had been so greatly improved and extended under the high prices which prevailed during the war that every abundant harvest produced a glut, and two or three such harvests caused " an enormously inconvenient accumulation." [1] Parliament laboured in vain to find a remedy ; and owners as well as occupiers of land listened readily enough to Cobbett when he suspended his usual vituperation of these classes to instruct them that the price of wheat would soon fall permanently to 32s., that rent would disappear in two years, that agriculture was being crushed under a weight of taxation which benefited nobody but placemen and pensioners,[2] and that the only remedy for this evil was parliamentary reform. Country gentlemen did not hesitate to act on this suggestion, and some 500 petitions had been presented from landlords and tenants by May 1822.[3] The agitation for reform was again centred—where it had originated in the days of Wilkes—amongst the county freeholders ; but the conception of reform which appealed to men of this class was Whig, not Radical ; and Lord John Russell, in supporting his motion of April 25, said that a few years ago all the petitions were for universal suffrage, whereas at a recent meeting of the county of Middlesex, " when a venerable advocate of the cause of reform proposed a petition for universal suffrage he could find no one to second him." [4]

[1] Tooke, quoted by Smart, ii. 8.
[2] It was stated in Parliament that a certain nobleman had left sums of £200 to £500 a year to members of his family " until they should be better provided for by Government in some other manner."— Smart, ii. 59 note.
[3] Smart, ii. 57 ; Walpole, ii. 30.   [4] Hansard, N.S., vii. 53.

More important than any specific factor in promoting the spirit of reform was the increase in wealth and knowledge, and consequently in the number of those who were capable of taking an interest in politics. Russell in dealing with this part of his subject adduced some interesting figures. Before the war the average exportation of British manufactured goods was £13,000,000. Now it was £40,000,000. In 1790 the number of newspapers published in Great Britain and Ireland was 146. In 1821 it was 284, and the total issue amounted to 23,600,000 copies. The *Edinburgh Review* and the *Quarterly* were believed to have " a greater circulation than all the periodical works of thirty years ago put together." In 1770 there were only four circulating libraries in London. Now there were one hundred, and throughout the country nine hundred, in addition to nearly two thousand book-clubs.[1]

To reduce the ratio of illiteracy to population had hitherto been the sole aim of those who instructed the poor ; but something more was now proposed for the masses than the mere rudiments of knowledge. We have seen that the controversy between Bell and Lancaster as to which of them had invented the system of teaching by monitors had developed into a question whether the Anglican religion should be taught in the schools, and that the National Society, with Bell as its director, had been established to promote this object. Bell was by no means an apostle of enlightenment, having decided in conformity with his patrons that writing was a dangerous accomplishment for the poor ; but the British and Foreign Schools Society which had come to the aid of Lancaster was less illiberal, though its reading lessons were, it seems, confined to the Bible, and about 1814 it proposed to apply the monitorial system to secondary as well as primary education. This scheme, which had originated with Place, was warmly supported by Bentham.

[1] Hansard, N.S., vii. 53.

In his garden at Queen's Square was to be erected a school-house which, despite the inevitable din of children teaching children, was to be but one huge room with nine concentric rows of desks, and a master in the middle turning his gaze in all directions from an elevated revolving chair—in short, a scholastic Panopticon ; and the course of study was borrowed from Bentham's treatise on useful education, disguised in his needless jargon as " Chresto-mathia." The Quakers, Dissenters and free-thinkers interested in this project were, however, too much at variance to permit of its completion. In 1817 little more than half of the estimated cost had been subscribed, and, three years later, owing to the growing reluctance of Bentham to sacrifice his garden, the scheme was given up.[1]

Though Place had failed in his endeavour to bring secondary education within reach of the masses, he succeeded a few years later in promoting a scheme for their technical instruction. Unknown as yet in London, an institute of this kind had long existed in Glasgow. John Anderson, who had been appointed to the Glasgow Chair of Natural Philosophy in 1760, was an ardent admirer of the French Revolution ; and—probably after his return from a visit to Paris in 1791—he showed his sympathy with the people by admitting workmen to his lectures, and finally by establishing in their interest a " gownless " class. A guinea subscription and an un-popular hour of meeting must have limited the range of this venture ; but the innovation was important, especially as there was a distribution of free tickets ; and the Professor, who died in 1796, made it of permanent value by providing in his will for the founding of the scientific college which still bears his name. George Birkbeck, an Englishman who had studied medicine at Edinburgh and London, was appointed the first professor of Natural Philosophy in this college. At that time there was only

[1] Wallas's *Place*, pp. 98–112.

one philosophical instrument maker in Glasgow, who, moreover, was not reliable ; and Birkbeck, being thus brought into contact with the workmen who made instruments under his direction, and observing their desire for knowledge, was induced to follow the example of Anderson, but on a more liberal plan. The class he established was gratuitous and met on Saturday evenings. It opened with seventy-five members, but within a month the number had increased to five hundred, and more would have attended had there been room. Birkbeck having left Glasgow in 1804 to practise as a physician in London, the mechanics' class was continued by his successor, Dr. Ure, who in 1808 added greatly to its popularity, which had then somewhat declined, by forming a library and allowing it to be managed by the mechanics themselves. The Library Committee had apparently some reason to complain that their constituents were rather discountenanced than encouraged. At all events in 1823 a number of the workmen seceded, and, with Dr. Birkbeck as their patron, founded the Glasgow Mechanics' Institute, which proved an immediate and permanent success. In its second winter the membership had grown to a thousand, whilst the number of those who attended the parent institution had not materially diminished.

The work of Dr. Birkbeck at Glasgow was first made widely known through an article in the " Encyclopædia Britannica " of 1817, and his example was followed elsewhere when the distress, which was then but beginning, had passed away. A school of arts with lectures and a library was established at Edinburgh in 1821 ; but it was conducted rather for than by the workmen, whose subscriptions of fifteen shillings accounted for less than half of the income. A year or two later, during the prosperity which preceded a commercial crisis, mechanics' libraries, with or without lectures, were so quickly and so generally formed that they are said to have " sprung up as if by magic." But the fullest and most direct development of Birkbeck's idea was that which was carried out under his own supervision in London. The *Mechanics' Magazine,* a weekly journal intended to familiarise workmen with the principles of their crafts, was founded there in August 1823. It circulated widely, being sold at the popular price of threepence ; and in the seventh number there was an account of the Glasgow experiment and a proposal that London should adopt the same scheme. The most influential patron of this project was Brougham, but its " main promoter " was Place, who had now retired from business, and was thus able as well as willing to give up to it " the whole of his time from morning to night." The London Mechanics' Institute was formed at a public meeting in November, one of the regulations being that two-thirds of the Committee should be workmen, and in February 1824 Dr. Birkbeck, as president, delivered the inaugural address.[1]

The zeal of Brougham for education was of no recent origin, for he had presided at the first meeting of the British and Foreign Schools Society in 1813 ; and we have seen that a few years later he was exerting himself in Parliament to rescue educational endowments and to provide elementary instruction for the poor. In January 1825 he published his " Practical Observations upon the Education of the People," which went through twenty editions in twelve months. The greater part of this pamphlet, which was dedicated to Dr. Birkbeck, consisted of a review and commendation of Mechanics' Institutes ; but it opened with certain suggestions for " the encouragement of cheap publications " ; and these were realised four months later, when Brougham, Lord John Russell, Dr. Lushington [2] and others founded the

---

[1] Godard's *George Birkbeck*, pp. 15–31, 34, 41 ; Wallas's *Place,* p. 112.

[2] The eminent civilian and broad Churchman.

Society for the Diffusion of Useful Knowledge. An introductory volume on the study of science, written by Brougham himself, was published in the spring of 1827, and was the first of a sixpenny series, issued at intervals of a fortnight and devoted in the first place to physics, which in a few weeks had a circulation of ten thousand. A much more ambitious scheme was, however, adumbrated by Brougham at the close of his pamphlet, where he says that " some of the greater cities of the kingdom, especially the metropolis, must not be left destitute of the regular means within themselves of scientific education." [1]

The first announcement of a design to establish a university in London is commonly supposed to have been made in a letter of Thomas Campbell the poet to Brougham, which appeared in *The Times* of February 9, 1825. Priority in this respect must, however, be conceded to William Frend, a barrister and distinguished mathematician, who published several letters on the subject about 1820 in a short-lived periodical edited by John Thelwall. These letters must have attracted some notice, for they led to discussions in which Frend, Campbell and Brougham took part ; but Campbell's letter, published after he had assured himself of influential support, was the real starting-point of a movement which had been suggested to him by a visit to the German universities, then a focus of liberalism, in 1820. · Dissenters and Jews, being debarred from Oxford and Cambridge, naturally favoured the scheme, and were well represented by John Smith and Isaac Lyon Goldsmid ; but amongst the promoters and subscribers were at least a hundred Churchmen, and of course the Benthamites, including the inevitable and invaluable

[1] *Edinburgh Review*, xlvi. 235, 239–243 ; Brougham's *Speeches*, iii. 151, 293 ; Martineau, ii. 347. The venerable Christian Knowledge Society, founded by Dr. Bray in 1698, had by this time established 1200 parish libraries, and was beginning to issue popular manuals of science.—*Quarterly Review*, xxxii. 425.

Place. Either exclusion or comprehension was obviously the only solution of the religious problem ; and the former was adopted. At the instance of Edward Irving, who regarded learning and science as " the natural enemies of religion," the Dissenters were at one time disposed to insist on rival theological chairs ; but Campbell, backed by the Churchmen, had no great difficulty in carrying the original decision, which was defended on the ground that, as students were to be non-resident, they could have religious instruction at home. On April 30, 1827, the foundation-stone of University College or, as it was then called, the University of London, was laid in Gower Street, where Goldsmid, without waiting to consult more than two of his colleagues, had secured a suitable site ; and the first session opened on October 1, 1828. Augustus de Morgan, son-in-law of Frend, was appointed Professor of Mathematics and John Austin Professor of Jurisprudence.[1]

" Happily," said Brougham in concluding his pamphlet on education, " the time is past and gone when bigots could persuade mankind that the lights of philosophy were to be extinguished as dangerous to religion ; and when tyrants could proscribe the instructors of the people as enemies to their power." [2] It soon appeared, however, that obscurantism, though less potent for mischief, had lost none of its venom. As the existence of Trade Unions had just been recognised by Parliament, the *Quarterly Review* thought it useless to oppose Mechanics' Institutes, contenting itself with the remark that " men who come together professedly to discuss the mystery of their own craft may digress into the mystery of politics or the more serious mysteries of religion " [3] ; but the *St. James Chronicle* considered that the effect of these institutes would be to set up " the

---

[1] Beattie's *Thomas Campbell*, ii. 438–443 ; *Memoir of Augustus de Morgan*, pp. 22–24.
[2] *Speeches*, iii. 150. [3] *Quarterly Review*, xxxii. 414.

labourers as a separate or independent class," and declared that "a scheme more completely adapted for the destruction of this empire could not have been invented by the author of evil himself."[1] The Useful Knowledge Society had not announced its intention to issue anything but purely scientific treatises when a proposal was made, but never carried out, to counteract its publications,[2] much as Hannah More in her "Cheap Repository" had combated the writings of Paine. But the greatest opposition of all was aroused by the proposal to establish a "God-excluding seminary" in London. Wilberforce said that to keep the most influential class ignorant of Christian evidences in order to obtain the support of the Jews "appears to me rendering a measure abominable in itself still worse by the motive assigned for its adoption"; and he was not at all satisfied when provision was made, as the result of this protest, for teaching apologetics as an optional subject.[3] Humanism being as abhorrent to Evangelicals as was Dissent to High Churchmen, the two parties took measures for their common defence; and, before the London University opened its doors in October 1828, steps had been taken to form a rival institution, which in the following year was incorporated as King's College on the principle that instruction in Anglican Christianity "shall be for ever combined with other branches of useful education."[4]

The attitude of religion, or of those who claimed to speak in its name, towards the establishment of a university for London was significant of a temper which survived till comparatively recent years as an obstacle to freedom of thought. Not only was theology to define at pleasure

[1] Godard's *George Birkbeck*, p. 73.
[2] *Edinburgh Review*, xlvi. 230.
[3] *Life of Wilberforce*, v. 257.
[4] The University of London was established as an examining body in 1836; and the earlier institution was thenceforth known as University College.

the domain of science, which indeed it had never scrupled to do, but science, even within these bounds, was to lose all that could commend it to the genuine student by being prosecuted with an eye to other interests than its own. Here are the injunctions imposed by no mean authority on the teachers of science. " It is their duty, if not to teach religious principles, to keep in view that there are such principles, and that they are all important." And again—" Every mode of instruction which so teaches learning, science or art as to make them seem all in all and fails to connect them with the higher object of all education, the fitting man for his ultimate destiny, we consider to be both incomplete and pernicious." [1] An antidote to intellectual or æsthetic enthusiasm might conceivably have been useful at Rome or Florence during the Renaissance ; but it could never have been needed by Englishmen, and least of all at a time when they were entering on a period of great material prosperity and power. Half a century later, Sir John Seeley was to write thus : " England surely is the country where the largest number of people lead, for mere superfluous wealth, a life that they themselves despise ; the country where vocations are oftenest deliberately disobeyed or trifled with, where artists oftenest paint falsely and literary men write hastily for money, and where men born to be philosophers or scientific discoverers or moral reformers oftenest end ignominiously in large practice at the bar." [2]

The influence of a more enlightened public opinion at this period is to be seen in the social as well as in the

[1] *Quarterly Review*, xxxii. 422.
[2] *Natural Religion*, 1882, p. 134. Stuart Mill and John Austin might have been quoted to much the same effect ; and similar testimony is borne by a recent President of the British Association. " It is a lamentable fact," said Sir Arthur Evans in 1916, " that beyond any nation of the West the bulk of our people remains sunk not in comparative ignorance only—for that is less difficult to overcome—but in intellectual apathy." This, however, requires qualification.

P

intellectual sphere ; and several humanitarian projects which under less favourable conditions had failed or only partially succeeded were now revived. In 1800 and in 1802 an attempt had been made in Parliament to put down the savage sport of bull-baiting ; and in the latter year it was mainly owing to Windham that the attempt failed. Windham was the only Whig of intellectual eminence whom Burke had succeeded in converting to his own horror of the French Revolution ; and on this occasion he did not hesitate to assert that the torture of bulls was essential to the stability of the constitution. He began by minimising the practice as " decreasing all over the country " and as too insignificant to merit the attention of Parliament, but soon showed that he thought it not cruel, or at all events not sufficiently cruel to outweigh its political value. If the masses were to be deprived of such amusements as this, they would become graver and more serious, and consequently an easy prey to Methodists and Jacobins who, if not fellow conspirators against the established order, had at least this fault in common, that they taught the people to read ; for " it was amongst the labouring and illiterate part of the people that Jacobinical doctrines had made the smallest progress." To interfere with this ancient sport would be to impair the " respect for antiquity "—one of the best safeguards against innovation ; and Windham, whilst belittling the petitions in favour of the Bill, made much of one against it from Stamford, because " it came from sober, loyal men who attended to their several vocations and never meddled with politics." Courtenay, who followed Windham, said he was surprised that the latter had complained that the time of Parliament was wasted on this theme, " for he had proved incontrovertibly that bull-baiting was the great support of the constitution in Church and State " ; and another member, whose humour was more blunt than ironical, said he thought " the right honourable gentleman, from being goaded by the terrors of Jacobinism, had run as wild as any bull that ever was baited." [1]

Erskine, who had been Lord Chancellor in the Ministry of all the Talents, was noted for his love of animals. For twenty years he had endeavoured to find some means of protecting them from ill-usage, and in 1809 he brought a Bill for this purpose into the House of Lords. A special object of his solicitude was " our unhappy posthorses." These, he admitted, must always in cases of urgent necessity be over-taxed ; but on the roads to London they were too often to be seen " panting—what do I say ! literally dying under the scourge," and this in the service of the idle rich, " to whom or to others it can be of no possible signification whether they arrive one day sooner or later and sometimes indeed whether they arrive at all." It appears that old and diseased horses were frequently bought on the chance that a few days' work might yet be got out of them before they were sent to the shambles ; nor did their sufferings end even there, for many of them were allowed to die of starvation—" gnawing one another's manes in the agony of hunger "—that the market might not be overstocked. Erskine did not meddle with bull-baiting, but left it to be determined in the courts whether this sport came under " the wilful and wanton cruelty " which he proposed to make illegal. It was the fate of this Bill—singular enough for such a measure—to pass the Lords with the commendation of Eldon and Ellenborough and to be thrown out in the Commons, where indeed Windham was lying in wait to attack it on grounds similar to those

---

[1] *Parl. Hist.*, xxxvi. 829. Jealousy of popular amusements as prejudicial to labour is said to have prompted this measure ; but there was a subtlety peculiar to himself in Windham's plea for indulging the masses in order to keep them in mental darkness and political bondage. His *Journal* is an interesting study in morbid psychology. Windham was one of the inglorious sixteen who voted against the abolition of the slave trade in 1807—" perhaps the most zealous of all its antagonists, not to be a planter."—*Edinburgh Review*, xlvi. 429.

'he had adopted in 1802. This time he did not venture to suggest that, if the " lower orders " were restrained from ill-treating animals, there would or might be a revolution ; but he argued that the Bill, if it became law, would be enforced rather against the poor than against the rich, and that Parliament, if it were to enact so unpopular a measure, would no longer be able to resist the demand for reform.[1]

Windham died in 1810 ; and in 1822—the period we have reached—Lord Erskine had the satisfaction of seeing his measure carried through Parliament on the initiative of an Irish member who, though a noted duellist, was to obtain the honourable appellation of " Humanity Martin." The Act imposed a maximum fine of five pounds or imprisonment for three months on persons who should be convicted of wantonly and cruelly ill-treating horses, cattle or sheep.[2] The considerable success of this law was due mainly to the exertions of its promoter, who stayed in London in order to lose no opportunity of enforcing its provisions. Bull-baiting, however, appears to have continued unchecked, though Martin made repeated attempts to put down both this practice and that of dog-fighting—notably in 1826, when he presented fifty-two petitions in favour of his Bill, and when also he endeavoured to extend the Act of 1822 to all domestic animals. The Attorney-General admitted that bull-baiting was punishable under this Act ; but a private member said he could not believe it had been prohibited so long as lands were held, as in some places they were, on condition of keeping a bull for baiting. In 1824 was founded, mainly through the influence of Martin, the Royal Society for the Prevention of Cruelty to Animals.[3]

We have seen that Mackintosh in 1819 had won a

[1] Cobbett's *Parl. Debates*, xiv. 553, 560, 563, 807, 1040.
[2] 3 Geo. IV, c. lxxi.
[3] Hansard, N.S., xiv. 647, 653, 655, 656.

signal victory for reform by carrying the appointment of a committee to revise the criminal laws, and that in 1820 a number of these laws, in so far as they created cápital offences, had been repealed. In 1821 he made a further attempt in this direction, but only to meet with discomfiture in the Lords. In 1822 he moved that early in the next session the House should take into its " most serious consideration the means of increasing the efficacy of the criminal laws by abating their undue rigour." The Government opposed this motion as wanting in detail and as " casting a censure on the whole of our criminal law "; but Mackintosh had concluded his speech amidst applause from both sides of the House, and his motion was carried by 117 votes to 101. Next year he sought to commit the House, in a series of nine resolutions, to the necessity of repealing many capital statutes. Sir Robert Peel, who had succeeded Sidmouth as Home Secretary, objected to proceeding in this summary fashion, and the resolutions were lost by a majority of ten. But Peel had announced his readiness to abolish the death penalty in many of the cases specified by Mackintosh; and an Act for this purpose was passed in the same session. Amongst the offences, about a hundred in number,[1] which now ceased to be capital and were to be punished only by transportation or imprisonment were shop-lifting, damaging embankments or hop plantations, cutting down trees,[2] and impersonating Greenwich pensioners. A great number of crimes, however, still remained capital; and, in order to obviate the necessity of sentencing many prisoners to death who were not likely to be executed, it was provided that in all capital convictions, except murder, where the prisoner was recommended to mercy, sentence should not be pronounced but merely entered on the record. Suicides

[1] Arnould's *Lord Denman*, i. 254.
[2] An execution for this offence had taken place within the previous sixteen years.—Hansard, N.S., ix. 425.

were no longer to be buried in highways with a stake driven through the body, but privately, and without such indignity, in a churchyard. Peel's next task was to consolidate and simplify the criminal law by repealing obsolete statutes and provisions ; and the result of this process was that by 1827 the death penalty had been confined to treason, murder, forgery of certain sorts, robbery by violence or intimidation, house-breaking, theft in a dwelling to the amount of £5, stealing of horses, sheep and cattle, fire-raising, destruction by rioters, and the causing or plundering of wrecks.[1]

We have seen that England stood alone among the nations in tolerating the use of " climbing boys " and spring guns ; and there was another and no less discreditable peculiarity in the administration of its criminal law. If a man was accused of high treason or of some minor offence which amounted only to a misdemeanour, he had the same facilities as in a civil action for rebutting the charge ; but, if the accusation was one of felony, that is, any serious crime except treason, he did not receive a copy of the indictment or a list of the witnesses who were to appear against him, and, worse still, counsel could address the jury for the prosecution but not for the defence. The prisoner's advocate might indeed contrive to influence the jury, but only under cover of raising legal points for the consideration of the court. "Humanity Martin" had tried more than once to abolish this anomaly—which had been condemned by Blackstone and even by the notorious Judge Jeffreys— in the case of a capital prosecution ; and in 1824 George Lamb, seconded by the foremost Whig lawyers, brought in a Bill to abolish it altogether. Scarlett, afterwards Lord Abinger, said he had often seen persons whom he

---

[1] Hansard, *passim* ; *Annual Register*, 1823, p. 85 ; 1827, p. 185. One notes with surprise that it should have been thought necessary so late as 1827 to legislate against the use of false lights and signals to bring a vessel into danger and the impeding of efforts made by shipwrecked persons to save their lives.

thought innocent convicted "for want of some acute and intelligent counsel to show the bearings of the different circumstances on the conduct and situation of the prisoner"; and Mackintosh asked opponents to point out a single nation, ancient or modern, in which a prisoner had not the privilege of defending himself by counsel. No such injustice existed in Scotland or in the United States. One argument brought against the measure was that the feeing of counsel would be an expense to the prisoner—"as if," wrote Sydney Smith, "anything was so expensive as being hanged." The Bill was thrown out on its first reading by 80 votes to 30. Lamb was even more decisively repulsed when he renewed his attack two years later; and the anomaly was not wholly removed till 1836.[1]

The movement for mitigation of the penal code which triumphed in 1823 had been inaugurated by Romilly in 1808. An attempt to diminish the misery and destitution caused by the protraction of civil causes had originated almost as early, and, though nominally more successful, was still as far as ever from having achieved its purpose. In 1810 Michael Angelo Taylor, who had joined the Whigs—when it was the fashion to desert them—at the crisis of the French Revolution, moved that the Commons should inquire into what Sydney Smith called "suitorcide delays" in the Court of Chancery. Next year and the next again he renewed his motion; and it was due mainly to his exertions, though not with his approval, that the office of Vice-Chancellor was instituted in 1813. This expedient did little to promote despatch, chiefly because so many cases decided in the new court were appealed to that of the Lord Chancellor; and in 1824 the whole question was re-opened on the initiative, not of Taylor, but of another Chancery barrister, John Williams. Melan-

[1] Hansard, N.S., xi. 180; Sydney Smith's *Works*, iii. 1–29; Arnould's *Lord Denman*, i. 226.

choly, indeed, were the facts brought to light in the
course of this two nights'·debate. Taylor, in supporting
the motion of his friend, said that thirty-four years
had elapsed since he 'began practice in Chancery, and
" gentlemen whom he then knew to be entangled in its
proceedings had not yet escaped from it." One man
who had a sum of only £90 at stake found that it would
cost £110 " to get it out." Another had won .a suit
for £2000, and had had to spend all but £700 in costs.
Of two pleas entered in 1812, one had been decided in
1823 and the other had not yet even been heard, though,
having been placed on the roll, it was costing £130 a
year in term fees alone. Nobody thought of questioning
the high legal qualifications, the honesty or even the
industry of Lord Eldon ; but he himself regarded the
whole movement as a reflection on his judicial character
—and not without reason ; for the congestion of business,
though explained to some extent by the growth of litigation, was due partly to his absorption in politics,
partly to his natural urbanity and patience in dealing
with counsel, but most of all to the habit of indecision
which caused him almost invariably to reserve judgment—a habit the more exasperating, as his decree,
however long deferred, was never known to differ from
his original opinion. So long did he hesitate, that a
case which had begun in 1792, and was still undecided,
had to be re-argued, " as he had entirely forgotten it."
" Eldonian doubting," it was said, " might give a good
illustration of eternity " ; and one of his judgments
began thus : " Having had doubts upon this will for
twenty years, there can be no use in taking more time
to consider it." [1]

The remedy adopted in 1824 was to appoint a
Deputy-Speaker in the House of Lords, in order that the
Lord Chancellor might have more time for the work of

[1] Campbell's *Lord Chancellors*, 1868, x. 223, 235 ; Hansard, N.S.,
ix. 706, 735, 736, 745.

his court; but this device seems to have been as in-effectual as that of 1813; for Dickens wrote, almost thirty years later, in the preface to " Bleak House ": " There is a well-known suit in Chancery, not yet decided, which was commenced before the close of the last century, and in which more than double the amount of seventy thousand pounds has been swallowed up in costs."

Legal reformers were frequently confronted with the plea that there was no general demand for a change in the law; and the same objection might have been made to a project of social as well as juridical interest which was now to achieve success. It has been said that the working classes since the Peace had been too much occupied with the movement for parliamentary reform to agitate against the Combination Laws [1]; but, as militant Radicalism was suppressed in 1820, it would be nearer the truth to say that their apathy originated in this cause and continued owing to the passing away of industrial distress.[2] That the Trade Unions should have been emancipated at a time when they were so little disposed to assert their freedom was a tribute to the personality, no less adroit and forcible than unob-trusive, of Francis Place. We have seen something of Place as an organiser in the populous constituency of Westminster; and it may be added that his first experience of politics had been gained as member and at one time chairman of the London Corresponding Society—an association of workmen, formed to corre-spond with other such bodies in sympathy with the French Revolution, which Burke had once denounced as " the mother of all the mischief." In 1789 he had begun work as a journeyman breeches-maker, and thirteen years later he had started the tailoring busi-ness at Charing Cross which, when he resigned it to his son in 1818, was yielding a net annual profit of some

[1] Webb, *Trade Unionism*, p. 85.   [2] See p. 200.

£3000. He had always been a hard student and a voracious reader, and was thus able to take full advantage of an acquaintance, which soon ripened into an intimacy, with James Mill and Bentham, for the latter of whom he prepared for publication the " Plan of Parliamentary Reform," and put into shape the anti-theological treatise, " Not Paul, but Jesus." Notwithstanding his wide and systematic information, the bent of Place's genius was, however, practical rather than intellectual ; and, after his retirement from business, he spent most of his days, from six in the morning to eleven at night, in the large and well-arranged library above his shop, studying social and political questions, and instructing rather than conferring with all who had matters of this sort to bring before Parliament.[1]

It has been well said of Place that he was a master in the art of agitation, permeation, wire-pulling, lobbying and drafting—in short, of " getting things done," and that the contempt for objects of vulgar ambition which made him leave to others the credit of his work assured him at all times of efficient support.[2] A sketch of his character published in 1826 begins with a saying of Archimedes : " Give me *place* for my fulcrum and I'll move the world " ; and the writer goes on to say that in the oratory of Burdett and Hobhouse, " in all that demonstration of frantic freedom, that tumultuous tide of popularity which they propel, he is the influential luminary, the *moon* which stirs up the waters." Place's most devoted disciple was not, however, one of the Westminster orators, but a Scottish member whose dogged insistence on economy is said to have originated the second word in the Liberal formula : " Peace, Retrenchment and Reform." Joseph Hume had been the schoolfellow of James Mill at Montrose Academy ; and the latter introduced him to Place, who at first regarded him

[1] Wallas's *Francis Place*, pp. 35, 84, 178.
[2] Webb, p. 86.

as anything but a promising pupil, but came at last to extol him as " the man of men." Office-seekers and pensioners who had an interest in public extravagance were never tired of gibing at " Old Joe " and of taunting him with " the tailor his master " ; but ridicule made no impression on the " imperturbable perseverance " of Hume ; and Place could have found no more capable agent for his campaign against the Combination Laws.

The Act of 1800 which revived and strengthened these laws had now been in operation for a quarter of a century, and, unjust in itself, had been administered in the worst possible spirit. Combination of masters against men was forbidden under a penalty of £20 ; but combination of men against masters was punishable, at the discretion of any two Justices of the Peace, by imprisonment for three months or with hard labour for two months. The men were continually being prosecuted ; and Place, who had collected a vast amount of evidence on this subject, said that what they had to endure on these occasions—" the gross injustice, the foul invective and terrible punishments "[1]—would in a few years scarcely be believed. Though many of the masters were prosecuted under the Act, not one was ever convicted,[2] and they treated it in consequence with open contempt. Thus the London type-founders had obtained no real increase in wages since 1770, and the reason was that their employers, being only ten in number, were so closely confederated that they had been compared to " the old decimal fraternity of Venice." In the kindred industry of nail-making, where the employers, owing to their greater number, had not been able to form so effective a combination, wages since 1770 had doubled. In 1804 some of the Scottish paper-makers left their employ-

---

[1] Considering the maximum, one hardly sees how the punishments can have been " terrible."

[2] Hansard, N.S., xii. 1302. Proof in their case was of course much more difficult.

ment and sought admission to better-paid trades, where upon the masters met and resolved that the names of their errant journeymen should be advertised, the public cautioned not to give them work, and the Justices of the Peace requested to proceed against them as vagrants. The sentence pronounced in 1810 on some of the *Times* compositors who had taken part in a strike began thus : " Prisoners, you have been convicted of a most wicked conspiracy to injure the most vital interests of those very employers who gave you bread " ; and in 1817 it was declared from the Circuit Bench at Chester that any master who conceded the demand of strikers for an advance in wages was an enemy to his country.[1]

The *Times* case made a great impression on Place, and in 1814 he addressed himself in earnest to the task of repeal. His project met with little sympathy from any but artisans, and only with discouragement from them, as they thought it both dangerous and hopeless ; but, after five years of ceaseless activity spent mainly in collecting information, exploiting trade disputes and contributing articles to the press, he found that a temper unfavourable to the prosecution of workmen was widely diffused and had permeated some of the leading newspapers, including even the *Times*. In 1822 Hume gave notice of his intention to move the repeal of the Combination Laws ; and two years later a Bill for this purpose was pushed, if not rushed, through Parliament in four days. It swept away all the statutes, thirty-five in number, which stood between the working classes and their industrial freedom, and secured to them the full enjoyment of this boon. No legal liability was henceforth to be incurred by " journeymen, workmen and other persons " who should combine to cease work, or to induce another to do so before the expiry of his term of service or the conclusion of his task ; to fix or raise the

---

[1] *Edinburgh Review*, xxxix. 316, 324, 326–329 ; Wallas's *Francis Place*, pp. 198, 200.

rate of wages ; to diminish the duration or output of labour or even to regulate the method or management of any manufacture or trade. On the other hand, a person who resorted to intimidation or conspired with others to destroy machinery or goods was to be punished—as he would be in any case under the common law ; but two witnesses were required, and the penalty was less than that which the Act of 1800 had imposed on the mere fact of combination—two months' imprisonment instead of three.[1]

. Had there been any debate on this measure, the wage-earners would hardly have obtained so full and elaborate a charter ; but Place and Hume had managed their business so well that it passed through both Houses without discussion. Next year the Prime Minister and the Lord Chancellor both declared that they would have opposed the Bill if they had been aware of its scope ; and cotton-weavers in Lancashire were being imprisoned under the old law some weeks after it had been repealed. Place believed that it was only the illegal power usurped by the masters that had caused the men to combine, and that their unions, being always expensive and now unnecessary, would soon cease to exist. " Combinations," he wrote, " will lose the matter which cements them into masses, and they will fall to pieces. All will be as orderly as even a Quaker could desire." The fallacy of this prediction might easily have been exposed on economic grounds, but it was demolished more effectually by the logic of events. As soon as the Act became generally known, the workmen hastened on all hands to take advantage of its provisions ; and the most attractive of these was naturally the one which empowered them to interfere with an employer in the management of his business. A Thames shipbuilder found to his surprise that four or five new hands were at work in his yard. Having intimated that they were not wanted, he was told

[1] 6 Geo. IV, c. 129 ; Hansard, N.S., xii. 1290, 1298.

that they had been sent thither by " a committee of delegates " ; and, on his refusal to employ them, the whole of his operatives threw down their tools. The first duty of delegates as defined by an association of Scottish miners was " to point out the masters they dislike." [1] Sailors in the coasting trade refused to put to sea unless the mate and the whole crew were members of their Union ; and one of the rules of this Union was that they should strictly confine themselves to their function as seamen. Accordingly, when a certain vessel laden with coal had run aground and required to be refloated, the men refused to shift the cargo ; and, this service having been performed by the crew of a passing ship, the owners had to pay £200 as salvage. The artisans of Sheffield demanded double the former wages for half a week's work ; and the *Sheffield Mercury* said—what had already been said in substance by the *Manchester Guardian*—that " almost the whole body of the mechanics in the kingdom are combined in the general resolution to impose terms on their employers."

When this statement was made in October 1825, the Act which had given rise to these excesses had been repealed ; and it is a striking testimony to the growth of a liberal spirit as well as to the skill of Place and the pertinacity of Hume that the right of combination had been restricted only, not abolished. The Act of 1825 repealed that of 1824 ; but it did not revive any of the thirty-five anti-combination statutes which had then been annulled. It enacted that the causing any person by violence or intimidation to cease work or the forcing any person to join or contribute to a Union should be punishable by imprisonment, with or without hard labour, for three months ; but the Act was not to extend to persons who should meet together or combine for the sole purpose

---

[1] Another maxim of this association with which we are more familiar at the present day was " that there should never be allowed to be any stock of coals in the hands of any of the masters."

of determining rates of wages and prices or the hours of labour.[1] The strictness with which the object of such associations was defined no doubt afforded room for oppression ; but we are told on competent authority that the Act of 1825 effected " a real emancipation " ; and Place, writing four years later, declared himself fully satisfied with the results of his work.[2]

The repeal of the Combination Laws had merely aggravated a tendency to social unrest which must in any case have made itself felt. We have seen that the condition of trade and manufacture had begun to improve in 1821, and it had gone on improving till in 1824 it was declared to be "flourishing beyond any example." Agriculture had also recovered ; for, as the result of two poor harvests, the average price of wheat rose steadily from 53s. a quarter in 1822 to 84s. in 1825 ; and Cobbett, having outlived his brief popularity with the farmers, had leisure to attack Bible Societies and the Reformation, which he called " the most unfortunate event the country ever saw."[3] These prosperous years had given rise to an accumulation of capital which was the more likely to be incautiously invested as in 1822 the interest on a considerable portion of the funds had been reduced, in terms of the original loan, from five to four per cent. Much of the speculation that ensued was legitimate enough, consisting mainly in large imports of cotton and wool[4] ; but persons who had no professional interest in these commodities soon began to participate in their purchase ; and now, as in 1809, a disastrous influence was exerted by the South American markets. We have seen that

[1] 6 Geo. IV, c. 129.

[2] Wallas's *Francis Place*, chapter viii. ; Webb, *Trade Unionism*. pp. 87–96 ; Hansard, N.S., xii. 1294, 1297, 1306. Mr. and Mrs. Hammond say that " under the new Act the Trade Unions were not allowed more than a bare existence."—*The Town Labourer*, p. 140.

[3] Smart, ii. 183. The cult of Cobbett finds no favour with Prof. Smart.

[4] That British merchants were " wool-gathering " in every quarter of Europe was a later witticism of Huskisson.

when these markets were opened at the outbreak of the Peninsular War, Brazil was inundated with huge quantities of unsaleable British goods ; and the independence of the Spanish and Portuguese colonies, which was practically recognised in 1823, caused large sums to be subscribed as loans to the New Governments and as capital for working the mines. Accounts of mineral wealth were of course grossly exaggerated ; and, according to Fowell Buxton, it was supposed that in Peru the commonest utensils were made of silver. Early in 1825 the excitement was at its height. The import of cotton from Egypt had risen from insignificance to twenty million lbs. ; and in a single year the import of wool had almost doubled. Numerous companies were formed to operate both at home and in Mexico, Brazil, Chili, the Argentine and Peru ; and, though most of the foreign enterprises dispensed with legislative sanction, the House of Commons in March 1825 had to deal with more than thirty Bills for the promotion of companies.[1] The inevitable disaster, foretold by M'Culloch in the *Scotsman* as early as the spring of 1825, was deferred till the close of the year and was precipitated by the failure of a great London bank. In this and the following year 63 out of 770 country banks were unable to meet their obligations, though most of them ultimately proved solvent. Lenders to South American Governments lost all but a dividend paid out of their own capital ; all but a few of the new companies collapsed ; and a great number of merchants and shopkeepers were ruined.[2]

It was natural that the workmen, confronted on all

---

[1] " The most wild and incoherent schemes were started ; projects which sprang with the dawn and expired before the setting of the sun, in whose beams they glittered for a few hours and then fell ; a puff of vapour sent them soaring towards the skies ; the puncture of a pin brought them to the earth."—Canning, quoted in Martineau, ii. 20.

[2] Tooke's *History of Prices*, ii. 142–167 ; Smart, ii. 182–190, 293–299.

hands with the profusion and extravagance which prevailed in 1824 and the greater part of 1825 should avail
themselves of the instrument for raising their wages
which Parliament had just placed in their hands, and
equally natural that they should use it to resist the fall
in wages which was inevitable when manufacturers
found themselves encumbered with stocks for which there
was no adequate demand. A strike of wool-combers
and weavers at Bradford in 1825 resulted only in the
break-up of their Union ; and another unsuccessful
strike of carpet-makers at Kidderminster in 1828 was
protracted for six months. These were years of deficient
and ill-paid employment ; and the failure of the masses
to improve or even to maintain their position by industrial effort caused, or was soon to cause, a revival
amongst them of the demand for parliamentary reform
which had been dormant since 1819.[1]

The liberal spirit which had shown itself in the attitude of Parliament towards industrial disputes was even
more manifest in the control of commerce ; but it should
be said here that the connexion with Continental auto-
cracy which had cast so dark a shadow on the Peace was
now severed or at all events much relaxed. In 1820
there was a popular outbreak in Spain, and similar risings
soon occurred in Portugal, Sicily, Naples and Piedmont.
Castlereagh, who had been Foreign Secretary since 1812,
conceded that, if Austria considered her Italian provinces
endangered by the Neapolitan revolution, she had the
right to suppress it ; and he even sent a squadron to
Naples to protect, if not to assist, the King. But, when
Austria, Prussia and Russia issued a joint circular from
Troppau, in which, irrespective of their national interests,
they announced their intention to put down all democratic
movements on the ground that changes in the government
and constitution of States ought to proceed only from
those " whom God has rendered responsible for power,'

[1] Webb, pp. 100, 101.

he intimated plainly enough that such a policy was in direct repugnance to the fundamental laws of Great Britain, and in any case " could not be safely admitted as a system of international law." Thus did he break away—much to the chagrin of Metternich, who had counted on his support—from associations formed under his own auspices at the crisis of the Napoleonic War ; and Canning, who was fond of presenting himself as the author of a diplomatic revolution,[1] had little scope for originality when, in consequence of Castlereagh's insanity and suicide, he succeeded him at the Foreign Office in September, 1822. But the new Secretary had a respect for nationality and a warmth of imagination and sympathy which were wanting in his upright but frigid predecessor— " so cold," said one of Castlereagh's friends, " that nothing can warm him " ; and a wave of liberal enthusiasm swept through both Parliament and country when Canning in 1826 sent troops to defend the Portuguese constitution against foreign attack and warned the Great Powers that this conflict might develop, like that of the French Revolution, into " a war of opinion."

We have seen that Adam Smith, long before the publication of his great work, expounded its principles to Lord Shelburne[2] ; and ever since Shelburne had proposed, and Pitt in 1786 had effected, a commercial treaty with France, there had been a political tradition in favour of non-interference with industry and commerce ; but during the war it could be applied only to production, and its revival after the Peace as a theory of exchange was due to the fact that the return of prosperity was so long delayed. On May 8, 1820, the merchants of London presented a petition to Parliament in which they asked for an inquiry into the " restrictive

---

[1] Canning was always unjust to Castlereagh ; and the misrepresentations of Stapleton, his private secretary and biographer, are exposed in Fyffe's *Modern Europe*, edition 1892, ii. 197.

[2] See p. 105.

system " on the plea that it might be shown to have
aggravated the prevailing distress.   Their own position
was a complete acceptance of what would now be called
the orthodox theory of free trade ; and it is remarkable
that, having no belief in the permanent efficacy of
retaliation, they maintained that impolitic restrictions in
this country would not be the less prejudicial to our own
capital and industry because foreign Governments persisted in retaining theirs, and " that, upon the whole, the
most liberal would prove to be the most politic course."
This petition and a similar one from Glasgow were cordially
received on both sides of the House ; but Baring, the
London banker, on presenting the former, said that
neither he nor the petitioners desired any immediate or
radical change ; and all were agreed in regaiding the
doctrine of Adam Smith as an ideal to be approached
gradually and only in so far as other than industrial
interests should permit.   Indeed the term " free trade "
was understood only as " open trade," that is, trade
subject to duties not heavy enough to be prohibitive.
A Committee was appointed to consider the best means
of promoting foreign commerce.   In 1821 an Act, which
has been described as " the first victory of free trade,"
abolished the preferential duty which had enabled
Canadian timber—much of it really came from the United
States—to compete with the nearer and much more
durable Baltic timber ; and next year a revision of the
Navigation Acts increased the facilities for the importation of Continental goods, and extended to South
America the right of importing native produce in
native ships which had hitherto been confined to Europe
and the United States.[1]

The Minister who introduced these measures—
Wallace, Vice-President of the Board of Trade—was in
full sympathy with their spirit, declaring that " no notion

[1] Smart's *Economic Annals*, i. 744–747 ; ii. 22–28, 33, 105.   Lord
Liverpool expressed his full concurrence in the Merchants' Petition.

could be more absurd or mischievous " than that we should endeavour to produce everything necessary for our own consumption and to render ourselves independent of the world." In 1823 Robinson, President of the Board of Trade, was transferred to the Exchequer and was succeeded, not by Wallace—who became Master of the Mint—but by Huskisson. The latter had always been closely associated with Canning ; and, though both were called upon to develop policies which had already been begun, Huskisson at the Board of Trade went much further beyond Wallace than Canning at the Foreign Office went beyond Castlereagh. It was Huskisson who was responsible for the repeal of the Combination Laws ; and from 1823 to 1825 he accomplished what Cobden in later days was to hail as " a commercial revolution." [1] The first reform effected was in regard to the Navigation Acts, which were reconstituted on a basis of reciprocity, that is, they were henceforth to be operative only against the shipping of States which put similar restrictions on ours ; and the commercial tariff was revised on a principle which provided that the duty on imported manufactures should in no case exceed 30 per cent. Thus the duty on cotton goods, which had ranged from 50 to 75 per cent., was to be 10 per cent. ; the duty on woollen goods, which had been nearly as high, and that on glass which had been higher, were to be respectively 15 and 20 per cent., and the prohibitive duty on paper was replaced by twice the amount levied as excise on the home producer. [2]

The statesman who had removed or diminished so many defences hitherto deemed essential to the thriving

---

[1] Morley's *Cobden*, i. 162. Historically the term may be justified ; but contemporary supporters of the movement were by no means satisfied with its scope. It was described as " no more than a very slight modification of the old system and merely the first steps towards a freer system " ; and the remark was made : " To talk of Free Trade as applied to this country is almost ludicrous."—Smart, ii. 489.

[2] Walpole, ii. 121, note.

of manufactures was naturally asked why he did not adopt a similar policy in regard to agriculture. Huskisson, though he parried the question as premature, did not hesitate to say that the Corn Laws, being quite erroneous in principle, must soon be revised, and he indicated significantly enough the extent of this revision by acknowledging that compensation would have to be given to the present landlords and farmers. The new tariff met with little opposition in Parliament ; but the *Times* may not have misrepresented public opinion when it referred to " that stun of surprise in the nation which imposes silence at first, but will shortly break forth in indignation and execration " ; and many Tories must have agreed with the opinion expressed in *Blackwood's Magazine* that Political Economy would " ruin this empire if reduced to practice by the Government " ; that it was republican and democratic in tendency, and " therefore unfit to be taught to the working classes." [1]

The spirit of the age had begun to disintegrate the ranks of its opponents ; and the change in foreign and commercial policy could not fail to intensify its action. The only secession which had yet impaired the solidarity of Toryism was that of Lord Grenville and his friends to Fox in 1806, and the seceders, as we have seen, returned to their allegiance in 1817 ; but from the beginning of the century there had been a rift of opinion in the party which steadily widened after the pressure of Radicalism was withdrawn in 1820. Grenville, Windham and Canning, then an Under-Secretary, had resigned with Pitt in 1801, when George III refused to consummate the Union with Ireland by admitting Catholics to Parliament ; and henceforth the Tories were divided into two sections, according as they favoured or disfavoured

---

[1] Smart, ii. 203, 288. Prof. Smart is mistaken in saying that " none of the great quarterlies gave any special attention " to Huskisson's measures. M'Culloch contributed two articles on the subject to the *Edinburgh Review*, Nos. 74, 75.

Catholic Emancipation. Both sections were admitted to office under Lord Liverpool in the long administration which lasted from 1812 to 1827. The pro-Catholic wing, now headed by Canning, was the smaller and naturally the more liberal; but there were notable exceptions; and the Duke of Wellington, Lords Eldon, Sidmouth, Westmoreland and Bathurst were almost the only Ministers who had not capitulated at some point to the pressure of the time. Thus the late Marquis of Londonderry, better known as Lord Castlereagh, who certainly favoured repression at home and was believed, more or less unjustly, to favour it abroad, was pro-Catholic, whilst Liverpool, who inclined to free trade, and Peel, who had reformed the criminal code and as early as 1820 had recognised the necessity of a "change in the mode of governing the country," were anti-Catholic. But the most characteristic product of that age of transition was Canning himself. In his youth an extreme Whig and a frequent guest at Devonshire House, he had entered Parliament as a Tory in 1793. Always a zealous, if not always a consistent,[1] advocate of Catholic relief, he steadily upheld the exclusion—by no means nominal—of Nonconformists from office. Far more emphatically, as we have seen, than Castlereagh, he protested against the claim of the Great Powers to maintain the peace of Europe by putting down popular movements. Yet he had vied with Castlereagh and Sidmouth in defending the Six Acts and would never advance a step—not even as far as Croker—in the direction of parliamentary reform. In 1826 the cleavage of Toryism had become so marked that the *Edinburgh Review* could refer to " the two great portions of the Liberal Party, those in office and those in opposition." [2]

In February 1827 Lord Liverpool was incapacitated

---

[1] In 1807 he was on the point of joining the pro-Catholic Ministry of Lord Grenville, and on its collapse joined the anti-Catholic Ministry of Portland.   [2] *E. R.*, xlvi. 421.

by an illness which soon proved fatal, and no statesman so conciliatory and representative could be found to fill his place. The anti-Catholics were a majority of the party in both Houses ; but Peel was their only man of outstanding ability in the Commons, and in these circumstances neither Wellington nor Peel could be induced even to think of forming a Government. The task had, therefore, to be entrusted to Canning, though George IV had never forgiven his defence of the Queen ; and Canning, being deserted by all but four of his colleagues, had to fall back on the Whigs. The liberal spirit of Canning's foreign policy and the inroads on protection made with his approval by Huskisson at the Board of Trade were far more congenial to this party than to his own ; and most of the Whigs, including Lords Lansdowne and Carlisle, Tierney, Lord Holland, Scarlett, Brougham, Lambton and even Burdett,[1] promised him their support. The first three consented, after some delay, to enter the Cabinet, and Scarlett was appointed Attorney-General. Lord Grey, on the other hand, held severely aloof, having worked too long and too hard for the conservation of the Whig party to countenance what he deemed " a negligent and unnecessary sacrifice " of its importance.[2] He had no love for Canning as a man and no respect for him as a politician ; and on the first opportunity which presented itself in the Lords he delivered an elaborate attack on his whole career. He said that Ministers need expect no general support from him, though equally far removed from the Opposition, if, as he believed, they had come to an understanding with the King not to bring forward Catholic relief as a Government measure. Insisting that Canning must share with his colleagues the credit of his foreign policy, he animadverted at length on its motives and method ; and finally, after asking what sort of

[1] Burdett was to end his career as a Tory—a change which he had foreshadowed as early as 1819.—Hansard, xl. 1455.
[2] *Early Correspondence of Lord John Russell*, i. 263.

liberalism it was which could demand the right of office for Catholics and refuse it to Protestant Dissenters, he declared that for thirty years the new Premier had identified himself with every measure inimical to civil liberty and the freedom of the press. " There is not any man who has less approved of his conduct than myself." [1] This unexpected disclosure of the passion which was always latent under the suave and stately exterior of Lord Grey [2] was condemned by most of the Whigs as " very atrocious " ; and the few members of Brooks' Club who still adhered to him were known there as " The Malignants." [3]

There was now both a Whig and a Tory schism—the former less openly avowed but scarcely less bitter, and one cannot but wonder that the controversy should have turned so little—if at all—on the question of parliamentary reform. The Canningite Whigs no doubt believed that they were securing the ultimate triumph of this cause by excluding from office the most reactionary of their opponents. " Anything to lock the door for ever on Eldon and Co." was their principle as expressed by Brougham.[4] Grey thought that even the return to power of " the old Tories "—which he deemed improbable —would have been " a much less evil " than the party split [5] ; and in his speech against Canning he said that the Whigs who had joined that Minister could not justly be reproached on the ground of " his known opposition to parliamentary reform " ; for they were not pledged, and their party was not agreed, on that question, and it

---

[1] Hansard, N.S., xvii. 720–733.

[2] " I wish you could see the veins of Lord Grey's forehead swell and hear his snorting," wrote Creevey on one occasion.—*Creevey Papers*, ii. 129.

[3] " I am what they call a Malignant : I am all for Lord Grey," said Creevey to the Duke of Wellington.—*Creevey Papers*, ii. 121. Mr. Butler has applied this epithet to the wrong side.—*The Passing of the Great Reform Bill*, p. 46.

[4] *Creevey Papers*, ii.

[5] *Early Correspondence of Lord John Russell*, i. 263.

had not "at present the public opinion so strongly in its favour as that it should be made a *sine qua non* in forming an administration." [1]

Canning had been far from well when he came into power ; and, after four months of physical illness and mental strain, he died on August 8, 1827. Lord Goderich, who succeeded him, proved quite unequal to his task ; and the whole Whig party was again in opposition when Wellington, with Peel as his lieutenant in the Commons, became Prime Minister on January 9, 1828. Though most of the Canningites remained in office, they were too few and too much distrusted to be of much weight, and the new Government was, on the whole, as ultra-Tory as it could well have been in the absence of Lord Eldon, who now retired from official, though not from political, life. But the liberal temper of the time was becoming daily more marked, and we shall find that even such a Ministry as this was compelled to fulfil its purpose.

[1] Hansard, N.S., xvii. 731.

CHAPTER V

THE Duke of Wellington would probably not have been greatly surprised if he had been called upon to deal with the question of Catholic Emancipation ; but it is significant of the difficulties which now beset a Tory Premier that as soon as Parliament met on January 29, 1828, he was confronted with another question of the same kind which had not been raised at Westminster for thirty-eight years.

The Dissenters in the latter half of the seventeenth century had refused, on the whole, to abet the designs of Charles II and James II against the Church ; and at the Revolution they were accorded—with exception of the Unitarians—the right of public worship on condition that their meeting-houses were registered, and that their preachers took the oaths and subscribed all but three and a half of the Thirty-Nine Articles. But they obtained no relief from the Corporation Act of 1661 and the Test Act of 1673 which, unless they had taken the Church sacrament, excluded them from corporations and from the meanest as well as the highest public offices— such as those of sergeant, exciseman, and even licensed hawker. The first of these Acts cannot originally have been meant to exclude the Dissenters, for it was passed before the restoration of Episcopacy ; and, when the House of Commons ordered its members to take the Anglican sacrament, only two out of fifty-four Puritans refused. The Test Act in their case was a great hardship. It was entitled " An Act for preventing dangers which may happen from Popish Recusants " ; all the Dissenters in Parliament had voted for it ; and in 1680 a Bill to exempt them passed both Houses, though it never received the royal assent.[1] The Presbyterians, having been in the habit of communicating occasionally in their parish churches, seldom scrupled to do so as a qualification for office ; and this practice, though the Baptists and Quakers always refused to adopt it, soon became usual—so much so that the Tories in 1713 procured an Act against it which continued in force for five years.

The prostitution of a solemn religious rite was of course more useful than edifying. One of the London churches was set apart for the benefit of those who had been appointed to minor offices. Such persons waited in an adjoining tavern till the service was over and the intimation was given : " Those who want to be qualified will please to step up this way." It is little wonder that men of principle refused to seek or accept office on such terms ; and the Corporation of London made them pay dearly for their scruples. In 1742 a certain Robert Grosvenor, who had been elected sheriff, declined to qualify, and his refusal was upheld as valid in the Court of King's Bench. In 1748 the Corporation passed a by-law imposing a fine of £400 on anyone who should refuse to be nominated as sheriff and of £600 on anyone who after election should refuse to serve ; and the funds thus raised were to be applied to the building of the present Mansion House. It then became the practice to nominate Dissenters who notoriously would not or could not accept office—one being blind and another bed-ridden. But in 1754, when a sum of £15,000 had been amassed, two of the victims resolved to raise the question at law. After thirteen years of litigation, when one was dead and the other dying, the House of

---

[1] It is said to have been " lost off the table of the House of Lords at the moment that the king came to give his assent ; an artifice by which he evaded the odium of an explicit refusal."—Hallam.

Lords decided in their favour; and Lord Mansfield in delivering judgment declared his abhorrence of the persecution to which they had been subjected. After the Whigs had come permanently into power on the accession of the House of Hanover in 1714, an Act of Indemnity was occasionally procured in favour of unqualified officials; and from 1743 to the period we have reached such an Act was annually passed. The best men amongst the Dissenters, however, were reluctant to avail themselves of this measure, partly as an indignity in itself and partly on account of its terms; for the Act professed only to grant further time to those who from illness, accident or absence had not yet qualified[1]; and Lord North declared as late as 1789 that any Dissenter who availed himself of this subterfuge " was guilty of mental fraud." In the case of Churchmen the Test Act was seldom enforced. Two-thirds, if not three-quarters of those employed in all branches of the public service had never complied with the law—some had never even heard of it; and Lord Goderich informed the House of Lords that he had never been called upon to qualify till he was made Chancellor of the Exchequer— " And why then he could not tell, except perhaps that the Chancellorship of the Exchequer was a very dangerous office." No such security for the national Church had ever existed in Scotland. In Ireland it had been abolished; and in 1824 an Irish member told the House of Commons that within the previous five years one of the King's Ministers had remarked to him that if the Irish Test and Corporation Acts were repealed, the Dissenters would speedily destroy the Church—unconscious of the fact, which he at first refused to believe, that they had been released from these Acts in 1782.[2]

[1] Thus, as Brougham pointed out, " the Dissenter was never pardoned unless he complied."—Hansard, N.S., xviii. 725.

[2] Hansard, N.S., xi. 1090; xviii. 682, 688, 719, 741, 750, 1472, 1474, 1507, 1595; Skeats's *History of the Free Churches of England*, 2nd edition, pp. 186, 348, 429–433.

The Dissenters did not submit without protest to the hardship of their legal position. In 1718, when the Act nullifying occasional conformity was in process of repeal, they endeavoured without success to obtain exemption from the Test and Corporation Acts ; and a committee was formed, mainly with this object, in 1732, consisting of two deputies from every congregation in and around London. A Bill to repeal the obnoxious statutes was introduced in 1736 ; but it was opposed by Walpole who, though closely connected with the Dissenters and personally favourable to their claim, did not venture to provoke the hostility of the Church ; and, after the rejection of another Bill in 1739, the attempt was given up. Its renewal was no doubt discouraged by the Annual Indemnity Act which dates, as we have seen, from 1743. But the Deputies, who had become a permanent body, were always ready to defend and, if possible, enlarge the legal boundaries of Dissent ; and a substantial victory was achieved— after two defeats in the Lords—in 1779, when Nonconformist ministers were released from their obligation —more or less obsolete—to subscribe the Articles, and were required merely to acknowledge the inspiration of Scripture. In 1787 the Test and Corporation Acts were again assailed ; and, two years later, a Bill for their repeal was lost in the Commons by only twenty votes. But the French Revolution, combined with the avowed hostility of many Dissenting ministers to a State religion, was now beginning to excite alarm ; and a relief Bill, introduced by Fox in 1790, was thrown out by 294 votes to 105.[1]

We have seen something of the Nonconformist agitation which resulted in the abandonment of Lord Sidmouth's attempt in 1811 to restrict the interpretation, if not the scope, of the Toleration Act [2] ; and within

[1] Bogue and Bennett's *History of the Dissenters*, 2nd edition, ii. 463–471, 477–482 ; Skeats, pp. 289, 338–345.   [2] See p. 132.

three days of this success it was resolved to form a new organisation which was to be called " The Protestant Society for the Protection of Religious Liberty," and the object of which was—within this province—to obtain the repeal of every penal law.   The leader of the society was John Wilks, member of Parliament for Boston, whilst William Smith, member for Norwich, who had supported Fox's motion in 1790, was chairman of the Committee of Deputies.   It appears that the Conventicle Act of 1664, and the Five Mile Act of 1665 which prohibited Nonconformists from coming within five miles of any corporate borough, were now, after more than a century of torpor, coming again into life, their victims no doubt being the Wesleyan itinerants ; and in 1812 Parliament was induced to rescind both of these statutes and also, on the motion of William Smith, to extend to Unitarians the protection which had been denied to them in 1689.   Encouraged by this discovery of its strength, the Protestant Society advanced rapidly in vigour and reputation ; and after 1820, when it was brought into close relations with the Whigs, we find among the chairmen at its annual meetings the Duke of Sussex,[1] Lord Holland, Mackintosh and Lord John Russell.   The question most frequently discussed at these meetings was when an attempt should be made to get rid of the Test and Corporation Acts.   In March 1827 a conference was held of the Protestant Society and the Committee of Deputies ; and it was then resolved that Russell should be requested to take up the cause in Parliament.   In order to keep supporters of the movement in touch with its progress, a journal called

[1] Sixth son of George III, and the consistent patron of every liberal cause.   Earl Grey thus gently rebuked his son, Lord Howick, for having declined a friend's invitation to meet the Duke.   " I have no reason to recommend any extraordinary pains to conciliate the favour of princes, but a proper respect is due to them, for which they have an additional claim when they behave well, which they rarely do."—Trevelyan's *Lord Grey of the Reform Bill*, p. 197.

the *Test Act Reporter* was established. No fewer than a thousand petitions are said to have been presented to the House of Commons ; but the project was eventually postponed to the following year.[1]

On February 26, 1828, after six hundred more petitions had been presented against the two Acts, Lord John Russell brought forward a resolution of which he had given notice at the opening of Parliament—that the House should resolve itself into a committee to consider the question of repeal. The substance of his speech has been anticipated in these pages ; and his exposure of the humiliating and inadequate protection afforded to Dissenters by the Act of Indemnity made a great impression. Reformers on this occasion had to combat an argument with which they were only too familiar. If they demanded the removal of an anomaly or grievance in times of public danger, they were told that the proposal was inopportune. If they waited till the danger was over—as the Dissenters had done in regard to the war and the first troublous years of peace—they were told that the anomaly must be harmless or the grievance imaginary, as otherwise they would long since have made themselves heard. But, apart from this common ground, the motion was opposed from several different standpoints. Sir Robert Inglis, who was now becoming conspicuous as a High Church Tory, maintained that the character of a man's opinions might just as reasonably exclude him from political power as the value of his property ; that the Test and Corporation Acts, tempered by the Annual Indemnity, were indispensable to the Church as a power in reserve ; and that in such matters we ought to defer to " the wisdom of our ancestors "—a theme which on recent occasions had too often been introduced " with a sneer." Our knowledge of physical science was daily advancing ; but the basis of morals had been supernaturally revealed ;

[1] Skeats, pp. 558–570 ; Hansard, N.S., xviii. 752.

and " the principles of political government " had been established by the Greek and Roman historians. Canning in the previous session had referred to the Dissenters as having " no practical grievance." Huskisson repeated this argument after it had been disposed of by Russell, and essayed the still more unpromising task of showing how he, a friend of the Catholics, could consistently uphold an Act which made not only the Anglican sacrament but the Act of Supremacy and a disavowal of transubstantiation the passport to office, and for the repeal of which the Catholics themselves had petitioned. Making the safe assumption that the feeling in favour of the Catholics was not " universal through all the Dissenters," he maintained—what proved to be quite a mistake—that, once their own object was won, the mass of them would strongly oppose the Catholic claims ; and he suggested that in the interest of the Catholics the safeguard now under discussion should be retained. Peel, who favoured neither Catholics nor Dissenters, turned this point against the latter, showing that Burdett's Relief Bill of 1825, whilst admitting Catholics to Parliament, left them under the suspended ban of the Test Act, which was now alleged to be so great a hardship. But Peel's assertion that the Indemnity Act had long since done away with the special church appropriated to office-seeking communicants was refuted by Brougham, who showed that such a church still existed and that over sixty " outrages " took place every year. Meanwhile Sir Thomas Acland,[1] who spoke after Peel and before Brougham, had utterly condemned the Acts as a scandal to religion as well as a political injustice, saying that he was more opposed to them as a Churchman than he could have been as a Dissenter.

---

[1] " Sir Thomas Acland, my old and kind friend. I was happy to see him. He may be considered now as the head of the religious party in the House of Commons—a powerful body which Wilberforce long commanded."—Lockhart's *Scott*, ix. 231.

The debate concluded with a Canningite speech from Lord Palmerston about one in the morning ; and Russell's motion was then carried amidst loud cheers by 237 votes to 193.[1]

The Government, having risked a battle and lost it, had now to consider the consequences of their defeat. Acland, though wholly in favour of repeal, had suggested as a compromise and experiment that the Acts should be suspended for a term of years. Russell refused to entertain such an idea ; but he and Peel agreed to another plan, also suggested by Acland and proposed in his absence by Sturges Bourne,[2] that repeal should be qualified by a declaration—to be taken by all persons appointed to municipal offices and to such national offices as might be specified by the Crown—that they should not avail themselves of their position to injure or subvert the Church. The Committee of Dissenters had no relish for this project ; but on Russell's assurance that the Bill without the declaration would not pass the Lords, they reluctantly gave way.[3]

Lord Holland, an old and tried friend of the Dissenters, took charge of the Bill in the Lords ; and it could hardly have been more cordially received. Bishop after bishop rose to express his abhorrence of the sacramental test, and the Bishop of Lincoln said that the only real security for the Church was " the hold which it possesses on the esteem and affections of the people."[4] But episcopal authority was of no avail to remove the scruples of Lord Eldon, who declared that he " would rather suffer death than have it told that he supported such a Bill."[5] On the second reading, which was agreed to without a division,

---

[1] Hansard, N.S., xviii. 676–781.   [2] *Ibid.*, p. 1181.
[3] Skeats, p. 574.   [4] Hansard, N.S., xviii. 1491.
[5] Even Lord Eldon was outdone by the clerical pamphleteer who declared that he would never " sanction that which may eventually unsettle ' the powers that be,' so long as one drop of loyal blood flows in these aristocratic veins."—Cassan's *Considerations against the Repeal of the Corporation and Test Acts*, 2nd edition, p. 60.

R

he contented himself with dissenting "from his heart and soul" and recording a protest which was signed by eleven other peers ; but he was very obstructive in Committee, moving some twenty amendments and speaking no fewer than thirty-five times.[1] He failed to have the declaration altered so as to express Protestantism and a belief in the inspiration of Scripture ; but he did succeed in inserting the words "On the true faith of a Christian." This excluded the Jews, who would otherwise have been eligible for corporations and from whom two petitions had been received ; and Lord Holland, who had dissented from the amendment, proposed without success an exemption in their favour. As Dissenters in Scotland and Ireland were under no disability, the Lords very properly restricted the declaration to England ; and, the Commons having accepted the amended Bill, it became law on May 9, 1828.[2]

The unity of the Government was not impaired by the repeal of the Test Act, to which all its members were equally opposed ; but the Canningites had all but parted company with their colleagues over the preparation of a new Corn Bill ; and a small attempt to purify the representative system was to bring to an end this ill-assorted alliance. The general election of 1826 had illustrated the familiar truth that "a state of venality supported by perjury" prevailed in more than half of the boroughs ; but two constituencies had made themselves so conspicuous in this respect that their misconduct could not be overlooked. Penryn in Cornwall had once been a nomination borough, the members being returned by two baronets and the electors being regularly bribed at the rate of twelve guineas a head. In 1807 the two hundred original freemen were more

---

- [1] Skeats, p. 576.

[2] *Lords' Journals*, April 24, 25, 28. As this movement receives little attention in our general histories, it has been treated with some fulness here. Walpole represents the measure as having originated in a taunt which "called up Lord John Russell."—*History*, ii. 472.

than doubled, and the result was—owing to greater publicity—that the borough was branded as delinquent thrice in twenty years. East Retford in Nottingham-shire, though now for the first time exposed, had been as long corrupt as Penryn and on a more lavish scale. For more than a year before the late election gratuitous refreshment had been provided for voters, and the crisis of the election had found them so " inflamed and besotted by liquor " that the assistance of cavalry had been required to suppress a riot. In 1827 a Bill for the disfranchisement of Penryn, though opposed by Canning as Prime Minister, passed through all its stages in the Commons ; and the same fate would probably have befallen East Retford—whose members were to be transferred to Birmingham—had not the session been too far advanced. Both these Bills were re-introduced in 1828, and Lord John Russell proposed to improve upon the former by giving the franchise of Penryn to Manchester.[1]

What was to be done to the offending boroughs in the event of their statutory condemnation was a question on which Ministers were by no means agreed. The majority wished to open these sinks of corruption to the adjacent freeholders or, in the graphic phrase of Brougham, to " sluice them with the hundreds "[2] ; but the Canningites stood firm for the substitution of towns ; and it was resolved by way of compromise that the freeholder solution should be adopted in one of the two cases and the town solution in the other. It soon appeared, however, that the evidence against Penryn—which, though none the less true, had been collected in the interest of a blackmailing conspiracy—would be deemed inconclusive by the Lords. Huskisson, the Colonial Secretary, had previously declared in Parliament that, if only one franchise were available, he should be

[1] Hansard, N.S., xvii. 1053 ; xviii. 83, 671, 1142, 1260, 1558.
[2] The hundred was a sub-division of the shire, and the name is still current in the " Chiltern Hundreds."

in favour of giving it to a town ; and on May 19, 1828, he fulfilled this pledge by voting against Peel on the motion that East Retford should be merged in the hundred of Bassetlaw. On the same night he wrote hastily to the Prime Minister what he intended as a mere offer of resignation ; but Wellington, though it seems to have been agreed at a Cabinet meeting that Ministers should vote as they pleased on this question, promptly accepted the letter as final ; and no subsequent explanations, laboured and protracted as they were, could induce him to recall his decision. The resignation of Huskisson was followed by that of three other Cabinet Ministers : Lord Dudley, Foreign Secretary [1] ; Viscount Palmerston, Secretary at War ; and Charles Grant, President of the Board of Trade. William Lamb, Chief Secretary for Ireland, also resigned. The withdrawal of the Canningites was hailed as a signal deliverance by Tories of the Eldon type, now represented in the Cabinet by Earl Bathurst. To quote *Blackwood* : " We have at last, thank God, got rid of the Liberals, [2] and once more have the satisfaction to live under a pure Tory Government. Not a remnant, we rejoice to say, of that bastard political sect, that cunning, cowardly, compromising, conciliatory school, has been left to divide and weaken the measures of the Cabinet." [3]

These and other notes of triumph were soon changed into ebullitions of wrath ; for the withdrawal of the Canningites, far from securing the so-called Protestant interest, was the immediate cause of its collapse. The

[1] " Ses affaires lui ont été étrangères," said somebody when the absent-minded Lord Dudley was appointed to the Foreign Office.— Walpole, ii. 446.

[2] The noun " Liberal " was applied to the Canningites, not because they were more liberal than the Whigs, but in order to distinguish them from their fellow Tories ; and Palmerston adopted the term in the enumeration of his party—eleven in the Lords, twenty-seven in the Commons.

[3] *Blackwood*, xxiv. 96 ; Bulwer's *Lord Palmerston*, i. 253–267, 278 ; Hansard, N.S., xvii. 1053 ; xviii. 1296.

appointment of Vesey Fitzgerald, a popular Irish landlord and a pro-Catholic, to succeed Grant at the Board of Trade, necessitated a by-election for Clare ; and nobody doubted that the new Minister would be returned. But he was opposed by O'Connell, the first Catholic to stand for Parliament ; no fewer than a hundred and forty priests are said to have been employed " to harangue the people from morning to night " as well as to canvass and bring up voters [1]; and clerical influence was decisive with the forty-shilling freeholders,[2] who had hitherto been at the disposal of their landlords. Unable to withstand so powerful a combination, Fitzgerald retired and O'Connell was returned unopposed. So long as Catholics were not returned for Irish constituencies, the question of their exclusion from Parliament could be evaded or postponed ; but, now that the issue had been raised between election in Ireland and rejection at Westminster, Wellington believed—and Peel agreed with him—that he must either give way or face the probability of civil war. A Bill to repeal the Catholic disabilities was introduced on March 5, 1829, and passed easily through the House of Commons, which in 1825 had declared in favour of concession ; and, Government influence having overcome resistance in the Lords, it became law on April 16. At the same time, as a counterstroke to the power of the priests, the Irish county qualification was raised from forty shillings to ten pounds ; and 70,000 voters, more than a third of the whole electorate, were thus disfranchised.[3]

Catholic Emancipation was essentially an Irish question,[4] and need be discussed here only in so far as

---

[1] Bulwer's *Lord Palmerston*, i. 307.

[2] This term had a different signification in all the three kingdoms—landowners in England, feudal superiors—about half of them fictitious—in Scotland, and tenants in Ireland.

[3] Hansard, N.S., xx. 1351.

[4] " The disqualification was National in its spirit, though Religious in its form."—*Edinburgh Review*, xlix. 267.

it illustrated the strength or weakness of liberal opinion in England. The movement was undoubtedly unpopular ; but the opposition it encountered was most powerful in the middle class and was raised to much more than its natural vigour by the exertions of the Church. A week before the Bill was introduced, 720 petitions had been presented to the Commons against relief and only 220 in its favour, including those of the Catholics themselves ; and the former were far the more numerously signed. Nine-tenths of the clergy were supposed to be anti-Catholic ; and in their zeal to obtain signatures they went from house to house and even exploited the schools and the prisons. Great use was made of inflammatory placards and handbills. One of these, issued by the Religious Tract Society and widely circulated, was entitled " Queen Mary's Days " and was illustrated by nine prints representing the burnings at Smithfield. Burke, the notorious criminal, who was executed on January 28, had unfortunately professed the Catholic faith, and the fact was thus turned to account : " No Popery. Englishmen remember the religion of the Edinburgh murderer." The agitation began and seems always to have been most vehement at Bristol and throughout the south-west, where the " Bloody Assize " provided a convenient historical background. All the persons sentenced to death as rebels by Judge Jeffreys in 1685 were reckoned as Protestant martyrs ; and the lists were headed " Murder " in letters described as so large that those who ran might read and those who could not read might learn to spell. It was hoped by the advocates of Emancipation that a less intolerant spirit would be shown in the industrial centres of the Midlands and the North ; but this expectation was only partially fulfilled. Nottingham was decidedly pro-Catholic and Sheffield almost equally divided ; but Protestant petitions signed by tens of thousands were received from Birmingham and Manchester ; and Lord Eldon, referring to a petition from Liverpool which he would have presented had he been able to lift it, said that " judging from its bulk, it could not contain less than a million names." Faber, a well-known Evangelical divine and interpreter of prophecy, wrote with great effect against Emancipation, though somewhat hampered by having substituted Napoleon for the Pope as Antichrist during the French war. Another of the same school was Edward Irving, who declared with more patriotism than modesty that, if the Catholic claims were conceded, " this kingdom will henceforth cease to be the intercessor between God and a guilty world " ; and to these names must be added Southey, the Poet-Laureate, whose testimony was cited in Parliament, Wordsworth and Coleridge.[1]

Educated opinion outside the Church, and the best opinion within it, were, however, not unfavourable to the Catholic cause. The controversy excited little interest in London which, half a century earlier, had been the scene of the Gordon Riots ; but a petition in support of the Government was voted by two-thirds of the Corporation, and another was signed by 327 out of 450 practising barristers ; and the barristers could claim to be disinterested, as they had petitioned to the same effect under the chancellorship of Lord Eldon. The Nonconformists, including the Quakers, who had once been hostile, but not the Methodists, fully repaid the assistance they had received from the Catholics in regard to the Test Act ; and their services were subsequently acknowledged by O'Connell from the platform of the Protestant Society. Peel, in consequence of his change of opinion, resigned his seat for the University of Oxford and was persuaded to stand for re-election. He was beaten by Sir Robert Inglis,[2] but

---

[1] Hansard, N.S., xx. 525, 573, 580, 598, 613, 637, 644, 652, 713, 907, 922, 937 ; xxi. 614 ; *Christian Observer*, xxix. 197.

[2] Sir Manasseh Lopez resigned his seat for Westbury in favour of Peel.

polled 609 votes as against 755, and amongst his supporters were eleven out of the fourteen professors. It is significant that the proposal of an anti-Catholic petition was quashed at Cambridge and that no allusion was made to the crisis in the *Quarterly Review*. The Evangelical school represented by Wilberforce and the " Clapham sect " had always been in favour of Emancipation ; and their organ, the *Christian Observer*, published and commended a long letter in its support from Daniel Wilson, who had ministered to most of them in his former chapel at Bloomsbury. Dr. Arnold published a pamphlet in which he advocated concession as a " Christian duty " and gave deep offence to his clerical brethren by denying their competence to decide questions which involved a knowledge of history—a subject " which they avowedly neglected to study." In one respect both the friends and the enemies of Emancipation were equally mistaken ; for it no more contented and pacified Ireland than it injured the Church. Those indeed were the wisest and most enlightened who put first, not the expediency or even the necessity of the measure, but its justice.[1]

The revolt of Ultra-Toryism could not fail to bring further discredit on the representative system ; for the malcontents did not scruple to use language which in earlier days would have earned for them the appellation of Jacobins ; and their opponents heard them, with more amusement than edification, lamenting the disrespect shown to popular petitions, taunting Ministers with their reluctance to face a general election, and upbraiding the representatives of nomination boroughs for sacrificing their convictions to the will of their patrons. The fullest-blown embodiment of Anglican Protestantism was the Earl of Winchilsea. One of the ten peers who had

---

[1] Hansard, N.S., xx. 707, 710, 897, 899 ; Skeats's *Free Churches*, pp. 581, 582 ; *Christian Observer*, xxix. 197 ; Stanley's *Dr. Arnold*, chap. v.

protested against the repeal of the Test and Corporation Acts, he issued in ´1829 a manifesto against Catholic Emancipation ; and his excess of zeal involved him in a duel with Wellington—which, it may be added, had so wholesome an effect on the latter that he became the leading spirit of the Anti-Duelling Association.[1] Earl Grey inquired of this Protestant champion whether he still retained his repugnance to a change in the representation ; and Winchilsea frankly declared that, whatever doubts he might once have had on this question, " late events had completely removed them," and that whenever Grey brought forward a measure of parliamentary reform he should heartily support it.[2] Another victim of disillusionment was the Marquis of Blandford, eldest son of the Duke of Marlborough. " That seven electors headed by the parish constable " should return the two members for Gatton seemed to him no longer proper or even tolerable now that boroughs of this diminutive type had furnished or swelled " that majority which lately overthrew the constitution " and was upholding " the odious principle of free trade." In June 1829, fearing that the Catholics might avail themselves of venal and nomination boroughs to build up a powerful interest in Parliament, he moved a resolution in which the existence of such constituencies was declared to be " disgraceful to the character of this House." The motion was seconded by one of the same school ; and William Smith, in supporting it, said that the Catholic Relief Bill had produced an effect not anticipated by the most sanguine of its friends, since it had " transformed a number of the highest Tories in the land into something very like radical reformers." Next year the Marquis renewed his exertions, supported by so stout a Radical as Joseph Hume.[3]

[1] *Political History of England*, xi. 251.
[2] Hansard, N.S., xx. 933. When Grey did bring forward a Reform Bill in 1831, Winchilsea opposed it.
[3] Hansard, N.S., xxi. 1675, 1676 ; xxii. 698.

The political future of both Nonconformists and Catholics had been determined, whilst that of East Retford still hung in suspense—the subject of a small but persistent controversy which, in the words of George Lamb, " had been almost as fatal in breaking up cabinets as the Catholic question itself." On May 5, 1829, it was moved for the third time that the franchise of this delinquent borough should be transferred to Birmingham ; and the motion was met by the no less familiar amendment that the right of election should be extended to the hundred of Bassetlaw, which comprised indeed some 2000 freeholders, but was so much a preserve of the aristocracy that it was known as " the dukeries." As in the previous year, Huskisson voted for the motion and Peel for the amendment ; but the former, though no longer a member of the Government, was at great pains to dissociate himself from " any revision of the representative system," and said that he favoured the enfranchisement of Birmingham merely because it was expedient in itself and because the refusal of this concession would outrage public opinion and " must pave the way for so fatal a measure as a general parliamentary reform." He even argued that the " congregated masses of population," if themselves enfranchised, might be converted into buttresses of the Unreformed Parliament. The motion was defeated by 197 votes to 111 ; but it was renewed in 1830 ; and then at last it was decided and enacted that the two seats should be used, not to bring a great industrial centre within the circle of representation, but to give a twofold franchise to a certain body of freeholders whose votes were more or less controlled by the Dukes of Newcastle and Norfolk, Earl Fitzwilliam and Lord Manvers.[1]

Wellington, having abandoned the line of the Church, was evidently determined to hold that of reform ; but meanwhile, with a change for the worse in economic conditions, an old controversy had been re-opened ; and

[1] Hansard, N.S., xxi. 705, 1087, 1091, 1103, 1119 ; xxii. 1320, 1394.

the commercial as well as the ecclesiastical policy of this
" pure Tory Government " was to prove a bitter disappointment to its friends. Four years after the commercial crisis of 1825, the nation was still suffering from
its effects. Prices and wages continued to be low, at
all events as compared with the high level reached in
1824 ; and early in 1829 the process which Canning had
called " hopeful but not confirmed convalescence " under-
went a sudden and somewhat mysterious relapse. An
over-stocking of markets, due to the fact that various
signs of revival had as such been over-estimated by
manufacturers and importers, appears to have been the
principal cause ; and this again was aggravated by the
continuous development of machinery which resulted
in accumulated supplies being undersold by those
produced later at a reduced cost.[1] Parliament had
scarcely disposed of Catholic Emancipation when its
attention was called to complaints of acute and widespread
distress. The manufacture most grievously affected
was that of silk—naturally the first to be injured by
diminished expenditure ; and the worst sufferers in this
and other trades were the handloom weavers, who indeed
were doubly afflicted because the power-loom, which was
equal to at least three hand-looms,[2] became their serious
competitor just about a year before the collapse of
prosperity in 1825. We have seen that Huskisson had
experimented with silk in the direction of free trade ;
and now that he and his friends were out of office it was
expected that the prohibitive system would be revived.
Fitzgerald, the new President of the Board of Trade,
dispelled this idea by rejecting the motion for a Select
Committee ; and he made it clear that the depression
of the silk industry was due not to foreign competition
but to over-production. In eighteen of the largest towns
from which returns had been received 300,000 spindles
were then unemployed ; but, even with this deduction,

[1] Tooke, ii. 213.   [2] Smart, ii. 332.

100,000 more spindles were at work now than in 1823.[1] The real enemy of the British silk manufacture was the smuggler—so much so that the illicit was believed to be at least double the legal importation ; and, as the revised tariff had not availed to put down smuggling, Fitzgerald proposed that it should be still further reduced. Accordingly, with the ready assent of Peel and, needless to say, of Huskisson, the duties on foreign silk were lowered from 30 to 25 per cent.

The first outbreak against the use of steam for weaving cotton and worsted fabrics had occurred in the spring of 1826, when about a thousand power-looms were destroyed in three days at Manchester and a considerable number at Bradford.[2]   Three years later there were similar scenes of violence ; but the workers, whether or not they had become reconciled to the power-loom, were now bent mainly on resisting the progressive reduction of wages, whilst the silk-weavers had a special grievance in the refusal of the Government to revive the prohibition of foreign silk.   The disturbances began at Spitalfields and Bethnal Green.   Materials belonging to the masters were destroyed 'in the cottages of their workmen, who were, or professed to be, overpowered by strikers.   The webs in thirty or forty looms were sometimes demolished in a night ; and this practice was introduced during a strike at Macclesfield on the arrival of two delegates from London, who showed the men how to cut the silk out of the loom and told them that " the destroying angel was the best ally they had."   Strikes and riots soon became general amongst the weavers in Lancashire and Yorkshire.   At Ancoats four factories were wrecked.   One of these was so completely burnt that not even a ledger was saved from the counting-house ; but it was remarked in the case of another that, whilst nearly all the hand-looms were destroyed, the power-looms were untouched.   At

---

[1] Hansard, N.S., xxi. 776.
[2] Hammond, *The Skilled Labourer*, pp. 126, 194

Barnsley the house of a manufacturer was fired ; and at Rochdale there was an encounter between the rioters and the troops, in which one of the former was shot dead and several were mortally wounded. Hunger, if not actual famine, was in most cases the impelling force. In a procession of strikers at Macclesfield a small loaf was carried at the end of a pole bound with black crape ; and at Huddersfield a committee of employers represented to Government " the agonizing condition " of their operatives and the " extreme patience " with which it was borne, thirteen thousand of them having no more to live on—it seems incredible—than $2\frac{1}{2}d.$ a day.[1]

Coventry, Manchester and Leeds were all suffering from the reckless extension of silk-making which had contributed to bring about the crisis of 1825, but none of them so severely as Macclesfield. In that year, when the population of the town was only about 20,000, the local silk-masters had advertised in the newspapers for between 3000 and 4000 apprentices and " to be built immediately, one thousand houses."[2] Recently there had been hardly any silk-looms in Leeds and now they were " innumerable "[3] ; but Leeds, being the metropolis of the cloth trade, had a security against general unemployment which was denied to many other textile centres. The power-loom had been applied simultaneously to the weaving of cotton, worsted and woollen fabrics, but, the thread used for broadcloth being peculiarly liable to break, it could revolve in this case no faster than the hand-loom ; and as late as 1858 or later the cloth-weavers in the villages round Leeds were still as self-sufficing and independent as they had been in 1795 [4] when they rode in on their ponies to vote for Wilberforce and the Sedition and Treason Bills.[5]

Agriculture, having obvious compensations in the

---

[1] *Annual Register*, 1829.   [2] Martineau, ii. 19.
[3] Hansard, N.S., xxi. 771.   [4] See p. 52.
[5] Hammond, *The Skilled Labourer*, p. 167.

event of a rise in the price of food, had frequently been an exception to the prevalence of distress; but it was not so on this occasion; and the farmers, like the silk-masters, believed that they were being sacrificed to the Moloch of free trade. The Corn Law of 1815 had pro-hibited importation so long as wheat was selling in the home market for less than 80s. a quarter, and in 1822 the restriction had been lowered to 70s. In 1828 Huskisson, whilst still a member of the Cabinet, had procured the adoption of a sliding scale which permitted importation at a duty falling with every rise in price from 52s. to 73s· when it was no more than a shilling; and the measure was passed just in time to provide against a very bad harvest, the effect of which must otherwise have been disastrous when depression set in about six months later. As early as November foreign wheat was being absorbed at the lowest rate of duty, and the total quantity imported before the next autumn was as much as 850,000 quarters. The new Corn Law was but a small concession to the disciples of Adam Smith, but the protection still assured to agriculture was qualified by the uncertainties incident to a new and wider market. The amount of wheat available at home and abroad turned out to be larger than had been anticipated, and farmers in 1829 suffered severely from the inevitable reaction in price. The crop of this year, though far from plentiful, was not so deficient as the last; but it fell below, instead of exceeding, the estimate; and, apart from losses due to this miscalculation, there was " the enormous expense of harvesting, which was attended with more interruption and delay and damage than in any season since 1816." [1] Thus from country and town alike came the disheartening tale of embarrassed capitalists and struggling or destitute workmen. The state of the peasantry can hardly have been worse than that of the artisans at Huddersfield; but we read of them as employed on the roads, with tools

[1] Tooke, ii. 194–199.

provided by themselves, at 3*d*. or 4*d*. a day; and it was reported from counties as far apart as Cheshire and Somerset that they were to be seen " harnessed to waggons and degraded to the labour of brutes." [1] We have seen something of the abuses in Poor Law administration which, with other causes, had brought the agricultural labourer to this plight [2]; and it has recently been shown that in the south of England, where wages had fallen to something like a shilling a day, the parish allowance was now but two-thirds of its original amount. For, whereas in 1795, when the Speenhamland system was introduced, the sum granted to a family of four persons was equal to seven and a half gallon loaves, it was now equal to only five. [3]

Since the close of the war there had been four economic crises—those of 1816, 1819, 1825 and 1829. In the first and second the sufferings of the people had found expression in a demand for parliamentary reform, whilst in the third they had been too much occupied in the industrial sphere with their new weapon, the Combination Act, to think of asserting themselves in politics. [4] The political movement was now to be resumed and was to culminate in what had long been regarded as a guarantee of the moderation essential to its success—a union of the middle and lower classes. The Radicalism which had expiated its sins in the purgatorial fires of Whiggism [5] was to make its first appearance at Birmingham; and there may be studied to most advantage the development of this change.

We have seen that in the days of the French Revolution Birmingham had boasted a " Church and King " mob; but this luxury was denied to the authorities

---

[1] Hansard, N.S., xxii. 958, 959, 1003.

[2] See p. 175.

[3] Hammond, *The Village Labourer*, pp. 183, 185.

[4] A correspondent of the Government wrote from Manchester in March 1826: " Certainly very different now from 1819 and 1820 when politics were mixed up with the distresses of the people."— Hammond, *The Skilled Labourer*, p. 126.   [5] See p. 187.

during the troublous times which succeeded the Peace. No other town had been so largely employed in the manufacture of munitions ; and the withdrawal of Government orders was so severely felt that one-fifth of the population is said to have been unemployed. In January 1817 the High Bailiff was requested to call a meeting for the purpose of petitioning Parliament. He refused, but the meeting was held none the less on Newhall Hill under the auspices of the local Hampden Club, of which George Edmonds, a schoolmaster and the proprietor of a weekly paper, was chairman. From 10,000 to 20,000 persons were supposed to be present, and Edmonds was the principal speaker. On the 28th occurred the assault on the Prince Regent [1] ; and the High Bailiff readily consented that the townsmen should meet to express their abhorrence of this outrage and their disapproval of petitioning at a time when it was likely to cause disorder. But the Radicals, resenting this imputation on their conduct, broke up the meeting, or at all events made things so unpleasant that " the respectable part of the assembly " withdrew. On July 12, 1819, Newhall Hill was the scene of a more famous demonstration—Edmonds being chairman—at which Sir Charles Wolseley was elected " Legislatorial Attorney." [2] We are told in a contemporary report that not a single person " holding a respectable situation in society " took a prominent part in the day's proceedings, and that when an actor in the theatre uttered the words " Perhaps some loyal hearts may yet be found," there was " one of the most astounding and long-continued bursts of applause we have ever heard." Edmonds was again in the chair when another open-air meeting was held to protest against the " Manchester Massacre." In November of this year the Constitutional Society was formed for the suppression of blasphemy and sedition ; and about a dozen persons belonging to " the dangerous

[1] See p. 147.   [2] See p. 152.

classes " appear to have been prosecuted and punished, including Edmonds, who was imprisoned for two years on account of the part he had taken in the election of Wolseley. Soon after his release he presided in July 1823 at a public dinner to Hunt ; and with this effort the Radicalism of Birmingham, in so far as it was confined to what its opponents called " the riff-raff and scum of society," may be said to have shot its last bolt.[1]

The new or Whig-Radical phase of the movement opened auspiciously in 1827 with the Bill introduced by Tennyson, one of the members for Warwickshire, to transfer to Birmingham the forfeited franchise of East Retford. Even the High Bailiff did not hesitate on this occasion to avow himself a reformer ; and the meeting convened and presided over by him in support of the proposal was the first to be held in Beardsworth's Repository, a building capable of accommodating at least fifteen thousand persons. Amongst those who addressed the meeting were the two bankers who were to be returned in 1832 as the first members for Birmingham— Thomas Attwood and Joshua Scholefield. The former had won a great local reputation in 1812 as the collaborator—outside Parliament—with Brougham in the agitation against the Orders in Council, on which occasion the artisans had contributed their sixpences to present him with a silver cup. He was now conspicuous as a writer on currency whose panacea for all ills was a large issue of inconvertible paper ; and, despite the Toryism of his family, he had become so complete a Radical that he said he " should be glad if the whole population were permitted to vote." Tennyson's proposal was defeated, as we have seen, in 1829 ; and, though the High Bailiff for that year consented to take the chair at a meeting in April to consider the prevailing distress, he refused to call another meeting in terms of a requisition addressed to him by Attwood and his friends in January 1830.

[1] Langford, *A Century of Birmingham Life*, ii. 413–439, 530.

This request for a meeting of merchants, manufacturers, tradesmen and artisans proceeded on a recital that the distress which now afflicted the country and had been more or less chronic since the Peace was due wholly to " the gross mismanagement of public affairs " and could be permanently cured only by "an effectual reform " in the House of Commons ; and that for the promotion of this object it was " expedient to form a General Political Union between the lower and middle classes." The reformers were not deterred by the refusal of official sanction. The meeting which assembled in the Repository at ten o'clock on January 25 and continued for seven hours is said to have been the largest yet held in any building in England. Muntz, an industrial magnate of Polish extraction, presided ; and the document embodying the objects of the Union and the duties of its members was adopted, with one dissentient, as " the act of the town of Birmingham." The thirty-six persons who had drawn up the articles of the Union were appointed its Political Council for the first six months ; and amongst them was George Edmonds, the veteran reformer who had presided over the original unauthorised meeting of 1817. The *Times* attested the importance of this affair, which it sought to minimise, by devoting to it four and a half columns ; and in the *Morning Chronicle*, which was more sympathetic, there was an even fuller report. Notices, long or short, appeared in every considerable journal ; and at a meeting of the Union in May, when a medal was approved expressive of its loyal and constitutional spirit, Attwood could say with some truth : " Be assured we have given the enemy a tremendous blow." [1]

The Cabinet had lost two men of first-rate ability—

[1] Langford, ii. 530–538 ; Dent's *Old and New Birmingham*, pp. 397–401 ; Butler's *Great Reform Bill*, p. 62. Unions modelled on that of Birmingham sprang up all over the country—one of the most notable being the Northern Political Union, founded by Attwood's brother, Charles.

to mention only Huskisson and Palmerston—in consequence of the Canningite secession ; and, the Catholic Relief Act having disgusted or rather infuriated the Ultra-Tories, it was now so weak and isolated that a much less " tremendous blow " than that of the Birmingham Political Union might easily have hurled it from power. The King's speech at the meeting of Parliament in February 1830 caused general dissatisfaction, because it referred to the distress as partial and for the most part inevitable, and declared that any attempt to relieve it must be made "with extreme caution." An amendment was moved to the address, and would certainly have been carried had not the Opposition leaders indicated that they did not wish to turn out the Government. Wellington was believed to be the only statesman who could control the caprices of George IV ; and, as the King's health had become very precarious and his death must be followed by a general election, there was no desire to precipitate a political crisis. Under these conditions Ministers were subjected to a process which was described in a contemporary pamphlet as that of " shaking them good-humouredly over the precipice and then setting them down on its edge " ; and, as anything could be discussed but nothing accomplished, it was remarked that during this session " more was said and less done than in any equal portion of parliamentary history since the Conquest." [1]

Such was the temper of Parliament—so cautious and irresolute—when those who had broken the bonds of Nonconformists and Catholics proposed to do the same for the Jews—a people who had been the victims of rapacity and intolerance in the Middle Ages and whose wrongs modern Christianity had done little or nothing to redress. The mediæval persecution of the Jews reached its climax during the period of the Crusades, and in this country ceased only with their expulsion

[1] *Edinburgh Review*, li. 574.

in 1290 by an edict of Edward I. In the time of the Commonwealth, or at all events in that of the Restoration,[1] they were again permitted to settle in England, and there was a synagogue in London at least as early as 1662 ; but the exercise of their religion, though covered by the Toleration Act[2] as extended to Unitarians in 1812, would seem even at the period we have reached to have been discountenanced by the common law ; for the courts, whilst admitting the right of Jews to the benefit of a charitable bequest, had refused to sanction a legacy to provide for their worship and religious instruction. On the other hand, they could present to church livings ; and—what is still more surprising—Lord Eldon, in a case where the parishioners had obtained the right of electing their vicar, was of opinion that Jews, but not Catholics, were entitled to vote. It was still doubtful whether they could legally own land. Most people who were aware of the ordinance of Henry III which deprived them of this right believed that, if ever valid, it had been implicitly repealed ; and so eminent a judge as Lord Ellenborough had shown in purchasing an estate from one of the brothers Goldsmid that he was satisfied with the validity of a Jewish title. Nevertheless the Solicitor-General affirmed in 1830 that an Act of Parliament was required to determine the question ; and a treatise intended mainly to prove the necessity for such an Act was published in that year. Jews who aspired to be more than labourers or artisans could find employment only in commerce or finance, and even these fields were but partially open ; for in London, which comprised two-thirds of all the Jews in England, they were not admitted as freemen and were debarred from retail trade. Moreover till 1828 they could not become stock-brokers without paying a considerable sum to the Lord Mayor,

[1] On this point see Blunt's *History of the Jews in England*, p. 72.
[2] The Toleration Act professed to relieve only Protestant Dissenters, but there was no Protestantism in the enacting clauses.

and their number as such was restricted to twelve. Jews could not be officers or officials, teachers, lawyers or members of Parliament, and voted only on sufferance, not because the law had intended to exclude them, but because the Oath of Abjuration which was prescribed in such cases concluded with the words " On the true faith of a Christian " ; and we have seen that the House of Lords by inserting this formula in the Declaration adopted by the Commons in 1828 had deprived them of the benefit which they would otherwise have obtained from the repeal of the Corporation Act.

Amongst the volunteers raised in London at the outbreak of the Napoleonic War were three hundred Jews ; and the constitutional maxim " No taxation without representation " might well have been applied to this community which, though poor enough in the main, included a few families of more than princely wealth. Benjamin Goldsmid, the friend of Pitt, had a mansion at Roehampton which was thought to rival Windsor Castle. Far richer was Nathan Meyer Rothschild ; and it was a reflection on the gratitude as well as on the justice of Britain that men of this type, whose financial resources and skill had been invaluable to their country during the French war, should be denied political and even civil rights. The Goldsmids and Rothschilds and Montefiores had, however, a still better claim to recognition in their benevolence and truly liberal spirit ; and one of them was referred to in Parliament as " at the head of no fewer than twenty-seven British charities, many of which were for the promotion of Christianity." [1]

Wellington, having made himself sufficiently unpopular by emancipating seven million Catholics, was not disposed to repeat the experiment in favour of thirty thousand Jews ; and the project was brought

[1] Blunt's *History of the Jews in England*, pp. vii, 118–122 ; Picciotto's *Sketches of Anglo-Jewish History*, pp. 30, 251, 254, 276, 3 44 ; Hansard, N.S., xxiv. 236, 793, 811.

forward by Robert Grant who, like his brother Charles, was a prominent Evangelical. An Act to dispense with the sacrament in the case of Jewish aliens who should apply to Parliament for naturalisation had been passed in 1753 ; and this paltry concession caused so great an uproar that it was repealed in the following year. On the present occasion, when it was proposed to admit native Jews to the full rights of citizenship, there were no petitions against the Bill,[1] and several of importance in its favour. Bristol and Southwark petitioned ; so did " every banker and almost every merchant of weight " in Liverpool ; so did a hundred and fifty members of the Bar ; and a petition from London with 14,000 signatures was enforced, or at least was expected to be enforced, by the votes of all the four members. Possibly the absence of popular protest may have been due to a belief that the Bill was not likely to pass ; for one can hardly account on any other assumption for the quiescence of the Church. Amongst those who spoke in favour of the Jews were Huskisson, Brougham, Lord John Russell, Mackintosh, Dr. Lushington, O'Connell, William Smith, Sir Robert Wilson and Macaulay, the last of whom delivered on this occasion his maiden speech. The *Annual Register* made unwilling obeisance to the rising star of liberalism when it said that the Bill was supported " on what were now commonplace grounds in all such discussions, viz. that it was persecution to look at a man's religion when speaking of his fitness for civil rights." One member indeed declared that, if any one had predicted, a few years earlier, what had been done and was now proposed to be done in the shape of religious emancipation, he would have been pronounced insane. Speeches in opposition—even that of Peel—were little more than an amplification of the theme that the passing of such

---

[1] Dr. Arnold was so much opposed to the measure that he was " more than once on the point of petitioning in his own sole name."— Stanley's *Arnold*, p. 193.

a measure would go far to " unchristianise " Parliament ; and Mackintosh did not greatly underrate the resources of opponents when he said that he had come down to the House unable to think of an argument that could be advanced against the measure and inclined to " advertise a reward for one that he might get it to refute." It was even objected to the Jews that they could not be whole-time legislators because their Sabbath commenced on the Friday evening. The introduction of the Bill was carried against the Government by the small majority of eighteen ; but on the second reading it was thrown out by 228 votes to 165.[1]

The state of indecision and suspense which had paralysed political life was now wearing to a close ; and the moderate Tories lost their last chance of averting the deluge when Lord John Russell was defeated in his endeavour to enfranchise the three largest unrepresented towns—Manchester, Birmingham and Leeds. On June 26, 1830, George IV put an end to his unpopularity by dying and making way for a sovereign whom other people than the Duke of Wellington could be trusted to manage. This event, long imminent, if not overdue, was succeeded by another which nobody had foreseen. France at this period atoned for the blow she had struck at British liberalism in 1792 by providing a revolution which could be cited as a precedent for moderate reform. Charles X was the counterpart of the English James II. On July 26, " by the advice of Jesuits and other wicked persons "—to quote the language of our own Bill of Rights, he issued a series of ordinances which our ancestors would have described as violating the original contract between king and people ; and a few days later, as the result of a sharp but decisive conflict on the 29th, he was supplanted by his cousin, Louis Philippe, who, in token of his popular title, was proclaimed King of the French. The general election, which

---

[1] Hansard, N.S., xxiii. 1287-1326 ; xxiv. 784-814.

was then imperative on the accession of a new sovereign, had already begun when these events became known in England ; and the *Edinburgh Review* indulged in no idle prophecy when it declared that " the battle of English liberty has really been fought and won at Paris." Enthusiasm for reform proved as disastrous to the Government in the large towns as Ultra-Toryism in the nomination boroughs ; and they also lost heavily in the counties, all of which polled late enough to be influenced by the tidings from France. On the other hand, a Ministry which had admitted Catholics to Parliament could not fail to do well in Ireland ; and no Ministry had ever failed to do otherwise in Scotland, " where men would enlist under Beelzebub's banner if he were First Lord of the Treasury." [1] The new Parliament met on October 26, by which date the tide of revolution had spread from Paris to Brussels. Eight days later, at a time when, as he himself afterwards admitted, " the country was in a state of insanity about Reform," [2] Wellington delivered the famous speech in which he described the representative system as so good that it could not be improved ; and on the 17th, having been defeated on a question relating to the Civil List, he resigned.

The task of forming an administration was naturally assigned to Lord Grey, the finest embodiment of aristocratic liberalism, who had succeeded Fox as Foreign Secretary in the Ministry of all the Talents and for forty years had been the consistent advocate of civil and religious liberty and parliamentary reform. Canningites as well as Whigs were prepared to accept him as their leader ; for Huskisson, the head of this group and their keenest Anti-Reformer, had been killed at the opening of the Liverpool and Manchester Railway on September 15 ; and their attitude had really been determined a few days later when Palmerston refused to rejoin the

[1] *Scotsman,* 1830, p. 729.   [2] Butler, pp. 85, 97.

Wellington Ministry, unless accompanied by Lansdowne and Grey.[1] Brougham, Durham, Holland and Lord John Russell were all provided for in the new arrangements, the first as Lord Chancellor ; but a Cabinet which included four Canningites and one Tory—the Duke of Richmond—and all the members of which, except two, were actual or prospective peers,[2] could not but confirm the suspicion of those who had maintained that no substantial reform would ever be attempted by the Whigs ; and, unhappily for the latter, the first duty imposed upon them was that of suppressing a popular outbreak.

The patience of the peasantry had stood the test of two bad harvests, and would probably have endured the rise in prices which foreboded a third, had they not been roused from stupor by the echoes of social convulsion in France. Thrashing-machines, in so far as they displaced hand-labour, were the agricultural equivalent of the power-loom ; and the labourers were treading a path not unfamiliar even to themselves when they began to destroy these appliances, as they did at Hardres in Kent on August 29, 1830. But the produce of the farm, unlike that of the factory, could not be kept under lock and key ; and the destruction of thrashing-machines was accompanied on a portentous scale by the firing of corn-ricks. These outrages, which spread through the south-eastern counties and soon became of almost nightly occurrence, were perpetrated with a secrecy and ingenuity unequalled since the Luddite riots[3] ; and the word " Swing," chalked on gate-posts and appended to anonymous letters, had the same ominous significance as " Ludd." No amount of watching and patrolling could ensure the immunity of a

[1] Butler, p. 93.

[2] Four Cabinet Ministers were members of the Commons ; but Palmerston was an Irish peer and Lord Althorp the heir of Earl Spencer. The other two were Charles Grant and Sir James Graham. Russell was not admitted to the Cabinet till next year.

[3] See p. 136.

farm-yard. Ricks are said to have been fired under the eyes of men stationed to protect them ; and some believed that the corn was first soaked in some inflammable liquid and then ignited from a distance by a mysterious " blue spark."[1] Notwithstanding the extreme poverty of the people, information was rarely to be had for money. In some cases as much as £1000 was offered, " and yet not one of the miserable beings have availed themselves of the prospect of becoming rich." There were serious riots in which several factories and two workhouses were wrecked ; and the whole countryside was infested with mobs of labourers who levied contributions, demanded higher wages and insisted on a reduction of tithes. The disturbances had not abated when the Whigs came into power ; and it was unfortunate for the rioters that the new Home Secretary was Lord Melbourne, who as William Lamb had discredited the Whiggism he was soon to discard by supporting the Habeas Corpus Suspension Act of 1817 and the Six Acts of 1819. We have seen that twenty-two Luddites suffered death in 1812. In this case fifteen persons were executed—all but three for arson—457 were transported and about 400 imprisoned.[2]

It was a severe, if not excessive, retribution for a rising in which the only life lost had been that of a rioter ; but the Government which had dealt thus with peasants, the great majority of whom were illiterate, was amply justified in prosecuting two writers who had encouraged them in their useless and suicidal course. Richard Carlile, who spent more than a sixth of his life in prison on account of so-called blasphemous and seditious publications, is justly regarded as having done much to vindicate the freedom of the press ; but it is impossible to defend the address, " To the Insurgent Agricultural Labourers," in which he extolled their exploits and

[1] Martineau, ii. 398.
[2] Hammond, *The Village Labourer*, pp. 308, 309.

assured them that they were waging war, and that " in war all destructions of property are counted lawful upon the ground of that which is called the law of nations." [1] For this address he was sentenced in January 1831 to a fine of £2000 and imprisonment for two years. The other offender was Cobbett. He had not directly encouraged the rick-burners, but had conveyed much the same impression by telling them " that their acts have produced good, and great good too," and that the wheat they destroyed could be no loss to them so long as their diet continued to be " potatoes and salt." Cobbett was not tried till July 1831, and, as the jury failed to agree, was then discharged. By that time Lord Grey's Government had introduced a Reform Bill which he thought worthy of his warmest support ; but that did not prevent him— consistency being no more his business than truth—from assailing the Whigs as " always the most severe, the most grasping, the most greedy, the most tyrannical faction whose proceedings are recorded in history." [2]

The severity of the Government towards agrarian disorder and its abettors cannot be fairly judged without reference to the great boon they conferred on the rural population by their reform of the Game Laws. Violations of these laws had become more frequent with every wave of agricultural depression since the Peace, till in the three years 1827 to 1830 they amounted to a seventh of all the criminal convictions [3] ; and at a time when great numbers of the peasantry were in such a condition that they must either poach or starve, the barbarity of the penalties to which they were exposed had become an intolerable scandal. The process of mitigation had indeed already commenced. Spring-guns, which proved

[1] Prof. Wallas would have done well to quote the words which induced " the Government of Whig rick-owners " to prosecute Carlile. —*Life of Place*, p. 255.

[2] Carlyle's *Cobbett*, p. 273 ; Arnould's *Lord Denman*, i. 331–335. ·' The Last Labourers' Revolt " is treated exhaustively by Mr. and Mrs. Hammond. [3] Hammond, *The Village Labourer*, p. 191.

more fatal to the innocent than the guilty,[1] were prohibited in 1827, and next year the Act of 1817, which
made it an offence punishable with transportation for
individuals to be found armed in an enclosure at night [2]
was repealed, and this penalty was reserved for those
who were convicted for the third time of actually taking
or killing game.   On the other hand, a party of poachers,
though no more than three, and only one of them armed,
might, if detected at night, be transported for fourteen
years.[3]   Sydney Smith had urged in 1823 that the best way
to discourage poaching would be to legalise the sale of
game, because the poacher would then " have to compete
with a great mass of game fairly and honestly poured
into the market " [4] ; and the same argument was used by
Peel in 1827.[5]   A Bill to make the selling of game legal
was brought into the Commons by Lord Chandos whilst
the peasants were still unsubdued, but the Government
objected to several of its provisions ; and their own much
superior measure was introduced in February 1831,
though it did not become law till the following October.
The monopoly of sporting hitherto enjoyed by landowners was abolished by this Act, which swept away all
legislation on the subject prior to 1820, and established
the present system of licences for dealing in and shooting
game.   The dealer was to forfeit £2 for every head of
game bought from an unlicensed sportsman, and the
same penalty was to be incurred by the sportsman who
sold to an unlicensed dealer.   Poaching by day ceased to
be a criminal offence, the landowner being left to protect
himself by an action for trespass ; but the clause which
altered the penalties for night poaching, and reduced the

---

[1] The frequency of accidents made no impression on Lord Ellenborough, who said : " The object of setting spring-guns was not
personal injury to any one, but to deter from the commission of theft ;
and that object was as completely obtained by hitting an innocent
man as a guilty one."—Hansard, N.S., xvii. 296.
[2] See p. 169.   [3] 9 Geo. IV, c. 69.
[4] *Works*, ii. 342.   [5] Hansard, N.S., xvii. 115.

maximum from transportation to one year's imprisonment, was struck out by the Lords, and the Act of 1828
consequently remained in force.[1]

The Game Act, even as thus crippled, was a liberal
measure, but far more creditable to the statesmanship
and courage of the Whigs, and also to their disinterested-
ness—for a third of the borough-owners belonged to this
party—was their scheme of parliamentary reform. The
Reform Bill was prepared by a committee consisting of
Durham as chairman, Lord John Russell, Lord Dun-
cannon, the Chief Whip, and Sir James Graham; and
the second of these, though not yet a member of the
Cabinet, had the honour of submitting it to the House
of Commons on March 1, 1831. Ministers had been completely successful in concealing, not only the details, but
the scope of their plan; and probably no great measure,
not in itself unexpected, has ever proved so complete
a surprise.[2] The ballot and quinquennial parliaments
which had been in the original scheme were indeed omitted;
but nomination, the dominant feature of the old system,
was neither curtailed nor counterbalanced, but abolished.
We have seen that only five boroughs had been punished
for corruption and that the only one to be disfranchised
was Grampound, the two members for which had in
1821 been transferred to Yorkshire; but now, for the
public good, and not for their sins, sixty boroughs with
less than two thousand inhabitants were to be suppressed;
forty-seven with less than four thousand inhabitants were
to be deprived of one member[3]; and forty-three cor-

---

[1] 1 & 2 Wm. IV, c. 32. The results of the Act were said in 1846
to be very disappointing.—*Westminster Review*, xlv. 413.

[2] " Members to half a dozen great towns " was Croker's forecast
of the Bill.

[3] As the criterion of population was found to have little bearing
on the number of qualified householders, it was subsequently given
up and replaced by no very intelligible rule. Downton, with a population of 3961, was wholly disfranchised, whilst Petersfield with a population of 1423 retained one member. Croker cited ten boroughs with
3000 electors which were to have two members and ten with 4000
electors which were to have only one.

poration boroughs were, as such, to disappear in consequence of the establishment in all towns of a uniform
householder franchise. Scarcely a year had passed since
Russell had sought to enfranchise only the three largest
unrepresented towns ; and now he was announcing the
intention of the Cabinet to assign thirty-four members
to such towns as well as eight additional members to
London and fifty-five to counties. Nor even by such
transfers was the gap caused by disfranchisement to be
filled up, for membership of the House was to be reduced
from 658 to 596.[1]

Reformers maintained that their Bill, though inimical
to the usage of the constitution, was a means—and
the only means—of restoring it to its original shape.
Nomination had prevailed for centuries, but had never
been more than a venerable abuse. To award, to
dispense with and to revive representation had at one
time been the prerogative of the Crown ; and, so long
as members were paid by their constituents and service
in Parliament was regarded rather as a burden than an
honour, it had been exercised with some regard to
population and wealth. In those days rising boroughs
were acquiring the franchise and decadent boroughs
were losing it—frequently through supineness or at
their own request ; and this process might have continued
indefinitely if the quickening of political life which
accompanied the Renaissance and the Reformation had
not led to its arrest—the Tudor and Stewart sovereigns in
their desire to counteract the popular spirit being far more
anxious to preserve and multiply decayed boroughs
than their predecessors had been careful to weed them
out. But the function which the Crown failed to discharge continued to be recognised. Thus under Elizabeth, when it was proposed to add two new burgesses to
the House, one of her Ministers replied : " It is thought

---

[1] The Bill is printed in Roebuck's *History of the Whig Ministry
of* 1830, ii. 427.

there are overmany already, and there will be a device hereafter to lessen the number for the decayed towns." James I admitted the necessity of disfranchising several such boroughs, including Old Sarum ; and the Protectorate Parliament in which members were allotted according to population was described by the Royalist Lord Clarendon as " a warrantable alteration and fit to be made in better times." The right of the Crown to control representation which had been so grossly abused was viewed with growing disfavour by the Commons ; and the last occasion of its exercise—which had then become extremely rare—was the enfranchisement of Newark in 1777. Not a few of the lapsed boroughs had by this time retrieved their position ; but the forty-five which were still in abeyance had now no chance of being restored ; and the last of their claims—that of Basingstoke—was rejected in 1693.[1] The membership of the House had thus become fixed just at the period of industrial expansion which preceded the Revolution [2] ; and, as Sir James Mackintosh very truly said, " The regulator of the representation, which had been abusively active in stationary times, was suffered to drop out of the machine at a moment when it was so much needed to fit the elective system to the rapid and prodigious changes which afterwards followed in the state of society." [3]

Uniformity in the counties,[4] diversity in the boroughs were the chief characteristics of the English franchise. The Reformers inverted this order, proposing to recognise several qualifications in counties—copyhold and lease-hold as well as freehold—and only one in boroughs ; and here they had more difficulty in vindicating the constitutional and even the popular character of their scheme. The common law assumed that the house-

---

[1] Porritt, *The Unreformed House of Commons*, i. 1, 2, 6.
[2] See p. 20.
[3] Hansard, 3rd S., iv. 678.
[4] County qualifications were various, including even church pews, but they were all based on the 40s. freehold.—Porritt, i. 22.

holder franchise which survived—effectively at least—
in only a few places had once been universal; but the
question was deemed of antiquarian rather than legal
interest ; and the diversity of electoral rights, far from
being regarded as an anomaly, had long been extolled
as securing the representation of many competing
interests. The rights of existing voters were assured
to them, with one exception,[1] for life, provided they
were resident ; but the qualification for new voters was
to be a year's occupancy of a house of the annual value
of £10[2] ; and this clause, though it greatly expanded
the suffrage, did in some cases contract it. " I think
it a fatal objection," said Peel, " that every link between
the representative and the constituent body should be
separated so far as regards the lower classes. It is an
immense advantage that there is at present no class of
people, however humble, which is not entitled to a voice
in the election of representatives." But he added with
characteristic candour, " I think this system would be
defective if it were extended further." And truly it was
limited enough, being practically confined—apart from
the freeman electorates which were largely fictitious
and non-resident—to Preston, which had something like
universal suffrage, Southwark and Westminster. The
unreformed House was essentially aristocratic ; but, in
virtue of this small popular element, its defenders were
able to contrast it favourably with what it would be
under the Bill. "The real fact is," said Lord Mahon,
" that under the present system all places are not
represented, but all classes are ; and that in the new
system every place will be represented, but only one
class." The best reply to this objection was that the

---

[1] Freemen admitted since March 1831—almost all in the Tory
interest—were disfranchised.

[2] In the original draft of the scheme, as a set-off to the ballot,
the qualification was to be £20. On that basis a certain town with
17,000 inhabitants would have had less than twenty electors.—
Hansard, 3rd S., viii. 239.

£10 franchise would be oligarchical in some boroughs, democratic in others [1]; but the point was frankly conceded by Macaulay, who enraged Hunt, one of the members for Preston, by arguing that the middle class should be admitted into the citadel in order to assist in holding it against popular assault. " That we may exclude those whom it is necessary to exclude we must admit those whom it may be safe to admit." [2] Anti-Reformers, though they differed from Macaulay on the point of admission, were at one with him on that of exclusion. Their one serious grievance was that representation, hitherto nominal, was—so far as it went—to become real ; and Sir John Scott, now Lord Eldon, had probably divulged the private opinion of many besides himself when as Attorney-General in 1794 he prosecuted Thomas Hardy on the ground that the society of which he was a leader had endeavoured to set up " a representative government, the direct contrary of the government which is established here." [3]

Nobody had supposed that a Whig Ministry, much less a Whig-Canningite Ministry, would propose such a measure ; and one of the main factors which contributed to that result has only now been revealed. When Grey became Prime Minister, the tide of liberal enthusiasm was at its height ; and it was generally supposed that he had returned under some degree of compulsion to the popular ideals of his youth. The public knew that he had once been one of the Friends of the People and their spokesman in Parliament ; but they also knew that in 1804 and for many years later he and his friends had been allied with a section of the

---

[1] " House rent does not indicate a social class. The City twenty-pounder, in a shop, sinks below any ten-pounder in a small market town."—*Westminster Review*, New Series, i. 34.

[2] Hansard, 3rd S., ii. 1193, 1209, 1346 ; ix. 370. Macaulay sat for Calne, which was to lose only one member, much to the vexation of Hunt, who called it " that rottenest, stinkingest, skulkingest of boroughs." In 1847 it had only 165 electors.

[3] Trevelyan's *Lord Grey*, p. 39.

T

Tories; that at the crisis of 1819 he had publicly denounced Radical reform as "radical subversion"; and that as late as 1827 he had said that reform was not so strongly supported in the country "that it should be made a *sine qua non* in forming an administration." His most intimate friends, with one exception, appear to have known no more—or rather to have known only this more, that he believed the Unreformed Parliament would last his life, and probably much longer. The exception was Lord Holland, to whom alone he had unbosomed his political soul. Writing to Holland on December 6, 1820, he stated that in his opinion no reform would be effectual or popular which did not comprise the following points: quinquennial parliaments; the admission of copyholders to vote in counties; and the transference to counties and large towns of a hundred members from "the most obnoxious boroughs"[1]; and fourteen months later he wrote again to Holland: "You may be assured that any nibbling at Reform will not now do." Thus early was foreshadowed the scheme which came to fruition in the congenial atmosphere created by the "July Revolution." With no such prospect to cheer him and constitutionally despondent, Grey may well have believed that he would not live to see his project realised; and, in deciding to do nothing for its fulfilment lest such an attempt should break up his party, he chose the safer but not necessarily the wiser or the better part. There were doubts and misgivings in the Cabinet even under the very favourable conditions of 1831. The policy of "nibbling" would still have been preferred by several of the Whig Ministers —not to mention the Canningites—and notably by Brougham, the most popular of them all, who maintained that "the close boroughs were not by any means the worst part of the representation."[2]

[1] Compare Russell's scheme of 1822, p. 197.
[2] Trevelyan's *Lord Grey*, pp. 180, 183, 275, 372.

Annual parliaments and universal suffrage were the watchwords of democratic reform ; but the Bill exceeded the expectation of the Radicals quite as much as it fell short of their demand ; and it was joyfully accepted by most of their leaders. Place had always hated and despised the " speech-making, gabbling Whigs," and had even exhorted his friends in Parliament not to turn out the Wellington Ministry at the cost of bringing the Whigs into power. " Here is hardly anything but imbecility. Who would be minister ? Earl Grey ? Look at him. Is he competent to do the duty ? " Place's foresight on this occasion was as much, though not so inexcusably, at fault as when he predicted that the repeal of the Combination Act would put an end to strikes He expressed himself as " delighted with the Bill," and wrote in his Diary : " None believed, none expected any such propositions." Cobbett, Bentham, Burdett, Hobhouse and Hume were no less agreeably surprised ; and the *Westminster Review* declared : " There is no doubt that the estrangement which had long been growing between the Whigs and the community at large has by one energetic step been removed." On the other hand, Hunt, whilst supporting the Bill as far as it went—and it went much further than he had expected—said it would be worse than useless without the ballot ; and Carlile, after asserting that no reasonable man could be dissatisfied with the measure, became himself so unreasonable a few months later that he denounced it as " delusive and dangerous." [1]

[1] Wallas's *Place*, pp. 250, 258 ; Butler, pp. 201, 210, 282 ; Hansard, 3rd S., ii. 1211, 1215. Sir Robert Wilson, to the astonishment of his party, voted with the majority against the Bill in Committee and resigned his seat for Southwark. Wilberforce, who belonged to a very different school, had retired from Parliament in 1825. Unlike most of his Evangelical friends, he approved generally of the Bill, but thought the franchise much too low—and no wonder, for he believed it to be equivalent to universal household suffrage. So did Lord Winchilsea.—*Private Papers of William Wilberforce*, pp. 156, 266 · Hansard, 3rd S., vii. 1141.

Aristocratic domination was even more hateful to the lower than to the middle class ; and it soon appeared that without their united efforts this incubus could not be removed. The Bill was read a second time in the Commons by only one vote ; and, a motion having been carried against the Government that the membership of the House should not be reduced, Parliament was dissolved and the Anti-Reformers suffered an overwhelming defeat. The Second Bill, substantially the same as that which the country had endorsed, was thrown out by the Lords on October 8, 1831. They treated the third Bill when it reached them next year with rather more respect, allowing it to go into Committee but endeavouring to save the rotten boroughs by postponing the discussion of their fate. Grey resigned, and was nominally out of office for a week, during which Wellington hunted for colleagues to assist him in carrying, not a substitute for the Bill, but practically the Bill itself. The failure of this attempt, which Peel discountenanced, was followed by a secession of Tory peers ; and on June 7, 1832, the Bill became law.[1]

We have seen that in January 1830, some nine months before the Whigs came into power, a movement for the formation of Political Unions had been inaugurated at Birmingham. The Birmingham Union, though its leaders belonged to the middle class, was composed mainly of working men, and was joined later by the wealthier townspeople ; but elsewhere this process was reversed ; and it was not till the Bill was rejected by the Lords in October that the artisans rallied in any great number to its support. From this period members of the Unions began to provide themselves with arms ; and, if Wellington had succeeded in supplanting Lord Grey, there would

---

[1] The struggle for the Bill in and out of Parliament is familiar to most readers of English history, and has been so fully narrated by Mr. Butler, Prof. Wallas and Mr. Trevelyan that it need only be touched on here.

unquestionably have been a rising in the midlands, supported by a demonstration in London sufficient to prevent the withdrawal of troops. The prospect of such an outbreak was welcomed by many who hoped to gain by this means the enfranchisement which was denied to them in the Bill. Several of the men who were to head the Chartist movement of 1839 were already at work; and under their influence unions were formed, especially in London and Lancashire, which comprised workmen only and were prepared to use force. "The great peculiarity causing a difference between the Political Unions and the unions of the working classes," said Place, "was that the first desired the Reform Bill to prevent a revolution, the last desired its destruction as the means of producing a revolution."[1] Place himself believed that the £10 householders included about as many of his countrymen as were yet fit to have votes; and even those who stood out for universal suffrage were quite alive to the fact that a uniform franchise, however limited, was capable—unlike the old system which nominally included all classes—of indefinite expansion.

The third and final edition of the Reform Bill was not so drastic a measure as the first. The Government had consented not to diminish the membership of the House and could therefore afford to be less stringent in the withdrawal of representation and more generous in its bestowal. Fifty-six boroughs—a reduction of four—were wholly disfranchised; thirty, instead of forty-seven, were deprived of one member; sixty-four members—an increase of twenty-two—were assigned to unrepresented towns and the new metropolitan boroughs; and the counties, which had been promised fifty-five additional members, were awarded ten more. In order to check the manufacture of county votes, it was provided that in future no one should be qualified who had the grant of a freehold for life of less value than £10 a year. But

[1] Wallas's *Place*, p. 290.

this provision was more than neutralised when Lord Chandos, supported by many Whig landlords, succeeded in enfranchising £50 yearly tenants—an amendment which Lord Grey announced to the Lords as not approved by the Government and likely in his opinion to revive a demand for the ballot.[1] The aristocracy had reason to congratulate themselves—the more so as the increase of county representation was much in their favour, and they had a promising field for their influence in seventy-six boroughs, some of them new, with a total electorate not much larger than that of Liverpool.

Of all the liberal movements which have been reviewed in the course of this work, the task of parliamentary reform was the first to be attempted and the last to be achieved. Seventy years had passed since George III exposed the anti-popular character of the representation by showing that as easily as in the days of the Tudors it could be perverted into an instrument of absolute rule. Most of the Whigs who then countenanced reform had combined with the Crown to suppress it when demanded by a few courageous spirits during the war with Republican France and by the masses after the Peace of 1815 ; and it was now accomplished under the guidance of a statesman who had been its advocate when it was less urgently needed as the recognition of a new adjustment of forces in the national life. The extension of electoral rights secured in 1832 corresponded indeed very closely to the area of advancement, geographical and social, as it had been determined by the industrial revolution. With few exceptions, the new boroughs were in London, the midlands and the north, whilst the boroughs defranchised or semi-defranchised were in the south and south-west. Brougham said that the £10 householders " in some country towns fill the station of inferior shopkeepers— in some, of the better kind of tradesmen—here they are

[1] Hansard, 3rd S., vii. 939.

foremen of workshops—there artisans earning good wages—sometimes, but seldom, labourers in full work."[1] As in the large towns they were admittedly of humbler rank, it is evident that the borough franchise included at least the aristocracy of labour—the men who had substantial sums in Savings Banks and a good many of those who were paying subscriptions of a guinea a year to Mechanics' Institutes ; and these were the only people below the middle class whose position the new methods of production had substantially improved.

Despite much that is disheartening, or even heart-rending, in the period we have traversed, it may be permissible to say that after the close of the eighteenth century the dominant or at least the most obviously growing spirit—the spirit which had abolished the slave trade and within a year was to abolish slavery, had repealed religious disabilities, extended the suffrage, liberalised the Foreign Office and removed or lightened the shackles of labour and commerce—was the passion for freedom ; but, unfortunately for the masses, the prevalence of this spirit in the economic sphere forbade any attempt, with one disastrous exception, to protect them from the hardships of industrial competition, at a time when these, owing to the progress of invention, were unusually severe and were aggravated by political repression and the privations or remoter consequences of war. The development of religion during these years followed, though less consistently, the same course. Evangelicalism was indeed little more favourable to political than to intellectual expansion, and, owing to its subordination of the present to a future life, was welcomed in certain quarters as an antidote to social discontent ; but it popularised as well as invigorated the Church, promoted sympathy and co-operation between the Church and Dissent, and maintained the philanthropic tradition which had descended by way

[1] Hansard, 3rd S., viii. 239.

of Methodism from the High Churchmen of the Revolution. Its most signal triumph, won in conjunction with the Quakers, was the abolition of the slave trade, which the *Edinburgh Review* pronounced " the greatest battle ever fought by human beings " ; but we have seen that something was done, under secular as well as religious auspices, to diffuse education, technical knowledge and thrift, to mitigate the barbarity of factories, prisons and the criminal law ; and, if philanthropy is too often rather well-intentioned than well-informed, one must admit that the enthusiasm and the intelligence which are both essential to social progress were happily exemplified in the apostolic fervour of Sharp and Wilberforce, the sober idealism of Romilly and Mackintosh, and the zeal for enlightenment of Brougham.

INDEX

Printed by SPOTTISWOODE, BALLANTYNE & CO. LTD.
Colchester, London & Eton, England

CPSIA information can be obtained at www.ICGtesting.com
Printed in the USA
LVOW011543021212

309766LV00023B/1945/P